Beyond Prince and Merchant

*Citizen Participation
and the Rise of Civil Society*

Edited by John Burbidge
for the Institute of Cultural Affairs International

Pact Publications

New York

ICA International
rue Amédée Lynen 8
B-1210 Brussels
Belgium

ISBN 1-888753-09-9

✿ Printed on recycled paper

The title of this book was inspired by an article written by Marc
Nerfin, "Neither Prince nor Merchant: Citizen. An Introduction to
the Third Sector," that appeared in *Development Dialogue*, Number
1, 1987, published by the Dag Hammarskjöld Foundation, Uppsala,
Sweden.

Dedicated to

Sir James Lindsay Kt FCIM CIMgt
Former President
Institute of Cultural Affairs International

Prince, Merchant, and Global Citizen

Contents

Acknowledgments

I f civil society is, as Michael Bratton reminds us, about participating in voluntary associations, embodying norms of trust, reciprocity, tolerance, and inclusion, and activating networks of public communication, then producing this book was surely an exercise in building civil society. An enormous amount of volunteer time and energy went into compiling, refining, and publishing this volume. Its creation was not driven by market forces or government mandate but by the desire of private citizens to share common wisdom on what makes for a vibrant, healthy civil society.

While many people participated in the publication of this book, I would like to acknowledge the contributions of a few in particular. Among these are the 20 women and men from 10 countries who took time in their already overloaded schedules to prepare a chapter. Not only has their work enhanced the quality of this book, it has made an invaluable contribution to the broader civil society dialogue as well. I would like to pay a special tribute to Goran Hyden, whose opening chapter on the origins and evolution of the concept and practice of civil society provides an excellent foundation for the book.

To my ICA colleagues, Richard Alton in Belgium and Martin Gilbraith in the United Kingdom, I owe special thanks. Without Richard's initial proposal and ongoing support, this book would never have happened. Martin's thorough critique of every chapter, in the midst of writing his own Master's Degree dissertation on civil society, deserves much more credit than a sentence here can offer. Sandra Powell in Costa Rica and James Troxel in the USA also provided extremely helpful feedback and personal encouragement throughout the editing process.

Dorothy Craig, who was an answer to my prayers for a copy editor, cannot be thanked enough. Apart from her finely-honed skills with the English language, her own involvement in and passion for civil society made her a source of much inspiration and reflection. I am also indebted to Robert Lanphear, whose empathy for and understanding of civil society enhanced his highly creative abilities as a graphic designer.

Finally, to my partner, Bruce Robertson, son Duncan, and our canine family member, Ganesh — "the remover of obstacles" — I owe my heartfelt thanks for their enduring patience and unfailing support throughout the editing of this book.

John Burbidge
Seattle, May 1997

Foreword

I n country after country, people are demonstrating they are no longer willing to leave it to mainstream political parties and corporate lobbyists to set the terms of the public policy debate. They are acting to reclaim their basic rights and responsibilities as citizens to create societies more responsive to the needs and aspirations of ordinary people. As they do so, they are reaching out across racial, cultural, religious, and national boundaries to build alliances with others similarly engaged. As this happens, we witness the awakening and formation of a politically and spiritually conscious, globalized civil society engaged in reclaiming citizen responsibility and sovereignty.

Civic engagement has many elements, but in its most basic sense, it is about governance and who makes decisions about how a community's resources will be used. The principle of civic engagement underscores the most basic principle of democratic governance, i.e., that sovereignty resides ultimately in the people — in the citizenry. It is about the right of people to define the public good, to determine the policies by which they will seek that good, and to reform or replace those institutions that no longer serve.

While "civic engagement" may be a relatively new term, it is a reality whose roots go far back to the dawn of human community. People have always organized themselves into tribes and villages and found ways to use available resources and technologies to grow food, harvest water, construct shelter, and treat their ailments. Forms of civic engagement are among the most natural and pervasive of human drives.

However, industrialization and urbanization have taken their toll. Monetized economies have tended to replace families and communities with markets, replace pathways where people meet with roadways where they isolate themselves in personal automobiles, and to redefine the active citizen as passive consumer. Modernization has tended to suppress the natural drive toward civic engagement. As that drive has declined, the power to govern has passed from people to distant institutions driven primarily by monetary imperatives. To create local habitats that serve their needs, people will need to reclaim that power and restore the rightful and necessary role of governance to civil society.

There is growing evidence that this reclamation and restoration is happening, not just in isolated pockets but in country after country around the world. Citizen groups are reaching out to form national and international alliances committed to transformational changes aimed at addressing root causes of global crises, particularly those of deepening poverty, environmental destruction, and social disintegration. An emergent social movement is coalescing around a shared vision of a world of diverse cultures and just and sustainable communities, of people living in balance with the natural world and joined in cooperative endeavor — not by a global economy ruled by powerful corporations but by an awareness of the underlying spiritual unity of the living world.

This movement gained substantial impetus from the Non-governmental Organization Forum of the United Nations Conference on Environment and Development held in Rio de Janeiro in 1992. This forum brought together civil society organizations from around the world to negotiate a series of citizen treaties for creating a just and sustainable world. It was here that the emergent movement began to become more aware of itself, as participants from widely diverse backgrounds came to realize the extent to which they shared common values and aspirations. The basic elements of this emergent consensus were recorded in The People's Earth Declaration.

Other United Nations conferences and international gatherings have built on this foundation and future possibilities for a new era of global civic engagement are being explored. Many groups are currently focusing their attention on citizen-led efforts to build locally-grounded policy agendas directed to the needs of the third millennium. We may expect that during the year 2000, civil society groups around the world will come forward to share their experiences, visions, and commitments toward creating a new era grounded in equity, democracy, and the celebration of life and spirit. Hopefully, these efforts will set the stage for a basic restructuring of the institutions of national and global governance to actualize the deep human yearning for democratic societies in which the institutions of government and market serve as extensions of the will of the sovereign people.

The Institute of Cultural Affairs is one organization that has embarked on this process, networking with other organizations similarly committed. Its 1996 Cairo conference on "The Rise of Civil Society in the 21st Century" was a small but significant step on the way down this road. This book — which highlights the historical roots of civil society, its diverse manifestations across the globe today, and some of the new frontiers of civil society we must tackle as we move into the future — is another important contribution to that task.

David Korten

Introduction

*Contrasting with governmental power and economic power
— the power of the Prince and the Merchant — there is an
immediate and autonomous power, sometimes evident, sometimes latent: people's power. Some people develop an
awareness of this, associate, and act with others and thus
become citizens.*

— Marc Nerfin

When I first began doing background research for this book, I went to the computer and typed in the keywords "civil society." I limited my search to articles and books published in the last five years. Within minutes, I was deluged with page after page of titles from all parts of the world. When I added other qualifying words, such as "democracy" and "development" I was inundated by even lengthier lists. The experience was daunting. I knew I was onto a "hot" topic.

As I extended my reading on the subject, I soon became aware that it wasn't just academics who were interested in civil society. I would pick up a newspaper or magazine and find civil society woven into many an article. I would switch on my radio or television and hear people discussing civil society. I noticed non-governmental organizations and research institutes conducting conferences and seminars on the subject. I discovered publications devoted to it and new positions being advertised incorporating the words in their title, not to mention Websites and Internet newsgroups focused on it.

Clearly, "civil society" had become a major theme occupying contemporary society, but why all this interest and what does it mean to its different proponents?

WHAT IS CIVIL SOCIETY?

Definitions of civil society abound, as this book testifies. In his chapter on "Indicators of a Healthy Civil Society," Robert Bothwell names four broad categories of definition commonly used.[1] One defines civil society in terms of the *results* or *behaviors* a healthy civil society produces; a second focuses on the *preconditions* or *foundations* for civil society; a third describes it as a desirable state for *all* society; and a fourth emphasizes the *composition* of civil society — who is and isn't included. Within these four broad categories are many variations.

In his opening chapter to this book, Goran Hyden adopts a historical perspective. He identifies four schools of thought on civil society, and traces them back to their roots in 17th, 18th, and 19th century Europe — the associational school, the regime school, the neo-liberal school, and the post-Marxist school.[2] Hyden emphasizes the essentially political nature of civil society, pointing out that "civil society is that part of society that connects individual citizens with the public realm and the state. Put in other words, civil society is the political side of society."[3]

Other commentators have played down the political dimension of civil society in favor of its more grassroots, community-oriented, citizen-based nature. One of the most widely quoted images of this understanding is the three-legged stool, developed by United States Senator William Bradley. In his 1995 address to the National Press Club, he said:

> Government and market are not enough to make a civilization. There also must be a healthy, robust civil sector: a space in which the bonds of community can flourish. Government and market are similar to two legs of a three-legged stool. Without the third leg of civil society, the stool is not stable and cannot provide support for a vital America.[4]

While some criticize Bradley's metaphor as being too simplistic, or even divisive, it projects a clear image of civil society as "the third sector" which is how many people use the term. However, there are those who challenge the notion of civil society being "third in line" behind the market and government sectors. Development researcher and writer Rajesh Tandon maintains that "the historical role of civil society and the democratic principle of people's sovereignty both point to the essential primacy of civil society as the only legitimate first sector."[5]

David Korten, author of *When Corporations Rule the World* and contributor of the foreword to this book, strongly endorses this position:

> The order of precedence among the three primary sectors is fundamental to the healthy and balanced function of society. A civic sector without government and an organized market is anarchy. This is why civil societies create governments and organize markets. Civil society is, however, the first sector. The authority and legitimacy of all other human institutions flow from it. Since government is the body through which citizens establish and maintain the rules within which the market will function in the human interest, government is appropriately viewed as the second sector. The institutions of the market appropriately function as the third sector.[6]

Given the variety of understandings and uses of the term "civil society," it is necessary to define it for the purposes of this book. The most helpful definition I have come across is that offered by Michael Bratton, Professor of

Political Science and African Studies at Michigan State University, USA. Bratton defines civil society as that "sphere of social interaction between the household and the state which is manifest in norms of community cooperation, structures of voluntary association, and networks of public communication."[7] He further breaks down the elements of this definition into the following components:

- Norms of civic community, such as trust, reciprocity, tolerance, and inclusion.
- Structures of associational life, voluntary in nature and ranging from local, informal associations to national and international political advocacy groups.
- Networks of public communication, both print and electronic media, including faxes and e-mail.[8]

While elaborating on each of these elements, Bratton has several words of caution.[9] First, we should not romanticize civil society as an arena in which conflicts are always peacefully resolved. The propensity to do this is evident in the writings of many "communitarians"[10] and those advocating greater civility in our dealings with one another. Second, while civil society stands apart from the state, it cannot exist without it. This theme is echoed in many writings on civil society, not least James Troxel's chapter in this book on the recovery of civic engagement in the United States.[11] Third, civil society is usually seen as opposing the state, but can also legitimize and support the political status quo. Bothwell underscores this point in his chapter on indicators of a healthy civil society.[12]

In describing the nature of civil society, Bratton highlights another key term, social capital. In contrast to economic capital (money and tools) and human capital (trained individuals), social capital refers to the values and networks that enable coordination and cooperation. Social capital is one of the definitive characteristics of civil society and appears frequently in the literature and throughout this book.

WHY NOW?

As Goran Hyden points out, the concept of civil society is not new, but has undergone a resurgence in the last decade or two, not only in Europe, but in almost every continent.

Many writers look to the wave of democratization that swept central and eastern Europe in the late 1980s and the early 1990s as a catalyst for strengthening civil society. The emergence of a democratic opposition to the authoritarian socialist state of the former Czechoslovakia, the fall of the Berlin Wall in Germany, the dismembering of the Soviet Union, and the demise of the Ceausescu regime in Romania[13] were pivotal events in changing the political landscape of Europe and ushering in a civil sector. However, in many of these countries, civil society is still embryonic, often more an idea than a reality.

Simultaneously, civil society began gaining currency in Africa, Asia, and Latin America. In *Citizens: Strengthening Global Civil Society* published by CIVICUS, the World Alliance for Citizen Participation, Miguel Darcy de Oliveira and Rajesh Tandon present detailed reports on the state of civil society around the world, region by region.[14] From the plethora of citizen-based initiatives described in their book, Oliveira and Tandon extract four common values:

- Solidarity and compassion for the fate and well-being of others, including unknown, distant others.
- A sense of personal responsibility and reliance on one's own initiative to do the right thing.
- An impulse toward altruistic giving and sharing.
- Rejection of inequality, violence, and oppression.

The globalization of civil society is one of its unique qualities at this point in history. Extensive networking has become standard operating procedure for many civil society organizations (CSOs). Nowhere has this been more obvious than at the United Nations global conferences of the last two decades, in particular the 1992 Conference on Environment and Development (UNCED) in Rio de Janeiro, the 1994 International Conference on Population and Development in Cairo, the 1995 Fourth World Conference on Women in Beijing, the 1995 Social Summit in Copenhagen, and the 1996 Conference on Human Settlements (Habitat II) in Istanbul. Before, during, and after each of these events, civil society organizations, most often in the form of non-governmental organizations (NGOs), have been a forceful presence, often commanding as much, if not more, media attention than their governmental counterparts.

One of the intriguing aspects of this worldwide resurgence of civil society is that the impetus for it seems to come from quite diverse roots in different societies. In many countries, the driving force is the struggle to attain or preserve basic human rights or the demand of disenfranchised minorities to participate fully in the society. Editor and activist Smitu Kothari isolates "six among thousands" of examples of civil society efforts which reflect these concerns. They are: [15]

- A 1995 meeting of 40 representatives of NGOs in Pakistan to discuss how they could move from being conventional development and social action groups to becoming a social and political movement to redefine the relationship between civil society and the state.

- The 1996 meeting in Nepal of the Assembly of the People's Plan for the 21st Century, an alliance of women's organizations, trade unions, fishing communities, indigenous and tribal peoples, farmers, child workers, and human rights organizations from across Asia.

- The 1995 peasant revolt in the Chiapas region of Mexico, which catalyzed a movement for radical political reform in Mexico and beyond and forced many to rethink the place of local economies in the global economy.

- The formation in India of the National Forum for Tribal Self-Rule, seeking the implementation of the government's recommendations on tribal self-governance that had been ignored, as well as their rights over productive natural resources and an end to being treated as trespassers on their own lands.

- The farmers' protests in India against transnational corporations — Kentucky Fried Chicken for its centrally-controlled mass marketing of an everyday food (with illegal chemical additives, it was alleged) and the Cargill corporation for aggressively marketing hybrid seeds at the expense of locally controlled and produced food crops.

- The unprecedented mobilization of "tens of thousands of women who had hitherto rarely moved out of their communities and villages" to make their voices heard at the 1995 UN Conference on Women in Beijing.

In other countries, the call to empower civil society seems to spring more from a deep cynicism about the role of government, a growing concern about a runaway global economy and the encroaching power of market forces, and the belief that voluntary associations which have been part of the bedrock of the society, are in decline. Many articles have been written on these themes but the one quoted most often by contributors to this volume and others is that by Harvard University professor Robert Putnam, "Bowling Alone: The Decline of America's Social Capital."[16] Putnam's basic thesis — that America's voluntary, associational life is on a downward slide as a result of the impact of television, the changing role of women in the work force, and several other key factors — has its supporters and critics, both in the United States and abroad. At the very least, this article and his other more detailed study on social capital in Italy[17] have raised the profile of the civil society debate to an unprecedented level.

In Britain, civil society and social capital are in the public eye, as well as under scrutiny by academics. In their report, "The Deficit of Civil Society in the United Kingdom," Barry Knight and Peter Stokes document the steep decline in church membership, trade unionism, and mutual aid societies as indicators of the diminishing stocks of social capital in Britain.[18] However, in spite of their conclusion that Britain is suffering a severe shortage of social capital, Knight and Stokes are optimistic that new forms of social capital are emerging. One is the Citizen Organizing movement made up of 60,000 people from faith communities, tenant associations, and community groups who have changed the policies of supermarkets, forced local councils to clear illegal dumping sites, campaigned for the homeless, and helped change policing tactics.[19] Another new form of social capital is Knight and Stoke's own Foundation for Civil Society, an organization which is built on the assumption that "a generation of decline in the quality of our civic culture will take another generation to repair."[20]

On the opposite side of the world, the state of civil society in Australia is also being examined. The focus for this was the series of nationally broadcast radio talks, the Boyer Lectures, presented each year by a prominent Australian at the invitation of the Australian Broadcasting Corporation. The 1995 series, "A Truly Civil Society," was delivered by Eva Cox, a leading social commentator, public servant, community activist, and academic. Although Cox picked up on Putnam's theme of declining social capital in the Australian context, she advocated a much stronger role for government in protecting and supporting citizen engagement, and encouraging active dissent and debate within a climate of trust and mutuality. Among her "Road Rules for Creating a Truly Civil Society," Cox makes a case for giving people more time to participate in public life and demanding a social capital impact statement before selling any public asset.[21]

WHY THIS BOOK?

In 1971, a group of people came together from around the world to examine what was happening in society so they could decide where to put their collective effort to really make a difference. They were students and teachers, writers and technicians, clergy and laity, men and women, old and young, from first and third world countries. They were, in short, a cross-section of the global civil society of its day.

Knowing they were stepping into uncharted territory, they created their own research methods based on an analysis of the fundamental dynamics of society — economic, political, and cultural.[22] Their research led them to the conclusion that the cultural dynamic most needed empowering, to counterbalance the dominant force of the economic and the weakened role of the political. As a consequence, they decided to devote their time, energy, and resources to revitalizing the cultural dimension of society and to call themselves The Institute of Cultural Affairs — the ICA.

They might well have called themselves The Institute for Global Civil Society, since the ICA has spent the last quarter of a century designing, applying, and refining a set of tools for enhancing citizen engagement. Beginning with its pilot project in the low-income, inner city neighborhood known as Fifth

City on the west side of Chicago, the ICA took its methods of civic involvement to thousands of communities across the globe — urban and rural, large and small, rich and poor. It also began using these same methods with business and government, as well as with other voluntary organizations.

One of the hallmarks of the ICA's work is its *Technology of Participation (ToP)* methods,[23] used today throughout the world in a variety of situations ranging from neighborhood planning associations to multinational corporations, from government departments to an international movement for Community Youth Development.

In September 1996, the ICA held its quadrennial global conference in Cairo, Egypt, on the theme of "The Rise of Civil Society in the 21st Century." With nearly 300 participants from 39 countries, the conference was a microcosm of global civil society. True to ICA tradition, it was a highly participant-driven event in which people shared experiences, exchanged lessons learned, and discussed issues of common concern. To ground the reality of civil society in the midst of the conference, a day was devoted to visiting a host of Egyptian civil society projects in Cairo and nearby rural areas.

WHAT'S IN THIS BOOK?

Although this book is in part an outgrowth of that conference, it is much more. It started well before the conference and has gathered input from people who were not present in Cairo, as well as those who were. It is not an attempt to "cover the waterfront" on civil society. That would be an impossible and perhaps fruitless task. Rather, it is an attempt to pull together some highly significant statements about what is happening in civil society across the world today, from those who are investing their lives in making it happen.

Goran Hyden, who delivered the keynote address at the Cairo conference, has written a comprehensive account of the evolution of the concept of civil society and the challenges we face as we promote civil society in different communities, cultures, and countries. At the other end of the volume, Alan AtKisson, former editor of *In Context* magazine and a young man with a deep passion for and commitment to citizen initiative, brings the book to a conclusion by making a compelling and inspiring case for "Why Civil Society Will Save the World."

Between these two presentations, the book is divided in half. The first half contains examples of creating civil society in local situations around the world. From India to Romania, Ethiopia to Bosnia, contributors have documented their experience in forging civil society and what they have learned in the process. The second half of the book focuses on new frontiers for civil society that still need attention and energy. These include increasing the role of youth in building civil society, articulating the values that underlie a robust civil society, and developing indicators for how we measure the health of civil society.

Among the many key elements of civil society mentioned in this book, two stand out from the rest. They are the need for inclusive participation to enhance civil society and the primacy of the grassroots as the locus of long-term social change.

"Participation" is a much-used word today, from business to government to rural development. People acknowledge that when they are involved in making decisions affecting their future, they develop a sense of ownership and commitment to carrying out those decisions. However, they often lack the knowledge and experience to elicit participation from those with whom they live and work.

"Grassroots" is also popular today among members of civil society organizations, academics, community developers, businesses people, and government officials. People decide the future of society daily in their homes and workplaces, with family, friends, neighbors, co-workers, and fellow citizens. It doesn't happen anywhere else. It is in the most local units of society that social change is born, develops, and dies.

While building civil society involves citizens working in partnership with government and business at all levels of society, it is essentially a bottom-up activity. As stated in a United Nations Development Programme document on sustainable human development:

> Social capital is not being formed by decree or by the stroke of a pen. The moral commitments that constitute the core of social capital evolve only in the context of meaningful human interaction. It has to come from the bottom up.[24]

This book acknowledges the efforts of countless people around the world who are morally committed to effecting positive social change in their everyday situations, and highlights some of the key issues to be dealt with in accomplishing this task. It underscores the need for citizens to experiment, share experiences, communicate, and network together on a global scale. In so doing, it is making a small but important contribution to citizen participation and the rise of civil society.

John Burbidge

NOTES

1. Robert Bothwell. "Indicators of a Healthy Civil Society." pp. 249-262.

2. Goran Hyden. "Building Civil Society at the Turn of the Millennium." pp. 17-46.

3. *Ibid.*

4. Bill Bradley. "America's Challenge: Revitalizing Our National Community." *National Civic Review.* Volume 84, Number 2, Spring 1995. p. 95.

5. Rajesh Tandon. "Civil Society is the First Sector." *Development.* Journal of the Society for International Development. 1992, Number 3. p. 38.

6. David Korten. *When Corporations Rule the World.* San Francisco: Berrett-Koehler Publishers and West Hartford: Kumarian Press, 1995. p. 99.

7. Michael Bratton. "Civil Society and Political Transition in Africa." *IDR Reports.* Volume 11, Number 6, 1994. Boston: Institute for Development Research. p. 2.

8. *Ibid.* pp. 2-3.

9. Michael Bratton quoted in "Civil Societies and NGOs: Expanding Development Strategies." InterAction's Civil Society Initiative. Report of Workshop #1. 9 February 1995. p. 3.

10. The communitarian movement is broadly defined by its concern that the moral fabric of society is in disarray and an ethic of unfettered individualism has taken over. Communitarians, of which there are many varieties at both ends of the political spectrum, call for a revitalization of civic life through communities, schools, workplaces, and religious institutions to help restore a sense of social bonding among citizens. Writers in this school include Robert Bellah, Amitai Etzioni, Michael Sandel, Philip Selznick, and Michael Walzer.

11. James P. Troxel. "The Recovery of Civic Engagement in America." pp. 97-111.

12. Bothwell. *op. cit.* pp. 254-255.

13. Alice Johnson and Barbara Wright. "Civil Society in Romania: An Evolving Partnership." pp. 143-160.

14. Rajesh Tandon and Miguel Darcy de Oliveira (Eds.) *Citizens: Strengthening Global Civil Society.* New York: CIVICUS, 1995.

15. Smitu Kothari. "Rising from the Margins: The Awakening of Civil Society in the Third World." *Development.* The Journal of the Society for International Development. September 1996, Number 3. pp. 11-13.

16. Robert Putnam. "Bowling Alone: America's Declining Social Capital." *The Journal of Democracy.* Volume 6, Number 1, January 1995. pp. 65-78.

17. Robert Putnam. *Making Democracy Work: Civic Traditions in Modern Italy* Princeton: Princeton University Press, 1993.

18. Barry Knight and Peter Stokes. "The Deficit in Civil Society in the United Kingdom." Foundation for Civil Society Working Paper Number 1, 1996.

19. Andrew Marr. "Do-It-Yourself Democracy." *Resurgence* Number 176. p.12. (First published in *The Independent* newspaper.)

20. Barry Knight and Peter Stokes. "Self-help Citizenship." *The Guardian.* 30 October 1996. Society Section. p. 2.

21. Eva Cox. "A Truly Civil Society." A series of radio lectures broadcast by the Australian Broadcasting Corporation's Radio National, November-December 1995.

22. For a more detailed description of the "Social Process," see appendix pp. 293-294

23. For a description of *The Technology of Participation,* see appendix pp. 294-295.

24. "Sustainable Human Development: From Concept to Operation. A Guide for the Practitioner." An edited report prepared for the United Nations Development Programme by a multidisciplinary team of consultants. August, 1994. p. 19.

Section I

ORIGINS AND CHALLENGES
OF CIVIL SOCIETY

1. Building Civil Society at the Turn of the Millennium

Goran Hyden

"Civil society" is a political concept because it is essentially about power, the power of non-state actors to participate in making decisions that have an impact on them.

— Leslie Fox

The 1990s have witnessed a marked reorientation of both academic and political discourse on development. For thirty or so years, the development debate focused on the state or the economic forces underlying a country's aspiration to make progress. This was as true for the modernization theorists of the 1960s as it was for subsequent generations of neo-Marxist and neo-liberal thinkers in the 1970s and 1980s. The intellectual trend in the 1990s is new in that it focuses on what generically is referred to as "political culture." This orientation differs from earlier structuralist theories in that it attributes a distinct role to human agency. At the same time, it differs from the neo-liberal "rational choice" theory in that it acknowledges that human choice is mediated by institutions.

More specifically, development discourse has in recent years come to focus on the relationship between democracy and development. An increasingly common premise of what is being said is that "democracy is good for development," that it may be a causal factor of development. It is in this perspective that the concepts of "social capital" and "civil society" have come to acquire relevance. The former refers to the normative values and beliefs that citizens share in their everyday dealings, what Tocqueville referred to as "habits of the heart and the mind." These habits provide reasons and design criteria for all sorts of rules. It is hard to imagine that constitutional arrangements, laws, and regulations would work without being embedded in, and reflecting, particular values and norms upheld by groups and communities making up a given society. "Civil society," therefore, is viewed as the forum in which habits of the heart and the mind are nurtured and developed. In this sense, both social capital and civil society are analytical categories in their own right, independent of democracy. However, it is assumed that investments in both social capital and civil society are necessary to achieve democracy and, by implication, development.

It appears as if analysts have arrived at this view of development from two different directions. One is the perception — based on a broad range of experiences — that a "top-down" approach to development does not work. For a long time, the basic premise was that the state is a rational instrument of controlling and promoting change. While the state is indispensable to achieve growth and redistribution in desired directions, by the 1980s, confidence in the state's ability to be such a powerful instrument had been replaced by disillusionment. From both a leftist and a rightist perspective, the state was viewed as an instrument of exploitation, preempting popular or individual initiative. As the pendulum has swung in the opposite direction, analysts now maintain that developmental wisdom is lodged not in government bureaucracies but in local communities and institutions. "Indigenous knowledge" and "popular participation" are examples of concepts that have come to occupy increasing prominence in the debate.

The other direction from which analysts of social capital and civil society have come is the problem of political apathy or lack of organization. Democracy requires organization; organization requires an interest in public affairs. During the 1980s, many people around the world adopted a cynical and distrustful attitude towards politics. Politicians suffered from a lack of credibility in democracies and autocracies alike. Robert Putnam's study of the evolution of civic values in Italy is an example of studies in this genre.[1] Contrasting what Edward Banfield[2] had identified as the "amoral familism" of southern Italy with the rich associational life of Emilia Romagna and other regions of northern Italy, Putnam concludes that the general difference in development between these two parts of the same country must be attributed to a difference in the presence of social capital and the strength of civil society. Thus, civil society is more than just society. It is that part of society that connects individual citizens with the public realm and the state. Put in other words, civil society is the political side of society.

The literature on social capital and civil society is not new. According to Sabetti,[3] the notion of social capital can be traced back to the democratic currents of the 19th century Italian Risorgimento movement, which conceptualized *valor sociale* (roughly translatable as social capital) as the educative feature of the growth and practice of self-governing institutions. Civil society can also be traced back to the period when modern ideas of democracy were beginning to take root. In order to fully understand and appreciate the current arguments about civil society it is important to first look at its philosophical origins. Following such a historical review, I shall examine the contemporary debate about civil society, suggesting that it takes its lead from the principal philosophical strands on the issue. The second part of the chapter is divided into two sections, one dealing with the question of where analysts locate their investigation when examining civil society, the other with the challenges that both analysts and practitioners face in operationalizing the concept.

PHILOSOPHICAL ORIGINS OF THE CONTEMPORARY DEBATE

The emergence of a concept of civil society is historically connected with the rise of capitalism and the evolution of a modern state in the Weberian sense of rational-legal structures of governance. Thus, it seems clear that civil society cannot be viewed in isolation from either market or state. For example, a totalitarian society in which the market is rendered inoperative leaves no space for the growth of civil society. Similarly, in societies where the state in the sense described above does not exist, civil society cannot develop. These points are not always considered by participants in the contemporary debate on civil society. Their significance, however, becomes clear if we take a closer look at the philosophical origins of the concept.

"Civil society" is currently part of a global development discourse but it is important to remember that it comes out of a European philosophical tradition. Drawing on the "founding fathers" of the civil society concept, it is possible to distinguish variations along two principal parameters. The first concerns the question whether civil society is primarily an economic or a sociological phenomenon: whether the focus is on the extent to which economic activity is privately controlled or the role associations play as intermediaries between individual and state. The second concerns the relationship between state and civil society: whether civil society is essentially autonomous of the state or the state and civil society are organically linked. Taking a more careful look at the philosophical pioneers of the debate about civil society, we find that each of the four positions listed above has a master advocate, as indicated in Figure 1.

State/Civil Society Linked

	Hegel	Locke	
Private Economic Interests			**Associational Life**
	Paine	Tocqueville	

State/Civil Society Separate

Figure 1. Different perspectives on civil society

Locke's position, reminiscent of Hobbes', is that the state arises from society and is needed to restrain conflict between individuals, but he emphasizes the need to limit state sovereignty in order to preserve individual freedoms derived from natural law. There must be a "social contract" between rulers and ruled which respects the natural rights of individuals but also allows the state to protect civil society from destructive conflict. Natural rights are not absolute and must be regulated to enable civil society to prosper. A constitutional arrangement that is being respected by both state and civil society is the cornerstone of liberal democracy. Locke's position might be called social-liberal in that it recognizes the need to balance the interests among different groups in society.

This is quite different from Thomas Paine's argument that societies become civil as commerce and manufacturing expand through division of labor. Writing in the tradition of the Scottish Enlightenment (David Hume and Adam Smith), Paine's position is particularly anti-statist. As the state expands to provide order and reduce conflict, the state may threaten the very liberties that cause civil society to flourish. In his libertarian view, civil society flourishes when individuals are able to freely exercise their natural rights. It is the market rather than the state that provides the best opportunity for the growth of civil society, because the limits of individual capacity to satisfy natural desires can only be transcended by commercial exchanges. Paine's focus on natural rights prevented him from recognizing that the state, even in its minimalist version, may be used by one segment of society to the detriment of another.

Tocqueville was alarmed not only by the prospect of a powerful state but also by the tyranny of the majority and treated associations as the strongest bulwark against this. Reflecting on the lessons of the French Revolution, he was particularly afraid of an unmediated popular will because it could lead to revolution. To prevent such outcomes, he believed an active civil society made up of self-governing associations is necessary. Such a civil society educates the citizenry and scrutinizes state actions. It facilitates distribution of power and provides mechanisms for direct citizen participation in public affairs. Without taking such a pro-market stand as Paine, Tocqueville nevertheless adopted a voluntarist view of civil society, that it is capable of protecting and promoting the interest of individuals regardless of their socio-economic position.

Hegel broke with the tradition of civil society as a natural phenomenon and instead regarded it as the product of historical processes. He recognized that division of labor creates stratification within civil society and increases conflict between these strata. In his account, civil society is made up of the various associations, corporations, and estates that exist among the strata. The form and nature of the state is the result of the way civil society is represented. Civil society thus stands between individuals and a legislature, which mediates their interests with the state. The conflicts these processes engender within civil society will lead to its destruction in the absence of a strong state. In Hegel's "organic" perspective, the state exists to protect common interests as the state defines them by intervening in the activities of civil society. Marx picks up on the theme of the destructive influence of the capitalist economic system and arrives at the conclusion that civil society is equated with the bourgeoisie. Antonio Gramsci, the foremost Marxist analyst of civil society, bypasses the economic determinism of Marx by arguing that associations are the mechanisms for exercising control in society. By transferring the focus from the state to civil society as the key arena of conflict, Gramsci comes to the conclusion that the control the dominant class has over society can be overturned through the development of counter-hegemonic associations that represent alternative norms.

A few general observations on these four philosophical positions may be helpful before trying to demonstrate their links to the contemporary debate. The first is that those writing in the tradition of either Paine or Hegel are essentially trying to retain a political economy perspective. Civil society cannot be viewed in isolation from economic forces. In contrast, those following in the footsteps of either Locke or Tocqueville believe in the autonomy of non-economic forces. Constitutional arrangements reflect such factors as prevailing norms or the institutional set-up in civil society which, in turn, are viewed as independent of division of labor, technology, and capital.

Another observation is that discourse on civil society in Europe has been much more influenced by the Lockean and Hegelian traditions. The organic relations of state to civil society have rarely been questioned in the European debate, even with regard to developing countries.[4] The American debate on the same subject, on the other hand, has been much more influenced by the writings of Paine and Tocqueville. It has stressed the importance of the market and the active role of associations. As I shall indicate below, these differences are evident in the contemporary debate. For example, the Europeans have a more instrumentalist orientation towards civil society. Its only *raison d'être* is its ability to reform the state. American thinkers have a more fundamentalist view of civil society. It is good in and of itself because it is in civil society that democratic norms are lodged.

Still another observation is that the pioneers of the debate about civil society are all Western philosophers. The concept has evolved from the historical experience of European and North American societies and been formulated by individuals reflecting on these processes. Yet, today it is being discussed not only by members of these societies but also by others around the world. Civil society has become a global concern and challenge.

CONTEMPORARY DEBATES ABOUT CIVIL SOCIETY

The same basic differences which existed among the early writers on the subject continue in the contemporary debate about civil society. While being a meeting-ground of the political right and left, the discourse is reflective of points of contention that can be traced back to the four philosophical schools identified above. Thus, I propose that the contemporary debate is being conducted by four different schools, as illustrated in Figure 2.

State/Civil Society Linked

Post-Marxist **School** **(Hegel)**	**Regime** **School** **(Locke)**

Private
Economic ———————————— **Associational**
Interests **Life**

Neo-Liberal **School** **(Paine)**	**Associational** **School** **(Tocqueville)**

State/Civil Society Separate

Figure 2. Principal schools contributing to the civil society debate

Associational School

Perhaps most dominant is the group of authors who emphasize the importance of autonomous and active associations. Examples of writers who reflect this largely Tocquevillean position are Stepan[5] and Diamond.[6] More specifically, civil society is here defined as the "realm of organized social life" standing between individuals and political institutions of representation.

For instance, according to Diamond,[7] civil society acts to strengthen democracy by:

• Containing the power of the state through public scrutiny.
• Stimulating political participation by citizens.

- Developing such democratic norms as tolerance and compromise.
- Creating ways of articulating, aggregating, and representing interests outside of political parties, especially at the local level.
- Mitigating conflict through cross-cutting or overlapping interests.
- Recruiting and training political leaders.
- Questioning and reforming existing democratic institutions and procedures.
- Disseminating information.

Although the argument of this "associational" approach to civil society accepts that the development of civil society is not sufficient for the consolidation of democracy, its advocates have a generally high expectation of the role civil society can play in achieving democracy. A critical function of civil society is to promote the principle of citizenship, as reflected in the writings of Sztompka,[8] Calhoun,[9] and Putnam.[10] The authors belonging to the "associational" school are generally optimistic about the opportunity for civil society to make a difference to democracy and development.

This assumption is also reflected in the position taken by many non-governmental organizations (NGOs) whose development agenda in recent years has come to incorporate democratization goals. Whether expressed in terms of popular participation or human rights or both, this agenda presupposes an active civil society and thus an expectation that these NGOs themselves can make a difference to the conditions under which a developmental philosophy is being implemented. While the fear of mass politics seems distant in the contemporary debate, the arguments carry a distinct affinity with Tocqueville's view of civil society — active citizen participation is needed for the organization and functioning of development activities and communication of information and ideas is needed to encourage participation and to guard against abuses of state power.

The "associational" school can be criticized on at least two principal grounds. The first is that it is based on a rather simplistic version of pluralism — groups organize to pursue a shared interest and are countered by other groups that mobilize to pursue an opposing interest, so that policy emerges from the balance of power among groups. A fuller pluralism argument developed by Truman,[11] Dahl,[12] and others recognizes that resources are distributed unequally in society but also asserts that multiple, overlapping interests of individuals mitigate the impact of inequalities and reduce conflict over policy. However, this view occupies a relatively insignificant place in the contemporary debate. The second line of criticism leveled against this school, therefore, is its tendency not to explicitly acknowledge that an associational focus can blind its advocates to the risk of elite pluralism a society in which resource-rich interests dominate.

Regime School

A second approach in the ongoing debate draws its inspiration largely from Locke. This school focuses on the nature of the regime and how rules can be made more democratic. It recognizes that the consolidation of democracy may require changes in both state and civil society. The "regime" school, therefore, tends to be concerned specifically with the constitutional issue of how state-society relations can be organized to promote democracy. A constitution by itself, no matter how ingeniously designed, no matter what formal arrangements of checks and balances admirably arranged, will not limit authoritarian rule. To be effective, constitutions must relate to the realities of society. They must intertwine state and civil society in ways that permit the effective articulation and aggregation of societal interests. Like the American Federalists, advocates of this position do not treat the state and civil society as standing apart. They are concerned with instituting constitutional and legal mechanisms that limit the risks of abuse of political power.

Students of regime transitions are particularly prominent within this school. O'Donnell and Schmitter[13] set the tone for much of this writing by evaluating the Latin American experiences of transition from authoritarian to democratic rule in the early 1980s. The specific challenges of regime transition in Africa have been discussed by Bratton and Van de Walle.[14] Some of the literature on governance also falls into this category. Hyden, for example, discusses the challenges facing African countries in terms of managing regimes, here defined as the "rules of the political game."[15] The difference between the "regime" and the "associational" schools is that the former concentrates its attention on the framework within which civil society can grow, while the latter focuses on its content. One does not preclude the other, as many organizations working in this field recognize.

For example, many human rights organizations spend their efforts shaping and monitoring adherence to the law of the land without denying the importance of the strength of associational life for democracy. A regime orientation is also naturally prevalent among the many constitutional bodies that have been set up to facilitate the transition to democracy. In several countries, such as Eritrea, Ethiopia, South Africa, and Uganda in Africa, government-appointed constitutional commissions have made a special effort to involve civil society in constitution-making by holding special hearings and inviting submissions from societal groups. In all these cases, there is a recognition that while containing state power is important, constitutionalizing relations among groups in civil society may be equally important. Civil society is not automatically democratic. Many groups may be using the relative freedom of civil society only to pursue anti-democratic objectives. To the extent that state and civil society are viewed as linked to each other, citizens rights must be balanced by citizen obligations. Furthermore, not all groups in civil society are ready to accept the existence of others. Justice and tolerance, therefore, are principles that civil society must learn to accept.

Neo-Liberal School

The "associational" and the "regime" schools both share a relatively optimistic view of civil society and its ability to make a difference to development. By largely ignoring the role of social structures, they assume a lot of scope for human agency. In this respect, they differ from the remaining two schools which take a more cautious view of what civil society can achieve on its own. The "neo-liberal" school, which draws its inspiration especially from Paine, particularly emphasizes the importance of structural reform to allow the strengthening of private property.

The historical relationship between capitalism and democracy is well known and has been explored in many different ways ever since Max Weber's time. The issue became especially important again in the 1980s when development analysts realized that "social engineering" using the state was a failure. Many experiments based on Keynesian ideas in Europe and Latin America and on Leninist ideas in Eastern Europe and Africa had proved untenable — more costly than beneficial to society. This policy of economic liberalization and financial stabilization has been called "structural adjustment" in the past decade and a half. While not explicitly being introduced to foster democracy, it is seen by many as an important corollary to ongoing political reform efforts.

However, this economic aspect of structural adjustment has generally received less attention than the social costs perceived as associated with this approach. One reason may be that the relationship between the market and democracy is by no means decisively clear.[16] For example, in the 1980s economic reforms were initially most successful in countries such as South Korea, Chile, Indonesia, and Mexico, all of which at that time had authoritarian forms of government. One often-cited reason for their success was that these governments did not have to cope with the inflationary demands of strong pressure groups in society. A weak civil society, therefore, was a boon rather than a bane.

More recently, some economists have come around to argue that economic freedoms are good for economic growth and, therefore, by implication in the neo-liberal view, for development. The clearest lesson from the collapse of communism is precisely that. To prosper, an economy must be allowed to order itself spontaneously in the main, according to the principles of competition and voluntary exchange. The invisible hand, in other words, works better than the visible boot.[17] On top of that can be added the importance of security of private property, which analysts believe is more easily secured in a liberal economy. It is not surprising that this anti-statist view was most pronounced among dissidents under communist rule in Eastern Europe.

Neo-liberals believe that a liberal economy creates the conditions under which a civil society of associations autonomous from the state can flourish. An interesting twist to their argument is the notion that economic freedoms alone may be worth little unless supported by political ones. For example, drawing on the historical experience of Europe, Olson argues forcefully that democracy is far more conducive to long-term economic growth than dictatorship, even of an apparently benevolent kind.[18]

Post-Marxist School

Apart from the Gramsci school, Marxists used to have little to say on the subject of civil society. They were more interested in seizing state power and doing so without accepting a pluralist arrangement. It is mainly in recent years that people on the political left have accepted the significance of civil society. They have done so by transcending the orthodox Marxist canons.

Like their neo-liberal counterparts, these "post-Marxist" analysts recognize the importance of social structures formed by the dominant economy. In contrast, however, they have a more sanguine view of the influence of structural reforms. Such reforms might be feasible but their effect is to reinforce social stratification and thus enhance elite interests. The point made by this school is that the ability to organize and participate is related to socio-economic status, so policy-making is usually the province of a select minority who have sufficient resources. Lindblom,[19] for example, reflects Hegel, Marx, and Gramsci when he speaks of government as having two separate spheres of authority, and business having a privileged position in politics because of the necessity for the production of material needs and its ability to more thoroughly socialize individuals in its norms.

Authors like Bayart[20] and Fatton[21] echo this position when they analyze civil society in terms of the power and domination exercised by specific social classes. In general, such writers are skeptical of ongoing economic and political reform processes. For them, the democratic transitions represent only minor adjustments rather than radical changes. Fundamental relations of power and privilege remain solidified. Rueschemeyer, Stephens and Stephens,[22] for example, examine how the capitalist mode of production transforms society and the regimes that result from different power relationships between classes. They emphasize the important role the working class has historically played in consolidating democracy, but they also point to the important influence of transnational power structures in the contemporary global setting. In general, these authors maintain that only the emergence of strong social movements capable of challenging existing power structures provide hope for a more fundamental change. Such movements — feminist, ecological, and others — have been more evident in post-materialist industrial societies than in developing and democratizing societies elsewhere. However, their role in certain parts of the developing world, notably Latin America,[23] should not be underestimated.

In concluding this review of how the contemporary debate relates to the philosophers pioneering the civil society concept, it may be worth emphasizing that inherent in the four schools identified above are two distinct roles that civil society tends to play in the context of democratization and development:

- First, it helps mobilize resources in ways the state alone is unable to do. Development benefits from the freedoms that civil society provides because people can take initiatives they would not otherwise do.

- Second, it socializes individuals in a democratic direction. Civil society associations look at the power structure from the bottom up and as a result, they tend to instill a participatory philosophy which emphasizes checks on abuses of power. A vibrant civil society is a necessary although not sufficient condition for democracy.

To fully appreciate the challenges of building social capital through civil society, I will examine the various levels at which the relationship between civil society, democracy, and development can be analyzed.

LEVELS OF ANALYZING CIVIL SOCIETY AND DEMOCRACY

The discussion so far has confirmed that civil society means different things to different people. Although there is no single view of the phenomenon, there is a tendency for most analysts to define civil society as the realm of organized social life standing between the individual and the state. The consequence of this outlook is that civil society tends to be analyzed primarily in the context of a single country. The latter becomes the most common level of analysis. There are, however, at least two other levels of analysis which in the contemporary context of building social capital and strengthening democracy become important.

One is the associational level. To fully appreciate the task of building social capital, it is important to know what is going on within civil society associations. How democratic are they? What norms or values do they foster? How do they relate to other associations? The other is the global or transnational level. Many advocacy organizations operate across national boundaries. They interpret issues in a global context and are interested in fostering civic values that apply to the global arena. For example, many of the strongest development NGOs are international. What are the implications of this "globalization" of civil society? In this section, I shall explore some of the specific issues that arise at each of these three different levels of analysis.

Country Level

The task of building social capital is always mediated by existing social structures. It is not possible to induce individuals to cooperate or respect one other without first paying attention to the institutions that make up society. Neither pure self-interest nor altruism alone can explain why social capital forms or why civil society flourishes in a given country.

Role of Tradition

One issue that has attracted attention in the development literature is to what extent traditional institutions can form the basis for the growth of civil society. In their extensive review of the role of local organizations in development, Esman and Uphoff[24] found they often play a positive role. For example, the Naam movement in Burkina Faso grew out of existing institutions among the Mossi people. Traditional ways of organizing may also serve as a model for new associations, as Dirven[25] shows with reference to rural trade unions in Bolivia. Korten[26] also adheres to this position when he argues that, as much as possible, new institutions should be made compatible with existing traditions and norms. This cluster of authors all take the position that civil society cannot be created from the top down. It has to grow organically from below. Working within existing institutions, while at the same time adapting them to new tasks and striving to make them more democratic, seems to be the preferred approach.

Others, however, maintain that traditional structures are hindrances to the evolution of a strong civil society. While indigenous organizations do not have to be controlled by elites, Julie Fisher[27] for example, found that new organizations emerging from below are least likely to be dominated by the already powerful. One of the best concrete examples of how civil society associations can be fostered to overcome traditional patterns of non-cooperation is Uphoff's study of the Gal Oya irrigation project in Sri Lanka.[28] A group of outside facilitators (Cornell researchers and government staff from the Agrarian Research and Training Institute) managed to persuade farmers to cooperate to improve the irrigation system so that water distribution dramatically improved and productivity on the land rose. Their approach was to build on the lowest common denominator — the property the farmers held in common. In this case, creating social capital involved circumventing traditional norms and authority, which became possible by institutionalizing new, initially informal, relations among the farmers.

Confrontation with the State

Another prominent issue in the literature analyzing civil society at the country level is whether or to what extent associations should adopt a confrontational approach towards the state. This issue has arisen particularly in the literature on human rights advocacy organizations. Because such associations are primarily concerned with the defense of individual liberties against the state, they almost inevitably get into a confrontational relationship with the authorities. There is no scope for compromise on these issues; an individual either enjoys these rights or does not. Activist organizations like Amnesty International and various branches of Human Rights Watch uphold the principles of civil and political rights of individuals at any price.[29]

Others, however, suggest that taking an uncompromising approach towards the state undercuts the overall objective of building social capital and strengthening civil society. This position is more common among developmental organizations for which the scope for bargaining with authorities over policy issues is also greater. Although sometimes criticized as cowardly, this position has been common with NGOs working in developing and democratizing countries because it has prevented them from being banned. At stake here, therefore, has been the question of what to do when the associational space is limited and civil society threatened. The most common answer has been that it is better to move slowly and try to enlarge available space without invoking the rage of those in power. However, Hadenius and Uggla[30] argue such a position is also fraught with its own risks. Entering into a relationship that allows the state to influence associational priorities may undercut their autonomy. Civil society leaders, furthermore, may become tempted to join the ranks of government leaders. This debate underscores that civil society associations are likely to have very different perceptions of strategy and tactics in their relation with the state.

Balancing the State's Power

Yet another issue of importance in the context of building civil society at the country level has been the question of how the state can be made to loosen its grip on society. Two major strategies have been discussed. The first is associated with breaking state monopoly over resource mobilization and allocation. Strengthening the market economy has been one way of delegating authority to individuals and organizations outside the state realm. This is a conspicuous component of the strategy of the World Bank and other donors in their effort to promote more democratic forms of governance. Although this effort has been couched more often in the terms of limiting "rent-seeking"[31] by state officials, its implications also affect civil society.

The other strategy involves decentralizing developmental responsibilities to local self-governing institutions. Ostrom[32] has been a particularly consistent advocate of the need for building autonomous organizations at the local level. This strategy, however, also requires a parallel devolution of political authority to local government institutions so these autonomous grassroots organizations, many of which are quite limited in geographical scope, have a chance of influencing public policy-making. The importance of a decentralized government structure that provides opportunity for local communities to make decisions about resource allocation, management, and distribution on their own has also been stressed by Brautigam[33] and Fox.[34] As the latter argues, pluralist politics must be learned and sub-national governments make the best school.[35]

Decentralization, however, is not a panacea. If local traditional patrons, for example, are able to control the state apparatus at its lower levels — as they do in many parts of the world — they may actually constitute a strong impediment to the emergence of civil society associations. Decentralization sometimes becomes just another means of strengthening the central government by way of patronage. Instead of being fostered, civil society in this scenario is choked.

Associational Level

The analysis at this level has largely centered on two questions:
- What institutions make up civil society?
- What qualities must associations possess in order to foster the process of democratization?

Institutions of Civil Society

The answers provided in response to the first question can be divided between a "minimalist" and a "maximalist" position. The minimalist argument tends define civil society associations as only those that are explicitly political or "civic" in the sense of fostering the norms of democracy.[36] In this perspective, there is a tendency to exclude organizations engaged in economic or productive activities. Some make a distinction, once made by Aristotle, between human activities of "work" (*techne*) and "interaction" (*praxis*), suggesting a communicative metaphor of the public sphere juxtaposed against an instrumentalist reading of manipulative work processes. The latter is not congenial to the development of democratic norms or the evolution of civil society. Arendt, Habermas, and Weil have argued along this line that politics is a vibrant and unique human activity. Their critique of modern society aims at freeing the subject from the "unnatural" technical domination they resolutely associate with work. Taken to a practical level, this suggests explicitly political or "civic" associations possess an autonomous capacity to shape the political sphere that other organizations lack.

The maximalist position, on the other hand, makes no distinction between political and other types of organization. Here, the spectrum of civil society associations ranges from small, exclusively local organizations in neighborhoods to organizations with a national orientation and membership. Activities range from those with a social or cultural focus, such as drama groups and sports clubs, to profit-making or service provision, such as producer associations, trade unions, and private hospitals. Anything that takes place outside the state realm counts as part of civil society and contributes to building social capital. In this context, the writings of Putnam are of particular interest,[37] because he describes groups having little directly to do with politics that are instrumental in fostering civil norms and thus building social capital. In his attempt to explain the developmental differences between northern and southern Italy, he concludes that organizations like choral groups may have played an important role in building trust and thus cooperation.

Qualities of Associations

The second question focuses on the qualities of civil society associations. The point here is that not all these associations necessarily promote democracy. Civil society associations may be places for egotistical pursuits.[38] They may also be places in which authoritarian values are nurtured. In short, civil society can undercut democracy if its associations pursue values that go against tolerance and respect for others. For example, in many societies currently undergoing democratization, the objectives of civil society are being threatened by anti-democratic organizations. Russia is a case in point, where fascist tendencies have cropped up in the post-Soviet period. Many women argue that civil society associations remain sexist and thus hamper participation by women in public affairs. Yet others focus on the racial or ethnic exclusivity of some of these organizations, maintaining that they must be more inclusive in order to promote democracy. Although it is possible, in line with the maximalist position above, to argue that any association regardless of its internal characteristics is part of civil society, the tendency is to assume that these associations must have some distinct qualities in order to qualify as "civil" or "civic." In other words, analysts make a definite normative choice in favor of criteria typically associated with democracy.

Criteria for Defining "Civil" Associations

Analysts have identified several criteria they consider important for understanding which associations qualify to be part of civil society. One is autonomy. A civil society association should be independent of the state in terms of decisional competence, recruitment of leaders, and control of important economic and managerial resources. It is no coincidence that authoritarian regimes have tried to curb the activities of civil society by circumscribing the autonomy of its associations.[39]

A second criterion is that associations should be democratically structured. They should be microcosms of civil society itself, so members are socialized to internalize values compatible with democracy. The more horizontal the decision-making structures in an organization, the more likely it will foster democratic values. Organizations with a very hierarchical constitution or those dominated by patron-client relations are less likely to contribute toward a democratic civil society.

A third criterion important for fostering a democratic organizational culture is accountability. There must be procedural mechanisms for members to hold leaders accountable for their decisions and actions. Procedures, however, are not always enough. Action speaks louder than words and elected leaders must be ready to respect the principle of accountability and voluntarily accept its significance in the context of fostering a stronger civil society.

A fourth criterion is open recruitment. This is particularly important for the purpose of social or national integration. Exclusive and closed associations tend to be less democratically inclined. Such organizations become particularly problematic in societies characterized by cultural pluralism, where many ethnic, racial, or religious groups live together in the same nation-state. In countries where exclusive associations predominate, civil society is polarized, turning politics into a "zero-sum" game. Multiple affiliation through open recruitment enables individuals to be members of more than one association. Multiple or cross-cutting memberships encourage individuals to seek common ground in ways that foster tolerance and respect of others. In these respects, open recruitment promotes a democratic culture that strengthens civil society.[40]

This last point is particularly important to emphasize because there is a tendency to look at NGOs in developing countries almost exclusively in terms of how their role in development management can be strengthened. For example, the primary emphasis is on creating networks or other forms of linkages. While this is important, much of the debate on the role of NGOs is too instrumental and overlooks the inherent potential for democratization embedded in these organizations. They are not merely resource mobilizers or providers. They are also, at least potentially, serving an important role as socializing agents. If they are democratically constituted, they are likely to make a significant contribution to the formation of a vibrant civil society that is also tolerant, fostering democracy rather than autocracy.

In conclusion, one can argue that civil society is no better than the sum of its associations. Little social capital of value for democracy will be built unless the associations that make up civil society respect and adhere to democratic values in their own internal governance. Values and norms institutionalized at the associational level are likely to be the strongest bulwark against attacks by the enemies of democracy. In the historical experience of many countries, cooperative societies, trade unions, and grassroots movements have served as the vanguard of democracy. In such associational contexts, the social capital needed for democracy is formed.

Global Level

One of the most interesting developments in recent years has been the rapid growth of independent transnational organizations. The building of social capital to strengthen civic and democratic norms no longer takes place at the national level only. Two aspects of this globalization of the norms of democracy are particularly important. The first relates to the "universalization" of specific policy issues and the evolution of organizations serving as global advocates, such as Greenpeace and Amnesty International in the fields of environmental conservation and human rights respectively. Donor agencies are also increasingly pushing the democratic agenda in developing countries. On this agenda, the notion of building social capital through strengthening civil society has been very prominent. The consequence of the globalization of the civil society discourse is that pressures to democratize no longer come only from within a country but also from outside. The lobbyists for democracy are not only national but also international, a development which has interesting implications for the analysis of civil society.

In the context of this paper, it is important to note that transnational activist organizations are not merely seeking to change state policies or create conditions in the international system that enhance or diminish interstate cooperation.[41] They are influencing the whole of civil society, defined as the arena of social engagement which exists above the individual yet below the state,[42] encompassing a complex network of economic, social, and cultural practices based on friendship, family, the market, and voluntary affiliation. Increasingly, this concept is beginning to make sense not only at the national but also the international level, thanks to the proliferation of transnational collective endeavors and the intermeshing of symbolic meaning systems.

For example, market forces shape the way vast numbers of people in countries around the world think and act on specific public issues. Voluntary associations or social movements based on religion, such as Christian-based communities in Latin America, represent significant attempts to politicize public arenas and bring about change. Women are organized into movements on an international scale, as in the huge NGO Forum associated with the Fourth World Conference on Women in Beijing in September 1995. There is now a global alliance for citizen participation, CIVICUS, whose aim is to strengthen global civil society.[43]

Clearly, civil society is no longer just that slice of associational life that exists between the individual and the state at the country level but also across national boundaries.[44] When transnational activists direct their efforts beyond the state, they are politicizing global civil society, identifying and manipulating instruments of power for shaping collective life. In short, it is too limiting to think of NGOs in world affairs merely as transnational interest groups.

Their political relevance goes beyond this by forging new alliances across national boundaries, reconceptualizing public issues, and empowering local communities. They are building social capital through long-distance relations, thereby helping to promote a "global civil society."

Bilateral and multilateral donors are increasingly playing an important role in this process. By tying development aid to the readiness of developing country governments to accept democratic norms of governance, they help foster the evolution of a new form of global governance that encroaches on the previously sacred notion of state sovereignty. Such aid is often channeled through international NGOs, which strengthens their power vis-à-vis national governments, particularly in developing countries, and helps provide the political space that enables NGOs to influence not only governments, but also civil society in these countries. In fact, it can be argued that the influence of most international NGOs in developing countries tends to be more at the civil society than the state level. For example, many NGOs have had a marked influence on how people in these countries view development in new ways that have yet to be adopted by governments. In fields such as public health and environmental conservation, donor-funded NGOs have helped reshape the character of public opinion and public life.

The prominence of donors, however, is problematic in that many beneficiaries of their financial support tend to lose their autonomy. The donors are not rooted in domestic conditions in these countries and therefore their ability to sustain collective activities is often limited. Associational life in many places tends to be so dependent on donor funding that civil society is very fragile. Thus, there is sometimes a conflict between the ambition to foster civil society at the global and the national level. International NGOs tend to focus on the global level at the expense of their potential contribution in fostering associational life at the national level. There is a limit to how far democracy in developing countries can be built with the assistance of international actors, be they NGOs or donors.[45] This issue needs to be fully recognized and further studied.

CHALLENGES

The challenge of building civil society can be meaningfully studied at the same three levels previously outlined — country, associational, and global. It is also important to recognize that efforts at these different levels interact with each other; they do not take place in isolation. For example, the emergence of a social movement like the Greens with a democratic self-governing agenda influences the nature of civil society in a given country but also invites alliances with similar movements in other parts of the world. It would be wrong to assume, however, that civic norms spread evenly throughout the world or that building civil society consists of a linear process from transition to consolidation. Strengthening civil society is essentially a political task and as such likely to be contested by those threatened by an open and accountable associational life. The evolution of civil society has been a long and contradictory process. It is going to be no different as the process extends to regions of the world where the concept is still new and foreign.

However, more and stronger social forces are geared up to fulfill this task than ever before. The past two decades have witnessed remarkable progress for democracy. Since 1972, the number of democratic political systems has more than doubled, from 44 to 107. Three out of five of the world's 187 countries have adopted a democratic form of government.[46] With the collapse of communism, democracy has reached every region of the world for the first time in history and, as Huntington[47] has noted, it has become "the only legitimate and viable alternative to an authoritarian regime of any kind." Civil society has been both a cause and a consequence of this process. In many places around the world, the rise of civil society has contributed to the emergence of democratic government. In others, its rise has been facilitated by the introduction of a democratically elected government. Democracy has provided the political space in which new forms of social capital can be built.

Because of these complexities, the challenges of building civil society are bound to vary from place to place. The challenges are greatest outside North America and Western Europe. In Latin America, for instance, civil society has been particularly threatened in the past thirty years. In much of Africa and Asia, it is a novel concept that is viewed with suspicion by those in power. This does not mean that civil society is not a challenge in North America and Western Europe. In the former, associational life has, at least according to Putnam,[48] been threatened by a growing tendency among people to do things on their own; "bowling alone," as he calls it. Although others question the extent to which this is a dominant trend, individualization is a potential threat to the vibrancy of civil society in the United States. The challenge in Western Europe is related largely to the contraction of the welfare state. Most West Europeans have grown accustomed to a benevolent state which has largely pre-empted the need for autonomous associations catering to citizens' material needs. As this system is no longer financially sustainable, the question is how far citizens in these countries are ready to take responsibility for these matters through civil society associations.

Turning to the other regions, three basic scenarios can be sketched out to describe the range of challenges the world faces as it moves towards the 21st century. The first focuses on limiting the role of the state in the public realm. In this scenario, civil society is already relatively strong and capable of autonomous action to achieve this end. The second centers on the task of strengthening civil society. Here, civic associations are weak and rarely able to challenge state authority. In the third scenario, the challenge is a dual one. Here, both state and civil society are weak and need developing.

Limiting the State

This scenario takes on special significance in Latin America where much recent democratization can be attributed to the failure of an authoritarian state to solve economic and other social problems. In these countries, democracy is not a new ideology or practice. In fact, most Latin American countries have had at least one, in some cases, two spells of democratic governance prior to the "wave" that began in the early 1980s. Although the pattern varies from country to country, the Latin American region has a tradition of relatively strong trade unions. In the past two decades, civil society has also been enriched by the emergence of social movements. These include Christian-based organizations drawing on liberation theology, feminism, and environmental conservation, notably of the bio-diverse Amazon basin. The frequent human rights abuses by previous dictatorial regimes have also served as an impetus for the emergence of civil society associations. Civil society has continued to grow in strength in opposition to a powerful but illegitimate state.

The "attack" on the state has taken two forms. One has been the effort by civil society associations to constitutionalize power relations in new ways. They have facilitated the introduction of democratic regimes in which civil and political liberties are guaranteed and public accountability effectively secured. Particularly good cases in point are Argentina and Chile, where the legacy of excessive abuses of power by the military in the 1970s provided a rationale for the calls by civil society associations to limit the powers of the executive. In both countries, the democratic transition in the past decade has been quite successful. In other Latin American countries, such as Brazil, it has been more problematic, yet not unsuccessful. Elsewhere, countries where a strong civil society has played a catalytic role in the democratic transition include the Philippines in the 1980s and South Africa in the 1990s.

The other form has been the effort to privatize the economy to reduce the role of the state in development. The Keynesian tradition of an interventionist welfare state was inherited in many Latin American countries, such as Argentina, Chile, Mexico, and Uruguay, for the same reasons as in Western Europe — to manage economic growth and control distribution of benefits and resources. Part of the transition in the past in that part of the world has centered on liberalizing the economy by reducing state control. Although this transition has been resisted in many places and has happened slowly, some countries like Argentina and Chile have created greater opportunities for private business and reduced the opportunity for state officials to seek "rents" added to the cost of providing public services. In spite of the strong support in many of these countries for a state-led strategy of development in the past, the failure of both military and civilian authoritarian governments to bring back economic growth in the 1970s and early 1980s, has reinforced the demands for regime transition.[49]

This scenario also applies in different ways to Eastern Europe and the former Soviet Union. In this region, there was no real tradition of a strong civil society, but particularly in the 1980s, underground movements were developing in many communist countries and challenging the totalitarian governments in the field of human rights. Solidarity in Poland and Charter 77 in the former Czechoslovakia are the best known of these organizations. Another difference is the communist economy proved incapable of sustaining itself as division of labor became increasingly complex. Transaction costs became so heavy the economy collapsed under their weight. The withering away of central planning and direction paved the way for economic reform which in turn opened the doors for civil society associations to grow in importance.[50] Again, the situation in the mid-1990s varies from country to country in this region, but it seems reasonable to suggest that civil society rests on a stronger foundation in Latin America than in Eastern Europe and the former Soviet Union. The prospect of bringing about economic and political reform, and thereby strengthening civil society, seems easier and brighter in the former as compared to the latter region.

Strengthening Civil Society

Not all governments in developing countries see democratization as a positive phenomenon. This is especially true of governments in the Muslim world and in many East and Southeast Asian countries. Western attempts to motivate and pressure these countries to adopt democracy have met with little success. A growing sense of solidarity among these countries makes it difficult for the international community to isolate or effectively pressure any single country. Nonetheless, governments in Asia are coming to recognize that popular sovereignty is a key component of political legitimacy. At the non-governmental level, especially in Southeast Asia, there is a growing political consciousness and increasing support for both democracy and human rights. The values of democracy and human rights are thus becoming part of the domestic political discourse and can no longer be excluded by fiat, except in a few places in the Muslim world. Perhaps most important, nearly all governments now embrace the principles of a market economy. Because economic growth frequently leads to greater political openness, economic liberalization is likely to have the greatest potential for inducing democratic change in these countries.

A strong reason for the reluctance of leaders in East and Southeast Asian countries to accept more pluralist forms of governance is that the state has proved to be a catalyst for development in ways it has not in Africa or Latin America. Economic growth in the Asian context has been achieved with a strong and interventionist state. The economic successes of these countries were reached with strategies that contradict those the international finance institutions have been trying to get governments in other regions of the world to adopt. Civil society has played a minor role in paving the way for economic and social development in these countries. Their trade-based growth strategies have largely relied on state initiatives and regulation.

Most Asian leaders would agree that economic reform must precede political reform. That is why, for instance, Singapore's senior minister, Lee Kuan Yew[51] has been campaigning against a blanket introduction of Western democracy in Asia. Lee and others have been particularly skeptical of Western advice on this issue and have insisted that only incumbent governments can decide on issues like the pace of reform and the sequence to be followed in developing their countries. To them, discipline matters more than democracy. Strengthening civil society, like democracy, therefore, is not a top priority in these Asian countries. This is clear, for example, from the final declaration of the Asian regional human rights conference in Bangkok, in which government representatives attest to the high premium they place on sovereignty and non-interference in domestic affairs.[52] The same position is also widely embraced by governments in the Muslim world, where religious dogma is often invoked to prevent the growth of civil society associations. In an orthodox Islamic perspective, there is no scope for action outside the religious realm dominated by appointed leaders. That is why not only civil society is marginalized but also why the relations between temporal and spiritual authority remain unsettled.

Although government leaders resist and often outright oppose the idea of building a stronger and more democratic civil society, there is a small but growing constituency for doing precisely this — even in countries like Indonesia, China, and Burma. Despite being labeled a "threat from the left" by the Indonesian government and a "threat from the right" by the Chinese government, democratic governance has become part of the contemporary political discourse in these countries. The Tianamen Square incident in 1989 shows there is a constituency for strengthening civil society in China, although it is difficult to gauge its size. It is also worth noting that the meeting of Asian NGOs that preceded the regional intergovernmental human rights meeting in Bangkok endorsed the significance of civil and political rights. Their starting point was the citizen, not government; civil society, not the state.

The existence and work of these organizations and individuals, in the face of grave danger to their lives, families, and property, at least partially refute the position taken by the governing elites that democracy and human rights are Western concepts with no resonance in Asian political culture. Although these constituencies are becoming more salient, their importance should not be exaggerated. These groups are still relatively small. Through repression, co-optation, and control over the funding and activities of these emerging associations, governments in these countries closely control civil society, both informally and formally.

In the short run, therefore, the prospects of these groups influencing the system of government are limited. Compared to the state, civil society remains weak and will need to be strengthened in order to obtain greater respect for democracy and human rights in these countries. In the long run, this may prove possible, particularly during a "crisis of authority." Economic growth, industrialization, higher levels of education, and the accompanying growth of the middle class are likely to sharpen the public's political consciousness and increase its awareness of the importance of popular sovereignty. These, however, are only long-term consequences and there is no guarantee they will lead to greater acceptance of democracy and human rights unless NGOs take deliberate measures to strengthen civil society. The latter objective is likely to be a prerequisite for reducing authoritarian tendencies in these countries.

Strengthening Both State and Civil Society

Civil society presupposes the existence of a public realm in which there is a clear delineation of rights and obligations between individual citizens and the state. There needs to be a legal and constitutional framework which applies equally to everyone. A society lacks in civility if some members believe they stand above the law. In states where this is the case the rule of law is in question. In these countries, the task of building civil society cannot be seen in isolation from building the state. If the latter lacks what Max Weber referred to as a "legal-rational" foundation for its authority, building civil society is bound to run into special problems. This is the challenge particularly in sub-Saharan Africa.

The reason for this complication in Africa is the prevalence of what political analysts refer to as "neo-patrimonialism."[53] Drawing again on Weber,[54] patrimonialism can be characterized as a system of rule in which all governmental authority and the corresponding economic rights tend to be treated as privately appropriated economic advantages and where governmental powers and the associated advantages are treated as private rights. Historically, this form of rule has existed everywhere. Kings and chiefs alike saw no difference between the public and the private realms. Taxes, or tributes, as they typically were called, were retained by the ruler as part of his household even though it was collected by titular officials. Remnants of the system are retained in the titles of British government officials. By reining in the powers of kings and constitutionalizing relations between different groups or actors in society, a public realm was gradually established. It was in this space the modern state arose and civil society was built.

"Neo-patrimonialism" exists in societies where the impact of the modern state has been felt but where prevailing social norms make no such distinction between private and public realms. It is particularly common in former colonies, especially those in sub-Saharan Africa, where the influence of the modern state was confined temporally to 60-70 years and spatially by virtue of the limited number of colonial officers employed in the enterprise. Here modern bureaucratic norms coexist with patrimonial ones. Public policy is mediated by the struggle between these two sets of norms. This situation is different from the patrimonialist society of the past, where there was no such contestation between norms upholding a public as opposed to a private realm. For example, in seeking legitimization, the neo-patrimonialist state refers to public norms and universal ideologies. These provide a facade behind which patrimonialist values can be pursued. That is why "corruption" in neo-patrimonial states is from the point of view of imported public norms, not by the prevailing private norms in these societies.

At the core of neo-patrimonialism in Africa is the tendency of rulers to personalize power relations. This has been going on ever since independence as part of the desire to indigenize the rule of these societies. For a long time, the rest of the world saw no reason to react to this trend, either because it was believed to be a matter of state sovereignty or that African societies must find their own way to develop and thus they should be allowed to experiment. In recent years, however, the position of the outsiders has changed. There is no longer the same willingness to let the Africans continue on their own, especially since these outsiders believe the limited impact of their foreign aid can be attributed to inadequate forms of governance. Neo-patrimonialism, therefore, is on attack from the outside. Many Africans too, however, are fed up with the private accumulation of wealth and power that has taken place in these neo-patrimonialist regimes. That is why there is a growing interest among members of both the elite and the public at large in Africa to bring about the rule of law and the delineation of rights and obligations between state and individuals so the task of building civil society can become a reality in their countries also.

This task, however, is not likely to prove easy. Neo-patrimonialism is a phenomenon that cannot be disposed of overnight because the whole power structure in post-colonial African societies has rested on the assumption of its general acceptance. Thus, calling it into question or attempting to wipe it out is bound to be associated with political instability. The examples of Liberia, Rwanda, and Somalia are often invoked — not always correctly — to highlight the dangers of overthrowing neo-patrimonialism. Yet, this process is ongoing across the continent and the political battle lines in the past few years, and probably in the years to come, are not likely to be between the "right" and the "left" but between advocates of neo-patrimonialism and those of constitutionalism. The latter constituency is made up of those who believe that peace and stability, democracy and development are only possible with the creation of a strong public realm in which rights and obligations are known and protected.

Even in countries that have not collapsed, such as Cameroon, Kenya, and Nigeria, neo-patrimonialism is not easily dislodged. At the crucial junctures of elections, there prove to be too many ways those in power can rig elections to their advantage. Electoral monitoring by external or internal groups has not been able to prevent this happening. The ability of neo-patrimonial rulers to survive and continue their arbitrary rule has caused special concern among donors who disapprove of their behavior but who wish to aid the people of these countries because they are poor. The tendency has been to apply economic pressures on the governments of these rulers, but there is little evidence that this leads to a change of heart. Instead, as the case of Kenya illustrates, the whole exercise turns into a cat-and-mouse game, in which the mouse (Kenya) tries as much as possible to escape the claws of the donors.

Some of the same difficulties apply also to the large number of international NGOs that work in Africa. Unlike the donors, they cannot escape the whims of neo-patrimonial rule but have to learn how to live with them. Viewing themselves as part of the effort to build civil society, do they try to help reform African societies from within by accepting neo-patrimonialism or do they take a confrontational approach, refusing to accept these norms? The tendency among development-oriented organizations has been to work from within, using their development work as a catalyst to achieve change in the right direction. Rights-based organizations, on the other hand, have taken a much more uncompromising stand and typically have accused the neo-patrimonial regimes of serious human rights violations.

Both these stands make practical sense given the agendas of these types of organizations. However, there is no easy victory, because becoming part of local African society in ways that make the latter demand not only "goods" but also the right to decide on the rules for allocating these goods takes time and requires civic courage that has no precedent in these societies. In Africa, therefore, the task at the turn of the millennium is not to limit the powers of the state but rather to create a public realm in which both a state, in the legal-rational sense, and civil society can be built. However this double challenge is met is likely to determine whether African societies develop or fall further behind in the years to come.

CONCLUSION

The rise of civil society is for the first time a global phenomenon. It is no longer confined to a few economically advanced and privileged countries in the West. The idea that even the poor have rights and can exercise them is now being spread to all corners of the world. This is an important aspect of the ongoing process of globalization as the next century approaches. A hundred years ago, this idea was being embraced by social groups in Europe representing workers and women, who until then had been denied the right to participate in public affairs. After years of imperialism and colonialism, the principle that every human being has the democratic right to participate in public affairs through voluntary associations — in civil society — is finally being extended to those who have suffered most throughout the world. To be sure, it is being opposed and contested in many places but by being on the global agenda, it will not easily disappear. Rulers who deny the rights of their citizens are under increasing pressure to change.

Civil society is Western in origin and although the concept is now being used in all parts of the world, no doubt many will find difficulty making sense of it. Normative concepts such as democracy or civil society do not always "travel" well. In cultures different from the ones in which the concept first arose, one should expect that people will adapt it to their own circumstances. This means civil society will come to have many faces. There will be a struggle between the "universal" and the "particular," between the ideas that human values and norms are shared by all regardless of race and religion, and the idea that these norms and values are determined by specific cultures. One would expect this to be the case, particularly in countries where Islamic or Confucian principles reign. The same scenario may also be evident in African countries where local associations build on a strong self-help tradition grounded in African customs. Regardless of the particular circumstances prevailing in a country, building civil society requires the ability to empathize, to see the world from the side of those not yet convinced. It requires strategy but also the readiness to make tactical concessions. None of this is easy; the risks of mistakes are many.

Finally, civil society will never become a global reality without networking and exchange of ideas. Local perceptions of what is right and wrong or how to do things must be allowed a voice and be listened to by others before they are dismissed. Civil society is not built by ignoring others or by shouting them down. It comes about through tolerance and the readiness to dialogue with others. This is how the social capital that helps develop countries is being formed.

NOTES

1. Robert D. Putnam. *Making Democracy Work: Civic Traditions in Modern Italy*. Princeton: Princeton University Press, 1993.

2. Edward C. Banfield. *The Moral Basis of a Backward Society*. Chicago: The Free Press, 1958.

3. Filippo Sabetti. "Democracy, Social Capital and Unity of Law: Some Lessons From Italy About Interpreting Social Experiments." Department of Political Science, McGill University, Montreal, n.d.

4. (a) Jean-Francois Medard. "Conclusion: Etatisation et desetatisation en Afrique noire." in J.F. Medard. (ed.) *Etats d'Afrique noire: formations, mecanismes, et crise*: Paris: Karthala, 1991. (b) Jean Francois Bayart. *The State in Africa: The Politics of the Belly*. New York: Longman, 1992. (c) Dirk Berg-Schlosser and Ralf Rytlewski. "Political Culture in Germany: A Paradigmatic Case." in D. Berg-Schlooser and R. Rytlewski. (eds.) *Political Culture in Germany*. St. Martin's Press: New York, 1993.

5. Alfred Stepan. "State Power and the Strength of Civil Society in the Southern Cone of Latin America." in P. Evans, D. Rueschemeyer and T. Skocpol. (eds.) *Bringing the State Back In*. Cambridge: Cambridge University Press, 1985.

6. Larry Diamond. "Toward Democratic Consolidation." *Journal of Democracy*. Volume 5, Number 3, 1994. pp. 4-17.

7. *Ibid*. p. 6.

8. Piotr Sztompka. "The Intangibles and Imponderables of the Transition to Democracy." *Studies in Comparative Communism*. Volume 24, Number 3, 1991. pp. 3-20.

9. Craig Calhoun. "Civil Society and the Public Sphere." *Public Culture*. Volume 5, Number 3, 1993. pp. 267-280.

10. Putnam. *op.cit*.

11. David Truman. *The Governmental Process*. New York: Alfred Knopf, 1951.

12. Robert Dahl. *Who Governs?* New Haven: Yale University Press, 1961.

13. Guillermo O'Donnell and Philippe C. Schmitter. *Transitions from Authoritarian Rule: Tentative Conclusions about Uncertain Democracies*. Baltimore: Johns Hopkins University Press, 1986.

14. Michael Bratton and Nicolas van de Walle. "Neopatrimonial Regimes and Political Transitions in Africa." *World Politics*. Volume 46, Number 4, 1994. pp. 453-489.

15. Goran Hyden. "Governance and the Study of Politics." in G. Hyden and M. Bratton. (eds.) *Governance and Politics in Africa*. Boulder: Lynne Rienner Publisher, 1992.

16. Adam Przeworski. *Democracy and the Market*. New York: Cambridge University Press, 1990.

17. *The Economist*. "Democracy and Growth." 27 August 1994.

18. Mancur Olson. "Dictatorship, Democracy, and Development." *American Political Science Review*. Volume 87, Number 3, 1993. pp. 567-576.

19. Charles E. Lindblom. *Politics and Markets*. New York: Basic Books, 1977.

20. Bayart. *op. cit.*

21. Robert Fatton. *Predatory Rule: The State and Civil Society in Africa*. Boulder: Lynne Rienner Publisher, 1993.

22. Dietrich Rueschemeyer, E. H. Stephens and J. Stephens. *Capitalist Development and Democracy*. Chicago: University of Chicago Press, 1992.

23. Arturo Escobar and Sonia E. Alvarez. (eds.) *The Making of Social Movements in Latin America*. Boulder: Westview Press, 1992.

24. Milton J. Esman and Norman T. Uphoff. *Local Organizations: Intermediaries in Rural Development*. Ithaca: Cornell University Press, 1984.

25. Martine Dirven. "Rural Society: Its Integration and Disintegration." *CEPAL Review*. Volume 51, 1993. pp. 4-8.

26. David C. Korten. *Getting into the 21st Century: Voluntary Action and the Global Agenda*. West Hartford: Kumarian Press, 1990.

27. Julie Fisher. "Is the Iron Law of Oligarchy Rusting Away in the Third World?" *World Development*. Volume 22, Number 2, 1994. pp. 129-143.

28. Norman T. Uphoff. *Learning From Gal Oya*. Ithaca: Cornell University Press, 1992.

29. Ronald Cohen, Goran Hyden and Winston Nagan. *Human Rights and Governance in Africa*. Gainesville: University Presses of Florida, 1993.

30. Axel Hadenius and Fredrik Uggla. "Making Civil Society Work." in A. Hadenius. (ed.) *Democracy's Victory and Crisis*. London: Cambridge University Press, 1996.

31. "Rent-seeking" is a term that has grown out of the literature on transaction costs and is broader than bribery. It suggests that state officials are taking advantage of their position, thus adding to the costs of what is being done.

32. Elinor Ostrom. *Governing the Commons: The Evolution of Institutions for Collective Action*. New York: Cambridge University Press, 1990.

33. Deborah Brautigam. "Governance, Economy, and Foreign Aid." *Studies in Comparative International Development*. Volume 27, No. 3, 1992. pp. 3-25.

34. Jonathan Fox. "Latin America's Emerging Local Politics." *Journal of Democracy*. Volume 5, Number 2, 1994. pp. 106-116.

35. This was also the argument of officers in the British colonial administration in the period leading up to decolonization. The idea that local governments were schools for learning democratic norms, however, was deemed too paternalistic by African nationalists who at that time were more interested in seizing national power, paying only little attention to how it was achieved.

36. John Harbeson, Donald Rothchild and Naomi Chazan. (eds.) *Civil Society and the State in Africa.* Boulder: Lynne Rienner Publisher, 1994.

37. Putnam. *op. cit.*

38. Calhoun. *op. cit.*

39. Hadenius and Fredrik Uggla. *op. cit.*

40. Claus Offe. "Micro-Aspects of Democratic Theory: What Makes the Deliberative Competency of the Citizens?" in A. Hadenius. (ed.) *Democracy's Victory and Crisis.* Cambridge: Cambridge University Press, 1996.

41. Paul Wapner. "Politics beyond the State: Environmental Activism and World Civic Politics" *World Politics.* Volume 47, Number 3, 1995. pp. 311-340.

42. (a) John Keane. *Democracy and Civil Society.* London: Verso Publishers, 1988. (b) Jean Cohen and Andrew Arato. *Civil Society and Political Theory.* Cambridge, Massachusetts: MIT Press, 1992.

43. Miguel Darcy de Oliveira and Rajesh Tandon. (eds.) *Citizens Strengthening Global Civil Society.* Washington DC: CIVICUS, World Alliance for Citizen Participation, 1994.

44. Michael Walzer. (ed.) *Toward a Global Civil Society.* Providence: Berghahn Books, 1995.

45. (a) Michael Bratton. "International Versus Domestic Pressures for 'Democratization' in Africa." *Michigan State University Working Papers on Political Reform in Africa,* Number 12. East Lansing: Department of Political Science, Michigan State University, 1994. (b) Joel D. Barkan. "Can Established Democracies Nurture Democracy Abroad? Lessons From Africa." in Axel Hadenius. (ed.) *Democracy's Victory and Crisis.* London: Cambridge University Press, 1996.

46. Doh Chull Shin. "On the Third Wave of Democratization: A Synthesis and Evaluation of Recent Theory and Research." *World Politics.* Volume 47, Number 1, 1994. pp. 136.

47. Samuel P. Huntington. *The Third Wave.* Norman: Oklahoma University Press, 1992. p. 58.

48. Robert D. Putnam. "Bowling Alone: America's Declining Social Capital." *Journal of Democracy.* Volume 6, Number 1, 1995. pp. 65-78.

49. Joan Nelson. *Fragile Coalitions: The Politics of Economic Adjustment.* New Brunswick: Transaction Books, 1989.

50. Sztompka, 1991; and Michael Bernhard. "Civil Society and Democratic Transition in East Central Europe." *Political Science Quarterly.* Volume 108, Number 3, 1993. pp. 307-326.

51. Lee Kuan Yew. "Democracy and Human Rights for the World." *Media Asia.* Volume 20, Number 1, 1993. pp. 37-38.

52. Mutiah Alagappa. "Democratic Transition in Asia: The Role of the International Community." *East-West Center Special Reports No 3*. Honolulu, October 1994. p. 8.

53. (a) Jean-Francois Medard. "The Underdeveloped State in Tropical Africa: Political Clientelism or Neo-Patrimonialism." in C. Clapham. (ed.) *Private Patronage and Public Power: Political Clientelism in the Modern State*. London: Frances Pinter, 1982. (b) Thomas Callaghy. *The State-Society Struggle: Zaire in Comparative Perspective*. New York: Columbia University Press, 1984. (c) Bratton and van de Walle. *op. cit.*

54. Max Weber. *The Theory of Social and Economic Organization*. Edited with an introduction by Talcott Parsons. New York: The Free Press, 1947.

Section II

THE GLOBAL MOSAIC OF CIVIL SOCIETY

Introduction

People coming together and helping each other solve problems is by no means a novelty .... What is distinctive about today is the extension of the virtues of solidarity and responsibility to the public sphere on a global scale.

— Miguel Darcy de Oliveira and Rajesh Tandon

G lobality is one of the undisputed givens of our time. It is the context in which we all live and is intensifying daily. Therefore, it is not surprising that a concept such as "civil society" should find a home so readily in all corners of the globe today. Although the impetus for its being and the conditions for its acceptance vary greatly from place to place, civil society is one of the common threads of the human community as people demand a greater say in defining and controlling their destinies, seek greater accountability and responsiveness from governments, and challenge the growing power and value systems of the international market place.

The first half of this book reflects the diverse faces of civil society around the world. It does not attempt to provide a comprehensive coverage and analysis of civil society on all continents. Others have made useful strides in this direction.[1] Rather, this "global mosaic of civil society" describes a variety of methods and approaches being used to enhance citizen engagement in quite contrasting social and cultural settings. Different chapters emphasize different aspects of civil society — the power of voluntary associations; the norms or values of reciprocity, trust, tolerance and inclusion; and the use of networks of public communication — but all point to the close relationship between a vibrant civil society and a well-functioning state.

In his chapter on "Populism, Islam, and Civil Society in the Arab World," Saad Eddin Ibrahim reminds us that although the concept of civil society has Western European origins, its reality is much broader and deeper. He shows how contemporary Arab civil society is rooted in pre-modern Arab traditions of public participation through such mechanisms as merchant guilds, religious sects, and ethnic organizations. He also underscores the strong link between civil society and democracy, making the case that both are developing in the Arab world, just as they have in the West over several centuries in what has been a "long, arduous, and occasionally bloody march."[2]

Susan Fertig-Dykes illustrates just how long, arduous, and bloody that battle can be in her description of civil society initiatives rising Phoenix-like from the ashes of war in the former Yugoslavia. As one of thousands who have come to the region from outside to help carve out a civic sector in this battered and divisive society, she speaks about the complexity of building partnerships between foreign NGOs and indigenous associations, as well as among local organizations themselves. She also highlights the fundamental necessity of establishing the rule of law and the vital role played by a free media in allowing civil society to take hold.

In their focus on Ethiopia, Terry Bergdall and Frank Powell offer valuable insights into how civil society is manifesting itself at the grassroots in this ancient society, despite a history of feudal imperialism and centralized communism, and a dependency mindset reinforced by international relief programs. Through years of systematic application, they have demonstrated the power of participatory methods to transform perceptions, prejudices, and practices of both government officials and community members. In so doing, they point to the crucial role of working with both the public and civic sectors in a climate of trust, respect, and reciprocity to create civil society.

This relationship between citizens and governments receives even greater attention in James Troxel's chapter on the recovery of civic engagement in the United States. He makes a compelling case that both a radical renewal of citizenship and a concomitant transformation in the role of government are necessary for civil society to be revitalized in the USA. In contrast to the writings of Robert Putnam and others, he perceives a resurgence of associational life in America today. Although he acknowledges efforts to "reinvent government" in the United States, he maintains it is only when both these trends converge in a symbiotic relationship that a new form of civic governance is possible and civil society is revitalized.

In similar vein, but from a totally different setting, Marlene Kanawati argues that the challenge today is to unite communities and create a connection between the state and citizens to reconstitute civil society. From her experience in working with rural and urban communities in Egypt, she has found Participatory Rapid Appraisal (PRA) to be a highly effective methodology for doing that, especially among women, the poor, and the disadvantaged who are often denied a voice in decision-making. It helps people realize their power as individuals and in groups, a power they can use not only to fight for their own rights, but to influence public policy as citizens fully participating in their society.

Bhimrao Tupe describes another example of how ordinary citizens are discovering their power to change policy and practice in India's Maharashtra State, where a group of educators have come together in a fledgling social movement to breathe new life into the decaying structures of public education. Although the educators are employees of government and private schools, the impact of this story lies in their decision to pour themselves into renewing their schools in their capacity as citizens in voluntary association, on their own time and paying out of their own pockets. Like several preceding chapters, this one acknowledges the key role played by non-governmental organizations and participatory methodologies in building civil society.

Finally, we are reminded of the interconnected global nature of civil society today by Alice Johnson and Barbara Wright's description of an evolving partnership between private, public, and voluntary sector organizations in Cleveland, USA, and four regional cities in Romania. They emphasize the value of networking, not only across national borders but also among the private, public, and civic sectors at all levels of society. Indeed, the authors depart from the three-legged stool analogy of society and define civil society as the "communal infrastructure" that underlies all three sectors.

These seven examples of the emerging, global face of civil society are a small but powerful sampling of the hundreds and thousands that could have been chosen for this book. They are diverse in place, culture, methodology, and historical context. Perhaps their one common link is that they are written by men and women who are immersed in the very approaches and activities they describe. These are not the collected thoughts of armchair commentators. They are the real-life experiences of those working to create civil society in their own particular situations. Not only does this lend a stamp of authenticity to their writing; it gives us all hope that the future we long for may be just a little closer than we think.

NOTES

1. A good example of this is *CITIZENS: Strengthening Global Civil Society*, a report published by CIVICUS, the World Alliance for Citizen Participation, Washington DC, 1994. It describes the state of civil society region by region around the world.
2. Saad Eddin Ibrahim. "Populism, Islam, and Civil Society in the Arab World." pp. 53-66.

2. Populism, Islam, and Civil Society in the Arab World

Saad Eddin Ibrahim

The most significant impediment to further development of civil society in the Middle East may have little to do with anything exceptional to the region, but rather may derive from the simple reluctance of powerful states or state elites to cede privilege and prerogative and make space for civil society.

— Eva Bellin

The six months between the end of October 1995 and the end of April 1996 capsuled in the most dramatic way the promises and perils deeply embedded in the Arab/Middle East region. The drama opened in October 1995 with the Amman Economic Summit, attended by more than 3,000 business leaders, intellectuals, governmental officials, and several heads of states — including King Hussein of Jordan and Prime Minister Yitzhak Rabin of Israel — from 63 countries.

It was followed a few days later by Rabin's tragic assassination, followed by clean and hopeful presidential elections in Algeria (16 November), followed by disappointingly sad legislative elections in Egypt (29 November), followed by indecisive elections in Turkey (24 December), followed by the first and euphoric presidential and legislative elections in Palestine (20 January 1996). All these events were interspersed with deadly salvoes between the Israeli Secret Intelligence, MOSAD, and Palestinian Islamic Jihad and Hamas organizations.

Backstage in the region, Iraq continued to horrify the world with brutalities which were becoming intra-familial among Saddam Hussain's own clan. In Qatar, a son staged a palace coup d'état against his royal father and the father, exiled in a neighboring country, attempted a counter coup to reclaim the throne from his incorrigible son. Palestinian Islamic Hamas performed three successive suicide bombings in the heart of Israel (in Jerusalem and Ashkelon on 25 February and in Tel Aviv on 3 March), which killed and wounded 100 Israelis. Much of the world sympathized with the victims and responded to Egyptian President Hosni Mubarak's hurried invitation for a World Summit of Peacemakers. Held at the Red Sea resort of Sharm El-sheikh on 13 March, the summit was attended by 30 heads of state, including United States President Bill Clinton and Russian President Boris Yeltsin.

With elections pending in Israel, and in the midst of charges by the opposition that Israel's Prime Minister was too weak to deal with the Arabs or to lead Israel in peace and war, Shimon Peres put on a show of brutal force against Palestinian civilians in the occupied territories, and an even more brutal one in neighboring Lebanon to the north, from 11 to 27 April.

There was no moment of boredom in the midst of this despotic, brutal confusion. Nor was there a loss of hope. Even in the height of bombing and killing in Lebanon, the Palestinians and the Israelis were carrying out some earlier mutual pledges for peace. On 24 April, the Palestinian National Council (PAC) removed from its covenant the clause calling for the destruction of the Jewish state. The next day, the ruling Israeli Labor Party removed from its political program articles of commitment banning it from allowing the establishment of a Palestinian state.[1]

The assassination of the Prime Minister Rabin was a shock not only to peoples of Israel, but also in the rest of the Arab world and the Middle East. It evoked diverse and contrasting feelings of sadness, fear, vindictiveness, and joy. The tragic event also has implications worth pondering for civil society and democratization in a new Middle East.

For the first time since its creation in 1948, Israel experienced the assassination of its top leader by one of its own citizens. It was an act incited by protracted, profound, and intense political divisiveness in Israel over the peace process. The Arabs in general, and the Palestinians in particular, have all known and experienced first-hand Israeli acts of violence and brutality of all kinds at the hands of the Israeli army, police, intelligence, and civilians. Occasionally, also, Israelis have used violence against one another. However, the Israelis had convinced themselves and the rest of the world outside the Middle East that they are far more "civil" than their Arab neighbors. With the assassination of Rabin, a "moral parity" of a kind was suddenly established. Neither Israelis nor Arabs have a monopoly on acts of political violence; neither side has a monopoly on the "moral high ground."

For the first time in the 100-year history of the conflict, Arabs genuinely and publicly grieved an Israeli leader. Conversely, Jews in Israel and in New York genuinely and publicly rejoiced over the same event. To be sure, there were Arabs who equally rejoiced, especially the pro-Islamic Jihad movement whose leader, Fathi Shakaki, was assassinated in Malta a week earlier, presumably by the Israeli MOSAD. The point here is that grief and joy were deeply and widely experienced by Arabs and Israelis alike.

For the first time, dozens of top Arab officials were seen on Israeli soil in an Israeli funeral, fully exposed to Israeli society with all its stresses, strains, and advances. It was a brief moment of such exposure for many of them. It was like that first American step on the moon — a small one for human beings, but a giant one for the region. There were many other "firsts" for Arabs and Israelis during those two days, from the moment of the assassination to the burial of Yitzhak Rabin. Many words were said and written about those 48 hours. For the purpose of this chapter, the "civil" dimensions of the tragedy are of most interest.

These events, along with many others, testify to the dynamism and profound dialectics in the region: the new quest for peace and economic cooperation vis-à-vis the old patterns of hostility and isolation; the fledgling civil society and democratic drive vis-à-vis entrenched ancient traditions and despotism. This chapter is an update of an earlier effort in which I examined the regional dynamics bearing on the topic.[2] A special look at Egypt, Algeria, and Jordan should elucidate the democratic-despotic and the tolerance-intolerance dialectics raging throughout the region. In all three cases, there is a three-way conflict among the authoritarian impulse of the state, the democratic impulse of the fledgling civil society, and the relentless quest for power by Islamic activists.

REVISITING THE CONCEPT OF CIVIL SOCIETY

As of 1985, the revised edition of the Social Science Encyclopedia[3] contained no entry for "civil society." The concept goes back to the 17th century and was widely used, especially by the "social contract" theorists. It was still being used in the early decades of this century. None of the 450 authors from 23 social sciences and humanities who wrote the encyclopedia felt the concept was important enough to deal with in the 1985 edition.

It is only in the late 1980s and 1990s that the concept of civil society has forcefully been re-incarnated. The collapse of the Berlin Wall and totalitarianism in Eastern Europe and the former USSR coincided with the powerful comeback of civil society. There have been other factors as well — the weakening of the nation-state, the failure or dismal performance of several development paradigms, the proliferation of multinational corporations, the mushrooming of non-governmental organizations (NGOs), and the sprouting of democracies in all corners of the globe. The concept of civil society is now so much used and so overloaded that there is a serious theoretical threat to its sharpness and utility.

Of 76 definitions I encountered in recent social science literature, the following seems to best capture the essence of the term:

> Civil society is the totality of self-initiating and self-regulating volitional social formations, peacefully pursuing a common interest, advocating a common cause, or expressing a common passion; respecting the right of others to do the same, and maintaining their relative autonomy vis-à-vis the state, the family, and the market.[4]

As such, "civil society" has emerged as an overarching concept which links "democracy," "development," and the peaceful management of conflict. The associational component of civil society encompasses a wide range of organized collective action, such as NGOs, clubs, trade unions, and political parties. Equally, it is the "normative" component which adds to the appeal of the concept, that is, civility in dealing with others, respect of differences, and a tacit or explicit commitment to the peaceful management of conflict.

Both the associational and normative dimensions of it have made many scholars postulate a close link between civil society and democracy. Both are rooted in citizenship equality, respect of the rules of the game, and peaceful conflict management. The 1990s literature on civil society has listed its attributes to include tolerance, respect, and protection of human rights, transparency, a check on state power, rule of law, accountability, promotion of citizenship, and practices of democracy.[5]

By the same token, many social scientists now equate "civil society" with "social capital." Harvard University professor Robert Putnam defines social capital as those "features of social organization which improve the efficiency of society by facilitating coordinated actions such as trust, norms, and networks."[6] The title, subtitle, and contents of Putnam's book, *Making Democracy Work: Civic Traditions in Modern Italy,* highlight the "holy trinity" of civil society, democracy, and development. Putnam's 20 years of painstaking empirical research concludes it is civic associations which have made the difference between "development" and "underdevelopment," between "democratic" and "undemocratic" practices in Italy.

Retrospectively, it seems clear that civil society emerged organically from modern socio-economic formations, such as classes, occupational categories, and other interest groups. In the West, this process unfolded simultaneously with capitalization, industrialization, urbanization, citizenship, and the nation-state. While the ultimate loyalty of citizens was supposedly to the nation-state as the natural sovereign embodiment of all society, sub-loyalties followed interests focused in class, occupation, and residential community. Volitional associations emerged and expanded around the saliency of many citizen interests — political parties, trade unions, professional associations, clubs, and community organizations.

While loyalty to the supreme sovereignty of the state was emotive, abstract, and only occasionally invoked, solidarities of volitional associations were interest-based, concrete, and more frequently invoked. While loyalty to the state was supposedly universal and consensual among all citizens, solidarity in a volitional association was particular and varied in intensity and duration. While citizens hardly ever change their membership in a nation-state, they frequently do so with regard to volitional associations such as class, occupation, status, and residence, due to vertical and horizontal mobility. With competing, or even conflicting, interest of various socio-economic formations in the same nation-state, governance gradually evolved in the direction of participatory politics, i.e., democracy. Some socio-economic formations were more conscious of their interest and quicker than others in organizing their ranks to retain, seize, or share political power within the state. Over time, the less conscious and less organized formations learned the art of associational life by emulation. Thus, the organizations of civil society in the West have multiplied in numbers and sophistication.

CIVIL SOCIETY IN THE MIDDLE EAST[7]

Some Middle East observers have contended that the lagging democratization of the Arab world is due to the absence or stunting of its civil society and its corresponding political culture. Some orientalists and ethnocentrists may totally dismiss even the potential for the evolution of an Arab civil society, and hence any prospect of genuine democratization. Propagators of this point of view often forget the long, arduous, and occasionally bloody march of civil society and democratization in their own Western societies. More than seven centuries passed between the proclamation of the Magna Carta in 1215 and the granting of suffrage to women in 1920 in the United Kingdom. What Huntington calls waves of democratization in the West during the last two centuries were followed by counter waves of authoritarianism in several European countries.[8]

Assertions about the inhospitality of Arab society and culture to democratization will be examined in both pre-modern and contemporary Arab realities to argue a counter proposition: despite noted distortions and time lags, the Arab world is currently building civil society and democracy. The relationship between the two processes is essentially the same; as modern socio-economic formations sprout and take shape, they create their civil society organizations which in turn strive for participatory governance. Two volumes edited by A. R. Norton[9] and the accompanying primer edited by Jillian Schwedler[10] elaborate and examine this relationship closely in several Middle Eastern countries.

Resilient Traditional Arab Civil Formations

Pre-modern society in what is now called the Arab world was fairly ordered around a political authority[11] whose legitimacy was derived from a combination of conquest and/or religious sources. However, public space immediately around that authority was shared by *'ulama* (learned men of religion), merchants, guilds, Sufi orders, and sects or *millets*.[12] Outside this first concentric zone, public space was populated by peasants and tribes. Political authority asserted itself most clearly in the first concentric zone of public space. Outside the first zone, its assertion varied markedly. In most cases, it was hardly felt. Other collectives, especially the tribes, were quite autonomous from the central authority, and sometimes outright defiant.[13] [See Figure 1.]

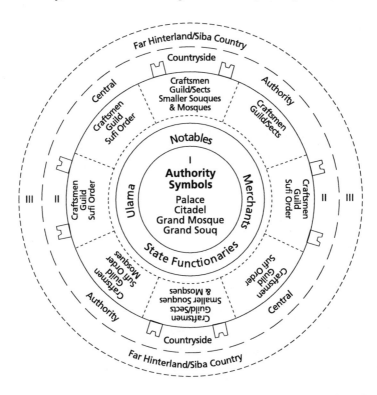

Figure 1. Political authority and civil formations in pre-modern Arab society

Even in the first concentric zone, often within city walls, various groups coexisted and interacted with a great deal of autonomy. Guilds, religious sects, and ethnic groups ran most of their own internal affairs through elected or appointed leaders. The latter were accountable to both the political authority and their own communities. No doubt tension existed within each category, but was of low intensity. Equally, tension may have existed between or among two or more of these communities, but was often resolved inter-communally; or occasionally warranted the direct intervention of the political authority.[14]

Leaders, elders, and notables of the above traditional formations performed several functions in the overall governance of pre-modern Arab society. Beside running intra-communal affairs and managing inter-communal conflicts, they acted as councilors and advisors to rulers. They were called "solvers and binders" — *Ahlu al-Hal wa al-akd* — and the important among them were the *'ulama*. In this capacity, they reduced the absolutist nature of the pre-modern Arab Islamic state. They spoke for the people in general and for their respective constituencies in particular. Solvers and binders equally mediated and legitimated the ruler's decisions to such constituencies.

This traditional equilibrium of governance was maintained by a multitude of mechanisms — clear hierarchies, occupational and residential aggregation, and autonomous resources, mostly from *Awkaf* or *Hobous* religious endowments. Social solidarities existed along primordial, occupational, religious, and ethnic lines. Central authorities collected taxes, administered justice through the *Shari'a*, maintained public order and defense, and occasionally patronized the arts and sciences. Social services and direct economic functions were not expected obligations of the state but mostly were left to local communities. In this sense, traditional Arab society not only knew the equivalent of civil formations but also survived because of them. Individuals relied on these formations for their identity and many of their basic needs. Civil society formations insulated them from direct dealing with political authority.[15] In the traditional equilibrium, the public space, in which civil formations interacted, coincided with the physical space in which they lived and worked.

The New Arab State and Civil Society: Expansion and Retreat

The birth of the new Arab states was midwifed by Western colonial powers.[16] They bore numerous deformities, ranging from the artificialities of their borders to the internal weaknesses of their institutions. Right from the start, they faced severe problems and challenges from within and without. Initially, the new states neither trapped the reservoir of traditional wisdom of pre-modern civil formations, nor adequately allowed enough public space for new ones to sprout and flourish autonomously. As a result, new Arab states found themselves embattled on many internal and external fronts for the first four decades of independence.[17]

The Arab world shared some, but not all, of the processes which had accompanied the emergence of the modern state and civil society in the West; for example, the erosion of traditional equilibria, rapid population growth, and urbanization. However, the processes of capitalization and industrialization lagged far behind. Hence, the new socio-economic formations which are the backbone of the modern state and civil society have not grown progressively or evenly.

The Arab world witnessed phenomenal socio-economic growth in the four decades following World War II, the birth period of most independent Arab states. But the growth was erratic or sluggish, resulting, among other things, in a distorted stratification. The bearing of this distortion on the development of Arab civil society has been detailed in other publications.[18] The most pertinent aspects of this distortion were listed by Schwedler in her primer.[19]

Four variables — socio-economic formations, the articulation of civil society, the state, and external factors — have been acting upon one another to produce a mini-wave of democratization in the Arab world. The interplay of these factors varies from one Arab country to another, which accounts for the degree of democratization empirically observed in each at present.

Civil society in the Arab world has revitalized itself in the last two decades due to internal, regional, and international factors. Internally, new socio-economic formations have been growing steadily, as the autocratic and/or populist regimes have not been able to accommodate or completely suppress them any longer. Regionally, protracted armed conflicts have weakened the state, exposed its impotence in managing such conflicts, and drained its resources. Meanwhile, other regional developments have unwittingly empowered new and old constituencies within each Arab state. Internationally, the patron-client relationship between Arab regimes and the two superpowers has either ended or been greatly altered. The global wave of democratization has also had a marked demonstrative effect on the expanding Arab middle class.

Sprouting civil society organizations in the Arab world have pressed first for greater liberalization to atone for the state's failure to meet socio-economic needs and, later, for its reluctance to respond to their political quest for

A. Age Categories	1970s	1980s	1990s
1. Less than 20 years	5%	11%	23%
2. 20 - 25 years	28	31	48
3. 25 - 30 years	61	53	24
4. Over 30 years	6	5	5
B. Formal Education			
1. Below secondary	5%	5%	9%
2. Secondary	8	12	29
3. Junior college	11	24	42
4. College & post-grad	79	59	20
5. Elite majors	51	27	11
C. Community of Residence			
1. Villages	0%	7%	18%
2. Shanty towns	8	16	36
3. Towns	37	43	31
4. Large Cities	55	34	15

Figure 2. Socio-economic profile of Egypt's Islamic militants

participation. The sluggish performance of the state vis-à-vis these demands has led many disenfranchised, lower-middle class young people to espouse Islamic militancy as a mode of protest. Figure 2 shows the profile of Islamic militants in Egypt between the 1970s and 1980s; they are getting younger and are being drawn more from small towns and slum areas. This changing profile signifies ever-widening alienation and social discontent. The sociological situation in Algeria is essentially the same.

During the 1980s and early 1990s, the Arab world has witnessed a three-way race to maintain or seize power among autocratic regimes, Islamic activists, and civil society organizations. In some Arab countries, one variant of the race has been the squeezing of civil society out of the public arena by autocratic regimes on the one hand and by Islamic activists on the other. In another variant, both the autocratic regimes and Islamic activists have attempted to win over or appropriate civil society organizations. The first variant is what public opinion in the Arab world and in the West associates with violent Islamic militants in Algeria, Egypt, and Palestine.

Palestine: Islamists' Fear of Democracy

Earlier in this chapter, I alluded to the Palestinian Hamas and Jihad which have been carrying on a lethal fight against Israel and, to a lesser extent, against their own Palestinian opponents, including Yassir Arafat's Palestine Liberation Organization and more recently, the Palestine National Authority, in an attempt to derail the peace process. Their argument is that Arafat is too weak to negotiate an honorable peace with the Jewish Zionist state; he will sell out or compromise Palestinian historical rights.[20]

Palestinian Islamic militants had an opportunity in January 1996 to put this argument to the test in the first Palestinian elections. They warned their people to boycott the elections and stay away from polling stations, but 85% of eligible voters went to the polls; Yassir Arafat received more than 87% of the vote; and his supporters swept the legislative elections. The whole democratic exercise in Palestine was a success for one of the Arab world's strongest civil societies. The latter had sprouted during many decades of Jordanian authoritarian rule (before 1967), and nearly three decades of Israeli occupation (after 1967). The absence of a national state of their own meant the Palestinians had to rely on their own civil society organizations. Hundreds of new NGOs sprouted in the occupied territories, along with old professional syndicates and welfare associations.[21]

Algeria: State Fear of Democracy

The Algerian case is somewhat different in that the Islamic activists, represented by the Front Islamique de Salvation (FIS), had accepted the challenge of democratic politics and had run for municipal elections in the spring of

1990 and parliamentary elections at the end of 1991. Their performance in both was so impressive, especially in the latter elections, that the Algerian Army could not bring itself to accept the Islamists forming a majority government. It rushed to take power into its own hands and forced then President Shazli Ben-Jadid to resign. The rest of the story is a case of an authoritarian regime unwilling to play by the rules of the democratic game.

The Algerian FIS felt justified in resorting to violence, since state violence had been used to rob it of its electoral victory. The country was plunged into massive armed internal strife. Six thousand Algerians are estimated to have been killed in clashes between the FIS and the GIA (Islamic Army Groups) on the one hand and the Algerian Army and security forces on the other. Another 30,000 perished between 1992 and 1995.[22] The irony in the bloody Algerian tragedy is that most casualties were civilians — journalists, teachers, and women activists in Algeria's budding civil society.

Four years after the bloodshed began, a presidential election was held in mid-November 1995. Algeria's Islamic militants warned their fellow countrymen not to participate, but most Algerians were not intimidated. Al-Amin Zeroual, the incumbent president, was elected by a 61% majority in an election judged by international observers as "fair and honest."[23] This act of democratic politics enhanced the regime's "legitimacy," and morally isolated the more militant Algerian Islamists, who are now quite splintered. Algeria in 1996 was a far cry from that of 1992. Civil society advocates may still have serious misgivings about the Algerian state but they are working closer with one another against forces of violence and anarchy than ever before.

Egypt: The Sterile Triangle

The triangulated conflict in Egypt is even more complex. Egypt was one of the earliest Arab and Third World countries to resume its second democratization process in 1976, after a quarter century of non-democratic rule since Nasser's 1952 revolution. However, several counter forces have impeded the process. Among these are the inertia of the authoritarian legacy (1952-1976), and the continued restrictive law of associations (Law 32 of 1964) which stunt the flourishing of Egyptian civil society. The first counter force has ingrained in the executive branch of the government the practice of election rigging in favor of the ruling National Democratic Party. The second counter force has meant, in effect, that the political parties would have weak cadres and political infrastructure, both of which can only be guaranteed by a robust civil society.

Along with a host of socio-economic problems bedeviling Egyptian society at large and the middle class in particular, one form of potent opposition force to the regime has been Islamic activism.[24] Since 1971, one wing of the Islamic movement has opted for peaceful means in pursuing its objectives of instituting an Islamic socio-political order. By and large, this has been the Muslim Brotherhood. Through teaching, preaching, and grassroots service provision, the Muslim Brotherhood has created new civil society organizations and penetrated or taken over many existing ones. For example, in the 1980s, the Muslim Brothers took over major professional associations such as the medical, engineering, and lawyers' associations through democratic peaceful means.[25]

The other more militant wing of the Islamic movement opted to use violence to destabilize the regime or overthrow it altogether. These militants have not only attacked the state but also symbols of civil society, killing police officers, other governmental officials, intellectuals, and journalists. The government attitude in turn has been mixed. As confrontations with the militants have escalated, the government has sought the support of civil society organizations. As soon as it has regained the initiative over the militants, the government has often turned its back on secular civil society organizations and harassed the more peaceful Muslim Brothers.

With the domestic situation well under government control in 1994 and 1995, the regime fell back into the same authoritarian practices of rigging elections,[26] arresting Muslim Brothers, and alienating many forces of civil society. The 1995 parliamentary elections were potentially the most promising. An unprecedented 4,000 candidates competed for 444 seats: two-thirds were independent, including 100 women and 60 Copts. President Mubarak repeatedly assured "clean elections."[27] Most Egyptians took the elections seriously. However, the elections turned out to be the worst in modern Egyptian history, since the first round of such elections on 26 November 1995. Sensing or observing governmental unfairness, many candidates and their supporters took the law in their own hands. Clashes broke out on large scale. Seventy-one persons, including a candidate, were killed and at least three times as many were reported seriously injured.[28]

It was not too surprising, therefore, that after two years on the defensive, Islamic militants began to strike against the heart of Cairo and Upper Egypt. In the first four months of 1996, they killed two police generals, scores of other policemen and officers, as well as 30 Greek tourists. This was essentially the same pattern as after the 1990 lopsided parliamentary elections which were boycotted by all major opposition parties because of the government's refusal to allow a complete judiciary supervision of the elections. The Islamic militants took advantage of the mass alienation resulting from the government's attitude and struck at the state symbols, starting in November 1990 with the Speaker of Egypt's People's Assembly. This ushered in a long period of intense confrontations with the state and civil society.

CONCLUSION

Another reading of the above account of Palestine, Algeria, and Egypt is that middle classes and other socio-economic formations are making a legitimate quest for participation in the public affairs of their societies. If they are not allowed to do so peacefully, they force their way into the system or against it violently. Islam, in this case, is merely a culturally legitimate vehicle to do so. King Hussain of Jordan, King Hassan II of Morocco, and the ruling Prince of Kuwait, Sheikh Jabber, have understood this fact and acted accordingly. Other populist authoritarian regimes have been either unable or unwilling to understand or to act accordingly. The price for this delayed understanding and reluctance to act has often been a heavy "blood-tax" paid by Islamic dissidents and the security forces, both of whom come from the lower middle classes.

This accommodation to increasing demands for participation contains the greatest promise for civil society and hence, for the democratization process. Importantly, it has provided ample bargaining power to civil society organizations when they deal with the state in attempts to gain concessions of a socio-political, reformative nature. It also has had a moderating effect on several Islamic activist groups. In Jordan, Kuwait, Yemen, and Lebanon, Islamists have accepted the principle of political pluralism, participating alongside other secular forces in national elections. Islamists are currently represented in those countries' parliaments. In Lebanon, Yemen, and Jordan, women have been elected for the first time, and the Islamists did not march out in protest.

So long as religious-based parties and associations accept the principle of pluralism and observe a modicum of civility in behavior toward the different "others," they can expect to be integral parts of civil society.[29] In this respect, even the Islamists may evolve into something akin to the Christian Democrats in the West or the religious parties in Israel. There is nothing intrinsically Islamic that contradicts the codes of civil society or democratic principles. This point was argued by Zubaida in his rebuttal of Gellner's theory of Muslim society.[30] Zubaida contends that social and political forms evolved by Muslims could be conducive to modernity and progress, for "Islam is a development ideology."[31]

The responses by Arab regimes to their civil societies indicate as many prospects for further democratization as against it. The modernizing monarchies, namely Jordan and Morocco, have impressively engineered a smooth transition toward more democratic governance. Their examples may tilt the balance toward greater democratic prospects in the entire region, prospects that promise to enhance the peaceful settlement of some of the region's protracted conflicts while also growing in strength from such settlements.

NOTES

1. *Time,* 6 May 1996. pp. 45-46.

2. Saad Eddin Ibrahim. "Civil Society and the Prospects of Democratization in the Arab World" in Norton, A. R. (ed.) *Civil Society in the Middle East.* Leiden, New York and Koln: E. J. Brill, 1995. pp. 27-54.

3. Adam Kuper and Jessica Kuper (eds.). *The Social Science Encyclopedia.* Second Edition. London and New York: Routledge, 1996. pp. 88-90.

4. *Ibid.*

5. Norton. *op. cit.* pp. 4-24.

6. Robert D. Putnam. *Making Democracy Work: Civic Traditions in Modern Italy.* Princeton: Princeton University Press, 1993. p. 167.

7. This section of the chapter is excerpted from the article by Saad Eddin Ibrahim, "Civil Society and the Prospects of Democratization in the Arab World." in Norton, A. R. 1995. pp. 28-32.

8. Samuel Huntington. *The Third Wave: Democratization in the Late Twentieth Century.* Norman: Oklahoma University Press, 1991. pp. 17-21.

9. A. R. Norton. (ed.) *Civil Society in the Middle East.* Leiden, New York and Koln: E. J. Brill, 1995.

10. Jillian Schwedler. *Civil Society in the Middle East. A Primer.* Leiden, New York and Koln: E. J. Brill, 1995.

11. Y. L. Rizk. *Civil Egypt.* London and New York: Routledge, 1992.

12. See (a) Manfred Halperin. *The Politics of Social Change in the Middle East and the Arab World.* Princeton, New Jersey: Princeton University Press, 1962. (b) Ernest Gellner. *Muslim Society.* Cambridge: Cambridge University Press, 1983. (c) Ilya Harik. "The Origins of the Arab System" in Luciani, G. *The Arab State.* Berkeley: University of California Press, 1990. pp. 1-28.

13. See (a) Ibn Khaldoun. *Al-Mukaddima.* Baghdad: Al-Muthanna, 1980. (b) Ernest Gellner. *Plough, Sword, and Book: The Structure of Human Society.* London: Collins, 1988.

14. Rizk. *op. cit.* pp. 40-48.

15. *Ibid.* pp. 141-142.

16. Saad Eddin Ibrahim. et. al. *Society and State in the Arab World.* (Arabic) Amman: The Arab Thought Forum, 1988. pp. 45-78.

17. Ilya Harik in Luciani. *op. cit.* pp. 1-28.

18. See (a) Saad Eddin Ibrahim. et. al. *Society and State in the Arab World.* (Arabic) Amman: The Arab Thought Forum, 1988. pp. 45-78. (b) Saad Eddin Ibrahim. *Civil Society and Democratization in the Arab World.* (Arabic) Cairo: Ibn Khaldoun Center, 1992. (c) Saad Eddin Ibrahim. "Civil Society and the Prospects of Democratization in the Arab World." in Norton, A. R. 1995. pp. 27-54.

19. Schwedler. *op. cit.* pp. 37-38.

20. Not surprisingly, this is the same argument used by Jewish extremists, including Yigal Amir, the confessed assassin of Israel's Prime Minister Yitzhak Rabin.

21. Ziad Abu-Amr. *Civil Society in Palestine.* (Arabic). Cairo: Ibn Khaldoun Center, 1995.

22. Michael Willis. "The Islamist Movements of North Africa." in Albioni, R., et. al. *Security Challenges in the Mediterranean Region.* London: Frank Cass, 1996. pp. 5-26.

23. *Civil Society:Democratization in the Arab World.* Monthly newsletter. Cairo: Ibn Khaldoun Center, December 1995.

24. Saad Eddin Ibrahim. "Egypt's Islamic Activism in the 1980s." *Third World Quarterly.* Volume 10, No. 2. April, 1988. pp. 632-657.

25. *Ibid.* pp. 637-647.

26. ICER. *Final Report of the Egyptian Independent Commission on the 1995 Parliamentary Elections.* (Arabic). Cairo: Ibn Khaldoun Center, 1995.

27. *Al-Ahram.* 30 November 1995.

28. ICER. *op. cit.* pp. 179-222.

29. See (a) Nazih Ayoubi. (ed.) "Rethinking the Public/Private Dichotomy: Radical Islam and Civil Society in the Middle East." *Contention.* Volume 4, No. 3, Spring 1995. pp. 100-101. (b) Ellis Goldberg. "Smashing Idols and the State: The Protestant Ethics and Egyptian Sunni Radicalism." *Comparative Studies in Society and History.* No. 33, 1991. pp. 3-4.

30. (a) Sami Zubaida. "Is There a Muslim Society?" and Ernest Gellner. "Sociology of Islam." in *Economy and Society.* Volume 24, No. 2, May 1995. pp. 151-188. (b) Ernest Gellner. *Muslim Society.* Cambridge: Cambridge University Press, 1983. pp. 88 and 92.

31. *Ibid.* p.184.

3. Sparks of Hope in the Embers of War: The Balkans

Susan Fertig-Dykes

The promise of the post-communist era rests largely on the potential for creating a more vibrant and deeply rooted network of organizations and institutions that mediate between the citizen and the state: the connective tissue of a democratic political cutlure.

— Daniel Siegel and Jenny Yancey

E ven in nations at peace, the concept of civil society spawns as many questions as answers in considering how to enable citizen participation in governance. Countries recently part of the communist bloc, where totalitarian governments were history's antithesis of civil society, face a particular set of challenges overcoming vestiges of those traditions.

War raises other, tougher questions about building civil society — even about the nature of civil society itself. In the new republics of the former Yugoslavia, many people felt the war was wrong but were helpless to influence their governments. Others, sadly, were drawn into the insanity of genocide and atrocities, either through their own perversions or through fear of repercussions for non-participation. Certainly, the conflict has had its share of demagogues, with at least some fanatic followers participating enthusiastically in their government's extremes, others acquiescing, and few openly protesting.

Now, after a first tentative year of peace has moved into a second, civil society seems far from a reality and, to some, even unattainable. In that context, even a modest achievement represents huge progress.

Some knowledge of the last few years as a frame of reference is essential to understanding the current challenges — particularly in Bosnia and Herzegovina (BiH) and in Croatia — and to envisioning the future of civil society there. [See box following.]

Bosnian Ethnic and Religious History

Yugoslavia refers to the South Slav region which in pre-slavic, ancient times (6000 BC - 100 AD) was populated by Illyrians. After the Roman conquest and rule from early in the millennium until about 400 AD, Slavic groups began to migrate into the area from farther east. Slavs are Indo-European peoples who speak the Slavic language. Current ethnic labels — Serbs, Croats, and Slovenes — came into use about the ninth century.

Bosnia is bordered on one side by Serbia and on the other by Croatia. The Bosnian people include Bosnian Serbs, who are predominantly Orthodox Christians, Bosnian Croats, who are predominantly Roman Catholics, and "Bosniaks" who are generally the same stock as the Serbs and Croats, may or may not have Turkish origins, but who are predominantly Muslim.

When Bosnia came under the rule of the Turkish Ottoman Empire (1400-1876), local nobles were allowed to keep their titles and property if they would convert to Islam. Others converted as a natural consequence of being conquered. Thus, their religious roots were probably more pragmatic than inspired. Until the last few years, the practice of the Islamic faith was hardly noticeable in a largely secular society. However, there has been some radicalization of the Muslim population, both in reaction to persecution and in response to criticism and demands of wealthy Arabic donor nations contributing to the cause and radical fundamentalists who came into Bosnia as Mujahadin (holy warriors) during the fighting.

In spite of ethnic cleansing in Bosnia and Herzegovina, Croatia, and Serbia, in each of the three are minority populations made up of the ethnic groups from the other two.

IN SEARCH OF A FRAME OF REFERENCE

All wars have their icons and rallying points. Perhaps because of the intensity and duration of its siege, Sarajevo, in the center of Bosnia and Herzegovina, glows brightly in the midst of a jumble of images associated with the "Balkan crisis." A chemist evacuated in 1993 after being wounded spoke bitterly of her forced absence. Struggling to adequately express the concept in her limited English, she said, "It is a big proud to stay in Sarajevo." Through the half-decade of war, the beleaguered city symbolized at once the ferocity of the conflict and the spirit of the people who endured it. That spirit, more than any outside influence, may be the best hope for the emergence of civility.

Sarajevo Now and Then

Sarajevo today is bustling. Streets so recently empty are choked with traffic. Zipping around and beside the military vehicles and convoys are spiffy sports cars, rehabilitated Yugo sedans, and a sleeker "4 x 4" than those used in the war.

In the spring and summer of 1996, carpenters and masons clambered up and down scaffolds and window glass began replacing the ubiquitous UNHCR[1] plastic. New businesses began to pop up daily, and the windows of shops filled with merchandise. Restaurants, cafes, and bistros are thriving as throngs of people move with an intense gaiety about the city again. The cafe society has quickly revived. But what about the prognosis for civil society?

When I first arrived in Sarajevo in 1993, it was a city under unrelenting attack from Serbs in the surrounding hills. I sensed danger the moment I put on the heavy flak jacket required to board the UN flight from Zagreb, where I lived. Back then, a flak jacket was fine for flak or shrapnel but useless against a sniper's bullet, for it would flatten a bullet and cause serious internal damage. The only ways to get into Sarajevo were to drive behind or hitch a ride with a relief convoy or to get on an UN Protection Forces flight. Often the plane, usually a big, Russian Illyusin-76 troop carrier/cargo jet, would be hit with artillery approaching Sarajevo.

Once on the ground, getting into the city meant a hazardous journey through various checkpoints as you passed from area to area controlled by different warring factions, and then running the gauntlet of "snipers alley" at 120 kilometers per hour, not stopping for traffic lights or pedestrians or anything else and dodging old wrecks and craters left in the roads by incoming artillery and mortar rounds.

Pedestrians scuttled from building to building hoping not to be a sniper's target. People had to decide whether to drop to the sidewalk or run faster when bullets zinged by. A person could be shot standing in line for bread or trying to fill a bucket with water. All day, the "ack ack ack" of automatic weapons and the "whomp!" of incoming mortars and artillery shells rang out. At night, it was one large, macabre fireworks display.

Food was scarce — one friend existed on a single candy bar for days. Water and gas lines were damaged in many parts of Bosnia and electricity was never on past 3:00 p.m. The trees of Sarajevo rapidly disappeared as people cut them to keep warm and families sacrificed their libraries for cooking fuel. Without water, unflushed toilets made office buildings smell like sewers. Since most windows were sandbagged, fresh air was not an option. Of course, in many places not at war similar conditions are normal.

What could never seem normal was the terror that pumped into my heart when I heard children playing outside. I wondered how their mothers could let them be out there, but what else could they do? Keep them inside for their entire childhood? Inside wasn't so safe either. Schools sometimes exploded around them. Children watched other children die and some witnessed their parents murdered or brutalized.

Pernicious Contradictions

Earlier in the war, non-Serb Croatia's capacity was severely strained by massive displacements of Bosnian Muslims and Bosnian Croats from Bosnia and from Serb-occupied areas in Croatia. Along Croatia's famous Dalmatian coast, nearly every tourist hotel was filled with refugees and displaced persons, with much of the expense borne by Croatia. Taxpaying citizens began to complain they could no longer obtain medical assistance and other benefits because the country's resources were stretched too thin.

Donors visiting from other countries wondered what was so bad about refugees living in luxury hotels and began to reduce contributions. A whole family of refugees might live for years in a single hotel room, without privacy or facilities to cook or launder. Trying to forestall internal political repercussions, Croatia restricted the right of refugees to work, forcing them into a life of dependence and boredom.

All this took place in the midst of chaotic economic conditions resulting from the shift away from communism. Doctors, teachers, and other professionals who made the equivalent of US $200 a month under the old system, now found their salaries unchanged but the cost of living soaring. With foreign embassies in Zagreb willing to pay rents of $US 6,000 a month for ordinary flats and houses, and with the UN paying exorbitant salaries for locally hired staff, an artificial economy built up quickly, with gross inequities and distorted values for different kinds of work. On the other hand, there were no jobs in some places, because of the collapse of industry in the wake of communism or in the swath of war. State-owned companies kept their employees but didn't pay them. As always in such times, a black market for stolen or confiscated relief shipments flourished.

In the midst of such chaos and gloom, instances of heroism and humanitarianism burst through — seeds of civil society, if you will. It may be a while before it is clear which have taken root, which will be hardy enough to survive the toxins of war. For the moment, it is enough that these vignettes offer models of courage and persistence as antidotes to despair.

Implications and Challenges

Civil society notions of citizen rights and participation in governance seemed as elusive as the smoke emanating from the smoldering buildings. Voters were not even sure where to vote, let alone how they could influence a system in which they have supplicant status. Whole populations of villages, towns, and cities were displaced, with people fleeing to other parts of the same country or becoming refugees in other countries. Families were separated and thousands still have not found one another. Large numbers of children, separated from relatives or orphaned, have been fending for themselves for years in refugee centers, yet they are still children with no appropriate means to care for themselves. For most, schooling has been haphazard at best. All have seen and endured things too difficult for any adult to bear.

For adults and children alike, one of the saddest repercussions of this war has been the loss of trust. Serbs, Croats, and Muslims lived side by side, attended school together, were friends, and intermarried. Then, suddenly, they were enemies, neighbor against neighbor, schoolmate against schoolmate, even brother against brother within a family which had intermarried. It is hard to imagine a member of one's immediate family coming home and announcing that our spouse must be gone by morning or our family will kill him or her.

The unspeakable and unthinkable occurred routinely. Documented cases which make it doubtful that civil society will ever be possible in this region — fathers at gun point forced to fellate their sons; Muslim men ordered to castrate each other with their teeth or be shot, and then shot after being driven to comply; raped Muslim women who killed their Serb babies at birth. The victims who lived are surely scarred spiritually as well as physically, but they will be responsible for shaping the society that is forming. They are coping in a post-war environment, with huge variations and fluctuations in economic conditions, one of which is a tentative experiment in something that resembles peace, but which could dissolve again into war.

In December 1995, preceded by psychological operations designed for intimidation, IFOR[2] troops arrived to enforce the peace agreed upon by the warring parties in Dayton, USA. The "psy-ops" efforts were effective in halting overt military activity. However, violent hostile acts have not stopped. These acts of destruction and injury are part of the smoldering ethnic enmities that have burst into flame time and again in the Balkans. They are perpetrated by every group — Muslims, Serbs, and Croats — in an effort to keep refugees and displaced persons of the other two groups from returning to their homes.

How does a society recover from such collective trauma and begin anew? For a while, the future will be written by those who wrote the past. Then it will depend on the resilience and spirit of another generation, one that innocently has borne the brunt of others' hatred, greed, and insanity. Even if peace holds, real change may have to wait for children yet to be born whose parents are children today. Maybe the oral tradition of generations of suffering and blame can stop when there are no more firsthand stories.

However, in the nearer term, the outcome may be more hopeful than could be reasonably expected, because of the efforts of organizations and individuals dedicated to building civil society in the embers of a war as terrible and senseless as any in history.

CITIZEN-BASED INITIATIVES

In the Krajina, that complicated part of Croatia where Serbs settled during the Austro-Hungarian Empire, Croatian Serbs came to think of themselves as a separate nation allied to Serbia. When the war erupted in the dissolution of Yugoslavia, they pressed for secession from the newly-recreated Croatia. Intoxicated with possibility, they expelled or exterminated thousands of their Croat neighbors. When the Croatian government recaptured the Krajina just before signing the Dayton Accord, thousands of Serbs fled, assuming there would be monstrous retribution, either from troops or from returning citizens. Shocked to find themselves not welcomed with open arms by Serbia, or "rump Yugoslavia," [see Figure 1] many were adrift.

Figure 1. The Former Yugoslavia

In the meantime, many displaced Croats have flowed back into the Krajina, reclaiming their homes or taking over those of the fleeing Serbs. Some Croats destroyed countless Serb homes, either to induce the Serb residents to leave or to keep them from returning. The "spontaneous combustion" of Serb houses was so widespread that American ambassador Peter Galbraith declared the Croats had changed from victim to aggressor. Weighted down under international pressure and criticism, the Croatian government feebly contends that Serb refugees should return, but shows no sincerity behind such assertions. In fact, it may be aggressively discouraging such returns.

A small, courageous group of Croats have taken a stand in the Krajina. In a burst of optimism and hope that our shared origins are more unifying than ethnicity is divisive, they formed local non-governmental organization (NGO) called HOMO, from the Latin "homo sapiens." With funding from OXFAM United Kingdom/Ireland, HOMO has set up centers throughout the area and is creating a safe environment for returning Serbs. The partnership between HOMO and OXFAM United Kingdom/Ireland began with a small grant to assist Serbs who stayed in the Krajina during its recapture by Croatia in August 1995, were imprisoned, and when finally released, were left without even the most basic necessities.

With a staff of only seven, including five volunteers, HOMO operates a center assisting individuals to reclaim their status as citizens and to reassert their rights. This might not seem so daring, until one realizes these are Croats helping Serbs in a highly charged environment where violence erupts frequently and where neither other citizens nor the authorities are sympathetic to the defeated ethnic minority. Volunteers are challenging their society and their government in a system that is not fully democratic and that can be harshly punitive towards nonconformists and perceived agitators. In so doing, they are dealing with a number of key points of leverage for civil society:

Gaining Equal Access to Government Services and Benefits. HOMO helps people acquire citizenship documents, such as identification cards, pension or social cards, employment papers and passports, even ensuring delivery or organizing transport for elderly to collect pensions. The loss or absence of documents has far-reaching effects. For example, it can be difficult to obtain death certificates for people who died between 1991 and 1995. Their families then cannot secure their property, which in some cases is now occupied by other people. For elderly returnees, the question of pension status is crucial but dependent upon records. The Center has assisted Serbs with pensions that have been blocked by the new Croat government, even after eligibility has been confirmed. The Center also collects information on prisoners, returnees, relatives remaining in villages, deaths, and missing people.

Shifting From Victimization to Empowerment. The Center is quietly establishing an understanding of civil rights and empowerment that lays a stronger future base for civil society. It is building confidence that people can decide not to be victims of their government and of one another. Many people the volunteers visit are extremely isolated and still live in fear of burglary or worse. The Center has seen looted property being carried off in cars without registration plates. All victims have been Serbs except for three Croat women married to Serb men. One 60 year-old Serbian complained that a police officer came in response to his burglary report, listened sympathetically, then took one of his cows when he left. An OXFAM report mentions possible police involvement in crimes and also describes drunk policemen shooting and throwing hand grenades. The Center regularly reports to the Croatian Helsinki Committee and the Human Rights Coordination Group in Zagreb.

Taking Charge of Infrastructure. In the village of Vrhovine, 32 Croat children — not enough to have their own school — were unable to get to school in Otocac. The HOMO Center convinced the Mayor of Otocac to reopen the school in Vrhovine despite the few pupils, by negotiating to have only one teacher for all subjects and all ages. The Center then worked with a Japanese NGO to rebuild the school building. OXFAM reports, "The success with the school is important, in that the Mayor of Otocac has recognized their intervention and has announced the rebuilding triumphantly. In addition, a few Croats have thanked them."

This latter comment is particularly pertinent. Since these Croat volunteers are visibly working with Serbs as well as Croats, many of their fellow Croats are angry. Further, they are more than a nuisance to the Croatian government, particularly the local authorities, and they risk official repercussions for their advocacy. Their investigation of missing persons is a further stimulus to retaliation from those who may have something to hide. Retribution has taken several forms. In an attempt to intimidate HOMO, offices have been set on fire, a Croatian staff member was severely beaten, and a director and visiting journalist were assaulted.

Two legacies of the communist tradition support the perpetuation of both: one is a lack of public will to resist or challenge established policy and the other is a government hierarchy comprised mostly of leaders and underlings who came from that tradition and who still collectively repress with impunity. When a group of Croats, such as HOMO, risks themselves to reintegrate Serbs into newly recovered Croat territory, they are setting an example that may inspire others — Croats, Muslims, and Serbs alike — to emulate them in building civil society.

Building Bridges of Mutual Need. In another part of Croatia, a different venture with some similar features is being carried out by Catholic Relief Services (CRS), one of the world's largest relief and development agencies. CRS has been working in Europe for 50 years and has been active in the former Yugoslavia throughout the war.

Croatian East Slavonia is adjacent to the Serbian border of rump Yugoslavia and was one of the four UN Protected Areas in Croatia. Early in the war, Croats were beaten, harassed, and killed throughout East Slavonia by the local Serbian population and by retreating Serbian soldiers. Those who could, fled, until today the region is almost exclusively Serbian, though it falls within Croatia's borders. This border was reaffirmed in the Dayton Agreement, with provisions for return of the area to Croatian control. But the question of resettlement of displaced Croats is not easy. Most would be afraid to return even now, and the Dayton Agreement cannot mandate that their Serbian neighbors welcome them.

CRS staff traveled to East Slavonia to hold conciliatory meetings with the generally Christian Orthodox Serbian population, to ascertain the level of hostility and the possibilities for peaceful reintegration. The slowly evolving dialogue in East Slavonia began with Serb threats and reiterations of hatred. CRS employed methods of conflict resolution in their meetings, as well as helping to rebuild community buildings and homes, providing trauma counseling, and developing parent teacher associations. In Vukovar, CRS rebuilt a convent and reconstructed a home for the elderly. Patience and consistent demonstrations of willingness to help rather than blame eventually led the Serbs to admit they would like their former neighbors to return.

Promoting Indigenous Partnerships. Relief and development work is carefully designed to avoid barriers and to promote partnerships with indigenous groups. The efforts are fully cognizant of diversity in origin, race, ethnicity, worship, beliefs, and expression, and encourage communities to embrace tolerance, a difficult assignment in a society emerging from war in which all sides have been damaged and each group has grievances against the others.

In Macedonia, the CRS program is based on strengthening the parent-school partnership. By trying to initiate communication between the lines of community conflict, they are bringing together Albanian Muslim and Macedonian Orthodox parents to improve schools for all children. CRS is also training local groups in NGO management and conflict resolution and has introduced Balkan-wide professional gatherings, hoping that professional ties will help bridge ethnic and religious divisions.

Sometimes it is hard to let go of either aggressor stance or victim status, especially when it may seem to afford the only protection or source of benefits available. In neighboring Albania, CRS has introduced tolerance training to address blood feuds in northern parts of the country. CRS ties reconstruction and other funding opportunities to participation as an incentive for an angry populace to explore new relationships together.

Moving From Shelter to Community. Much community development work would not be possible without the massive shelter programs carried out with money from the Office of the United Nations High Commissioner for Refugees (UNHCR) and other disaster funding. Resettlement projects would not succeed if people had no place to live when they returned. The United Methodist Committee on Relief (UMCOR) is one organization that has grown exponentially in Bosnia and Herzegovina over the last few years, primarily because of major UNHCR and USAID grants for shelter construction. Construction materials are procured through Bosnian manufacturers and companies to stimulate economic growth and build local capacity for long-term reconstruction and development. With UMCOR monitoring the process, these materials are then distributed through local government centers and provided to citizens for self-help home repairs.

At the same time, UMCOR works to overcome destructive ethnic divisions within the communities they are reconstructing. When UMCOR staffer Julia Demichelis started working in Gornji Vakuf, the town was bitterly divided between Bosnian Croats and Bosnian Muslims. Even after open warfare officially ceased, violent incidents occurred regularly. As she started meeting with individuals and small groups, she found hard-core hatred prevented meetings between the two ethnic populations. Initially by visiting families, she discerned that the community was split along geographic lines but mutually owned resources such as housing, schools, hospitals, and community facilities. Some facilities were isolated in the midst of an ethnic concentration, making access dangerous for the other ethnic group; others were between the two territories, making them natural places for possible joint use. Youth programs and a women's microenterprise project developed in consultation with the people provided an enticement to jointly use facilities.

Demichelis first helped individuals address their particular war experiences, then focused on motivating individuals to accept and acknowledge their own roles and responsibilities and those of their ethnic group in community and personal destruction. Finally, she focused on their ability to transform and be accountable for their environment. She progressed from family visits to joint groups, using herself and others as neutral advocates, and conducted meetings in neutral territory. She also used split government meetings to focus on shared interests.

At one point, the process began to break down so she made sure everyone understood that her presence would only continue if they wanted her there and desired to try to accomplish something together. After much discussion, the community resolved to keep her with them and to pursue the objectives they had developed. In her mind, there was little doubt about the value of her work:

> What we've done is extraordinary because we have found the difference between the will dictated by political leaders and will of the people. Teachers want to teach in the same school again, parents want their children to go to school in the same schools again, and they want their library back. My job is to strengthen the voice and the will of the people who have been separated by political and military means and to provide them with the physical conditions and programs to help them reintegrate.[3]

For everyone engaged in programs like these, the deep stress of the program itself — keeping the two sides talking, retooling after setbacks, adjusting for constantly changing conditions — is compounded by the underlying fear that funding will run out before the program becomes sustainable. Demichelis worried that when her funding ended and she had to leave, the program would be vulnerable to influence from those who do not want reintegration. However, when she returned to Gornji Vakuf after a short absence, she found the work she had begun continued apace.

Including Women in the Political Process. One of the most important developments in the Balkans today is the emergence of women in political life. While conservative Islamic forces seek to restrict women's participation in the public sphere, women themselves are making headway into this previously all-male domain. One example is Zena 21 (21 Women), a group of Bosnian women who banded together to help one another and other women during the war and grew into a sprawling but efficient organization of around 200 volunteers and fewer than a dozen paid staff. With the help of the American Ambassador to Austria Swanee Hunt and UMCOR among others, they launched the first Sarajevo International Women's Conference in June 1996. Women came from all over the former Yugoslavia to participate in this three-day event in which they workshopped issues and crafted solutions on political involvement and empowerment. In an emotional first day of heartbreaking and heroic stories, President Izetbegovic and Ambassador Hunt delivered the opening addresses. One outcome of the gathering was that three months later, the major political parties invited women candidates for the first time.

DEVELOPING A FOUNDATION FOR CIVIL SOCIETY

Ambivalence to International Assistance

Most NGO workers are inspired to help people who have suffered and who stand poised at the edge of democratic possibilities. However, there is scant reward for altruism in this environment. People take much for granted, including the huge amounts of money the world has infused into the situation and rarely show appreciation for dedication and hard work. Foreigners, always called "strangers" in official documents, are viewed as an exploitable source of income for exorbitant apartment rentals and other gouging techniques. Even foreigners having close friends in the local community often feel the community at large resents their presence.

An insular attitude among citizens and the authorities allows them to believe theirs is the most vital and urgent crisis in the world at any given moment, if not the only one. Coupled with an attitude that the world owes them assistance, this creates a disconcerting atmosphere for outside workers. The situation is further complicated by people's refusal to understand the donors' unwillingness to turn over funds in their entirety to local groups or governments.

The government has even contemplated legislation taxing non-profit organizations as much as 30% of incoming humanitarian goods and other aid.

Along with such local factors influencing the development community, global shifts are occurring. With all the crises around the world demanding attention from donors, combined with donor fatigue and the difficulty of achieving expected results in the confusing reality of Bosnia, it is hard to sustain funding or secure new funding. Even more serious for the Balkans, and for development work in general, a subtle shift in attitudes has occurred in the post "cold war" period: many nations feel less urgency about using aid as a diplomatic wedge. Many UN agencies have been facing serious shortfalls because of reduced contributions by donor countries. This places tremendous strain on projects when specific, funded objectives may be achievable but long-term stability demands more time than available funding allows, or worse, when funding commitments are broken in mid-stream.

Symbiosis Between International and Local NGOs

On the other hand, there are abundant inspirational stories of local citizens taking responsibility, forming volunteer organizations, and setting about to turn their world right side up. In the former Yugoslavia as elsewhere, these citizen initiatives have given rise to grassroots humanitarian organizations. Individuals and indigenous groups have emerged to care for one another in the vacuum left by the collapse of government structures and in the gaps not addressed by international organizations.

A case in point is a local NGO in Serbia, Hi Neighbor. Early in the conflict, child psychologist Vesna Ognjenovic decided to help war-traumatized refugee children. She offered her assistance to the local Red Cross but was told they had no program which could use her help. Undeterred, she marshaled support from other professionals and began to conduct workshops and organize activities for refugee children. Eventually, this work was noticed by UNHCR and other international organizations, enabling the group to expand throughout Serbia. After four years, Hi Neighbor became a registered NGO with more than 130 members and now offers training for teachers and other professionals working with refugee children.

Another local NGO which has expanded with assistance from an international NGO centers around a dynamic young psychologist, Dzenana Rustempasic. She was living in one of the most bombarded areas of Sarajevo, Heroes' Square, so named because more people died there than in any other part of the city. In the early years, Rustempasic, like everyone else, was consumed with her own family's survival. This extraordinary woman transcended her own trauma by focusing on the children around her who had lost friends and family members, had no schooling or social life, and were ill-equipped to cope with terror. She opened her home to these children and offered daily activities to introduce some measure of normalcy into their lives. Three years later, she is the director of Heroes' Children, an NGO that provides psychological support, educational assistance, and drama productions to the children living around Heroes' Square.

Working under a five-year USAID Umbrella Grant, International Rescue Committee (IRC) has been able to offer assistance to more than 50 local NGOs such as Heroes' Children and Hi Neighbor. This development package includes capacity-building training and financial assistance, including training for IRC grantee project managers in the *Technology of Participation™* methods[4] by the Institute of Cultural Affairs.

However, the long-term sustainability of indigenous humanitarian aid is in question because many needs addressed by grassroots organizations cannot be met by local governments. The international community's role in relation to this grassroots movement has been two-fold. In the early years of the war, the international community funded local NGOs. As the level of the NGOs' sophistication and the scope of their work increased, the need for capacity-building and organizational development followed. Now, with the imminent departure of the international community and without a local environment that supports this movement, both financially and politically, capacity-building will have little consequence.

Indeed, the Balkan environment raises complex issues for civil society. The current post-communist situation is only a few years old, so results cannot yet be considered sustainable, even where they seem well established. Most perplexing is the lack of viable, equitable government systems that offer some promise of continuity. Too many policies and practices are carryovers from the only available structures and laws, those derived from communist totalitarianism.

Introducing the Rule of Law

A fundamental pre-requisite for the effective functioning of civil society is an acceptance of the principle of the rule of law.[5] Over the past several years, the American Bar Association (ABA) has been active in Croatia and BiH, working with the local judiciary to establish the rule of law and government structures accountable to its citizens. ABA operates throughout Europe's emerging democracies under the name of CEELI, the Central and East Europe Law Initiative.

In December 1993, 100 judges from throughout Croatia came together to explore judicial ethics and develop disciplinary procedures against unethical judges, a concept for which there was no written code. Most of the judiciary in Croatia are held over from communist times and it will take years to move away from a judiciary reflective of the previous system.

The conference organizers from CEELI prepared a format of panel presentations and workshops that would be routine in democratic countries where participation is taken for granted. The presentations were not unusual to this group but workshops led by teams of Croatian facilitators were a new experience. People who were accustomed to exercising absolute control in their courtrooms suddenly became participants faced with unfamiliar egalitarian practices. However, most judges adapted and responded enthusiastically.

In Croatia, schoolchildren have been taught not to have opinions and adults have a deeply ingrained respect for authority, born in some cases from fear and in other cases from training. Ironically, most Croats love to orate at great length and to correct and inform their peers but "brainstorming" requires a mental and emotional adjustment. Thus, the workshops were strange both for participants and the Croatian facilitators. One of the facilitators, Zlata Pavic, who teaches English at the Law Faculty and Social Work School of the University of Zagreb and is the director of the ICA Croatia, described the experience:

> There was a lot of fear and suspicion how people so autonomous and dominant in the courtroom would respond to group methods. All my facilitation skills seemed insufficient and inappropriate. But the judges were very enthusiastic. We had to be careful to keep to the time schedule because everybody was anxious to contribute to the final product. Most said they wanted to apply the methods in the towns where they work as judges. One told us, "This is the first time I have been asked what I thought about a code of judicial ethics and disciplinary procedures."[6]

In addition to the rule of law, other basic tenets of civil society such as freedom of speech and an independent media have yet to gain widespread acceptance in the former Yugoslavia. However, working slowly but persistently, eschewing a requirement for measurable change, is the most likely way to bring about pervasive, sustainable change.

Birthing A Free Media

In building civil society, a free media is such an important tool for people to hold governments accountable that its independence from government control is a top priority. However, given that many Western European countries have government-funded, if not government-controlled radio and television, state-run media in the Balkans would seem normal to many. Once people have tasted free speech and free media, they are hungry for more and governments have little chance of retaining control and sustaining repression, although they may periodically try.[7]

From "studios" in the catacomb-like basement of the building housing the Organization for Security and Cooperation in Europe, an important broadcasting effort began when an international group called Search for Common Ground (SCG) partnered with a local NGO, the International Center for Help Communications and Relationships, to form Resolutions Radio. Their talk-show programs were designed to promote reconciliation and civil society in Bosnia by finding common ground on issues ranging from refugee return to inter-ethnic communications.

An initial difficulty for Resolutions Radio was the inability to arrange callers from both sides of the Inter-Entity Boundary Line established by the Dayton Accord, since the two sides, Republika Srpska (RS) and the Federa-tion (of Bosnian Croats and Muslims) had not decided to reconnect their telephone linkages to each other. People-on-the-street interviews in RS capi-tal of Pale helped address this problem.

When the RS minister of telecommunications refused to come to Sarajevo, an agreement was struck for the producers to provide his point of view. On the Federation side, a deputy minister from Mostar agreed to participate via phone and the Federation sent a telecommunications official to present its view. Dur-ing the program, other officials called in to be included in the discussion, and after the producer reported on the position of the Pale government, all guests agreed there was common ground on this issue and that, if the minister was unable to come to Sarajevo, they would happily meet him in the RS city of Banja Luka. In the delicate balance of power in BiH, this seemingly small accomplishment was an important step forward.

In Macedonia, SCG has brought together journalists from the country's leading Macedonian, Albanian, and Turkish newspapers in a team reporting project that required co-authorship and resulted in three multi-part series which demonstrated that all Macedonians share similar concerns about the economy, the health-care system, and the environment. Other SCG efforts in Macedonia have included joint television productions to foster use of conflict resolution methods among pre-teens, inter-ethnic roundtables eliciting consensus rec-ommendations for the Macedonian government, and a mobilization of Macedonian and Albanian students to clean up the country's monuments. SCG President John Marks commented:

> In the end, it is impossible to demonstrate conclusively if any of our activities have prevented violence in Macedonia. Validating preven-tion is like trying to prove a negative. The bottom line, however, is that Macedonia has not exploded. We believe the combined effort of the international community — including international organizations, gov-ernments, and NGOs like us — has made a real difference. At the same time, we are convinced that outside efforts would have been in vain if the political will had not existed among Macedonia's leaders to keep their country peaceful.[8]

This comment, and the stories recounted in this chapter, remind us that a strong, accountable state and a strong, responsive civil society go hand in hand. One is not possible without the other. However, whether in government or civil society, it is when individuals and small groups of people decide to risk forging the new rather than repeat the patterns of the past that society moves ahead. The initial steps being taken to create civil society in the Balkans may seem small and insignificant but they may well help decide the future of this society as it emerges from the embers of war.

NOTES

1. The United Nations High Commissioner for Refugees distributed massive quantities of plastic sheeting to cover bombed-out walls and windows. The plastic always had embedded in it the UNHCR cupped-hands logo or the acronym.

2. NATO's Implementation Force.

3. Quotation from Julie Dimichelis in a taped interview for an UMCOR documentary.

4. For a discriptionof the *Technology of Participation*, see appendix, p. 295.

5. See Robert Bothwell. "Indicators of A Healthy Civil Society." pp. 249-262.

6. Zlata Pavic. Personal communication.

7. The Milosevic regime's suppression of unfavorable election results in Serbia in December 1996 resulted in hundreds of thousands of enraged citizens protesting in weeks of peaceful but insistent street demonstrations. In January 1997, Milosevic acquiesced by acknowledging he suppressed election results and called for a coalition government. In Croatia, the role of a free media was highlighted during the November 1966 elections when the Tudzman regime closed an independent radio station, an act which resulted in citizen uproar and mass demonstrations.

8. John Marks. Personal communication.

4. Grassroots Empowerment in Ethiopian Villages

Terry Bergdall and Frank Powell

The state should not believe that it alone knows better than anyone else what the society needs. It should trust its citizens and enable them to share in a substantial way in exercising responsibility for the condition of society.

— Vaclav Havel

The community elders in the Atare Genda were extremely suspicious when they first met Wuditu Assefa. Wuditu introduced herself as a facilitator with a new pilot program being undertaken by the zonal government. The name was suspicious enough, the Community Empowerment Program, but God above only knew what a facilitator was. The leaders had a wealth of experience with nice sounding projects from the government which seemed only to result in hardship and frustration. Besides, Wuditu was a woman. How could she be of any use to them?

The elderly men Wuditu met in Atare Genda were the leaders of the local *kire,* one of the countless traditional self-help organizations in Ethiopia for arranging community activities around important cultural events like weddings and funerals.[1] The elders had been informed by the chairman of their peasant association (PA), that government officials wished to meet with them because they were handicraftsmen, but gave no other details. Wuditu explained that she was in Atare Genda to conduct a workshop with community residents to plan ways people living in the area could begin to solve their problems. This was part of a pilot program involving many *kires* in designated areas of the South Wollo Zone.

Suspicions or not, African hospitality is a fundamental prerequisite in the highlands of rural Ethiopia. After a few cups of tea and a lot of informal discussion, Wuditu and her team of facilitators began to learn about life in the area. A major conflict existed between the craftsmen of Atare Genda and the non-craftsmen farmers who lived around them. The craftsmen felt strongly that they had been the victims of social negligence by the leaders and other members of the PA. An ancient prejudice in Ethiopia considers handicraft work to be the task of those who have the "evil eye." This traditional bigotry continued to cause them a lot of trouble. They told the facilitators they had recently wished to build a church for themselves in Atare Genda but were forbidden to do so by their non-handicraftsmen neighbors.

The facilitators were sympathetic listeners and as time passed the conversation began to warm. At long last, the elders even told them why they were so suspicious; they feared the purpose of a government-sponsored workshop would be to organize a producers' cooperative. If the handicraftsmen organized such a cooperative, they were afraid they might be forced to give up the small agricultural plots which were an essential part of their livelihood. Past government policy during the "dark regime" of President Mengistu, popularly called the *derg*, had forbidden two incomes, and they were very unclear about future government policy.

This, the facilitators explained, was definitely not their purpose. They said they hoped to conduct a Community Participation Workshop (CPW), the sole objective of which would be to identify development needs according to the views of the *kire* members and then to enable people to create an action plan whereby community residents could begin to address those needs through their own efforts and resources. Satisfied that the CPW was not a risk for them, though not entirely convinced of its usefulness, the *kire* leaders agreed to call a meeting.

But Wuditu shocked them with another request. In order for the workshop to be held, it would be necessary for women and youth to attend in addition to the men. "Why?" they asked. "We speak for our women here." Nevertheless, they were told, women and youth must attend or, as Wuditu explained, she and her team would have no option but to go somewhere else to conduct the workshop. It was a fundamental principle of the program.

Reluctantly, the elders agreed to invite women and youth and set a date for the workshop in two days' time, but the surprises were not yet over. Wuditu said she and the other facilitators would need to stay with the craftsmen as house guests until the workshop was completed. In all their lives, the craftsmen of Atare Genda had never before received such a request from an educated senior government expert like Wuditu. She and her team were most welcome!

During evening conversations with their hosts, Wuditu and her team pieced together a general picture of the community. Atare Genda is located in PA 67 in the Debre Sina District. It is in the highlands, seven kilometers from the district center, Mekaneselam, and is bounded by the Legedaba River which flows into the Blue Nile after a 20 kilometer journey from Atare Genda. The population is predominately Christian, of the Amhara tribe, and consists of 150 households. Though all people are farmers in Atare Genda, most households also earn income through craftsmanship as potters, blacksmiths, tanners, and weavers. Agriculture is primarily subsistence and the major crops are teff, wheat, beans, and chickpeas. About half the households own an ox and working tools. The average family farm plot is about one acre. Health services are provided in Mekaneselam. About 30% of eligible children in Atare Genda attend school in neighboring Soye and Legemara. Those few who continue with intermediate school go to Mekaneselam. More than half the adults are illiterate.

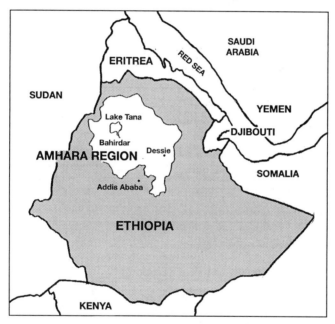

Figure 1. The Amhara Region of Ethiopia

The facilitators also learned about past development activities which had taken place in Atare Genda. The cleaning of springs and maintenance of the Legedaba River diversions for irrigation purposes were undertaken by local farmers. This work, however, was usually done in a disorganized way. Minimal cleaning of the spring was done only when pollution from animals and the washing of clothes became intolerable, and then it was done on an individual basis. Tree planting, forest protection, the construction of an adult literacy center, checkdams, and terraces had been accomplished through mass mobilization work organized by the lowest level of the government bureaucracy, the peasant associations. These mobilization campaigns, however, were extremely unpopular because people were forced to work on activities that didn't benefit them directly. Much of this work, the facilitators were told, had been destroyed recently by unknown persons. The facilitators were familiar with this story since they had heard about destruction and vandalism of mobilization work in most places they had visited.

As the evening talk wound down, the hosts talked more about their living conditions as craftsmen. People in Atare Genda had gone on a two-week strike the previous year by refusing to sell their wares when they felt they had been verbally abused by people at the market in Mekaneselam. The strike ended when members of the district council came and offered them an apology on behalf of customers and traders.

Information gained from the evening conversations contributed to an evolving picture of the situation in Atare Genda which had begun to take shape for the facilitators when they first arrived in the *kire*. They had already experienced several difficulties during preparations for the workshop. Following their usual procedure, they had first approached the PA leaders with an official letter of introduction from the zone and district administration offices. They then explained they wished to conduct a community workshop with Atare Genda craftsmen. This was important because they were expected to conduct workshops that represented the general geo-social composition of the district, which included doing workshops with craftsmen.

The PA chairman, however, did not like the idea of them going to the craftsmen since he thought they had little of value to contribute. Instead he suggested his own *kire* which he felt was much better informed and, furthermore, were "real" farmers. Finally, at the insistence of the facilitators, he agreed to meet with the *kire* leaders at Atare Genda and arrange a workshop for them.

Community Participation Workshop

The CPW was held on 25 May 1994. Since Atare Genda was to serve as the "craftsman *kire*," the craftsmen thought this was their big chance to speak on their own. Therefore, when the PA leaders and nearby farmers arrived at the workshop site, the craftsmen of Atare Genda insisted they leave. After a long debate, these unwelcome neighbors finally agreed to go. The PA chairman, however, insisted no meeting could be conducted in his area without his approval and that no one, therefore, could force him to leave. He said he would respect their request and not be a part of the discussions, but he would sit on the side as an observer. After these departures, 63 people remained, including 16 women, 36 men, and 11 youth.

The workshop was conducted following the standard format used by the facilitators to identify development needs, constraints, and solutions, and to create local action plans. The CPW took approximately six hours to complete on a single day. Key discussions in the workshop focused on the improvement of working tools, the need for non-craftsmen to respect the craftsmen's skills, and past planting of communal trees on land which they thought suitable for farm land.

The two actions plans created at the CPW involved terracing, which was suggested by the women, and the cleaning of springs, which was suggested by both men and youth. Interestingly, these plans were not directly related to their craftsmen concerns. This was due to the fact that even though they are craftsmen, subsistence farming still provides most people in Atare Genda with their basic foodstuff, and water is an essential element of any community.

As in all CPWs, the four-person facilitation team stayed in the homes of farmers while they were in Atare Genda. The facilitators had brought food with them and had invited their hosts to share in the meal; this was to avoid being a burden on the limited means of the people in the *kire*. When the CPW was over, the residents of Atare Genda prepared a meal and invited the facilitators to attend. During this feast, the people of Atare Genda expressed their deep gratitude about the way they had been treated with respect by the facilitators. They said even the fact that the facilitators had joined them in the closing meal caused them to have a "*huge* happiness." They further said they would look forward with pleasure to the day the facilitators returned.

Workshop Follow-Up

A follow-up meeting to the CPW in Atare Genda happened three months later. Due to heavy rains, only nine women and 25 men attended. The youth were absent because job applications and interviews for census takers were being done on that particular day in Mekaneselam.

At the follow-up meeting, the facilitators found that people in the *kire* were proud of their accomplishments resulting from their CPW action plans. Four springs had been cleaned and fenced (the project suggested by the men and the youth) and 18 kilometers of terraces had been constructed (the project suggested by the women). Both action plans had been completed in an exemplary fashion.

The reasons given for these successes by Atare Genda residents were that the community was working together and that everyone was involved in the planning. Surprisingly, even though they had insisted the PA leadership leave the CPW, they also said they had been successful because of PA support. This was in sharp contrast to their original complaints of social negligence by the PA prior to the CPW. The PA gave wood to build a fence around the springs. Some of this wood was sold by the project coordinators selected at the CPW to purchase nails and to pay for carpentry work at the springs.

In addition to the two projects planned during the CPW, a number of other activities had been completed by the follow-up meeting. Thirty-two check dams were constructed and 12,000 tree seedlings were planted. Both resulted from discussions that had taken place in the community after the CPW. Seedlings for the trees were mostly purchased at the market, 70 seedlings for one birr (6 birr = $US 1). Some had produced their own seedlings in household nurseries. The primary motivation for planting seedlings was the eventual use of the trees as building materials in private construction.

Another solution to one of the big concerns discussed at the workshop had also been initiated. A traditional savings scheme, *ekub,* had been started to provide funds for buying craftsmen tools. Common in rural areas, *ekub* involves a lottery in which everyone wins at some point during the year. The decision to use this system for purchasing craftsmen's tools was a new development.

In debriefing conversations with the facilitators after the follow-up meeting, people in Atare Genda said they had learned three key things about self-reliant development since the CPW:

- They cannot wait for external bodies to solve their problems; that is why they decided to start their *ekub* for buying tools.
- Direct personal benefit is a key to doing development work; that is why they had been successful in planting 12,000 tree seedlings.
- They gained renewed pride and self-confidence about being craftsmen as a result of their discussions during the CPW. This made them eager to do development and to pass on their skills to their sons and daughters.

The PA chairman appears to have taken a new relationship to handicraftsmen in Atare Genda. Even though he had first expressed contempt for holding the workshop there, and in spite of being forced to leave the workshop, the chairman did arrange practical support from the PA to help implement the action plans. People in Atare Genda recognized and appreciated this support. This seems to suggest some change in attitude on the part of the PA chairman. He could have easily ignored, or even taken retaliatory action against people in the *kire* if he had wished.

In December 1994, Wuditu and her team of facilitators returned to Atare Genda. After a warm welcome, she was taken to see a new onion plot. Six families had worked together to plant a half acre of onions as a new income-generating project. Their decision to start the onion plot was inspired by the results of the *kire's* initiatives after the CPW. Once they began to think about it, they realized there were many things they could do to improve their lives if they put their minds to it.

COMMUNITY EMPOWERMENT IN HISTORICAL PERSPECTIVE

The toddling steps toward self-reliant development taking place in *kires* like Atare Genda need to be seen in a wider context to appreciate their significance. The emergence of civil society, with its emphasis on voluntary associations and local initiative, is occurring in Ethiopia against a history of unquestioning obedience, passivity, and dependence. It is characterized by the feudal past of an imperial system, centralized planning under a communist regime, and a food aid culture arising from the benevolence of international drought relief.

Imperial rule in Ethiopia, when ended in the early 1970s, could be traced through a legendary chain stretching unbroken between King Solomon and the Queen of Sheba of biblical times to Emperor Haile Selassie in the 20th century. As with other traditional feudal societies, a local farmer's well-being depended upon positive relationships with powerful benefactors. Within this environment, a cultural etiquette emerged where peasants were expected to defer to those in authority. In response, powerful aristocrats were expected, more or less, to guard the peasantry's welfare.

The feudal society of imperial rule was replaced with the centralized planning of a communist state. A quota approach to development sprang from a command style of government. Central ministries set targets and apportioned them to regions and administrative areas until, finally, quotas reached the local level with dictates that terraces be dug, roads be maintained, and schools or health clinics be built. Peasant associations were directed to achieve these targets through mass mobilization, a practice which amounted to little more than forced labor. Regular work days were organized to complete projects, often requiring people to travel long distances from where they lived. Failure to participate brought severe penalties from the authorities.

The communist state was eventually overthrown, but a strong legacy still lingers. Though often softer in tone, the basic same model still persists and is the common interpretation given to the concept of participation. Development quotas continue to come from above and mass mobilization is still the primary means of meeting these targets. Even in their most enlightened forms, an overwhelming majority of current development activities in Ethiopia can be characterized as essentially expert-based and top-down.

This core relationship is maintained in many participatory programs. An example is the Local Level Participatory Planning Approach used by the Bureau of Agriculture in the Amhara Region. Soil conservation targets are typically set in zonal and district planning offices. Government development agents (DAs) — agricultural extension officers in other systems — are instructed to make surveys and gather information in large catchment areas, formulate proposed activities for the community's review, and share their conclusions at large meetings before organizing work days to accomplish agreed-upon soil conservation measures. This is a consultative approach to participation, but the DA's expertise is the key ingredient; people's involvement is supplementary.

When expert-based development is coupled with an authoritative history, unintended results often occur. Sasakawa Global 2000 provides a model for one of the most widespread agricultural programs in rural Ethiopia today. It consists of a package approach for upgrading agricultural production through improved seeds and fertilizers. In principle, this approach is accomplished voluntarily through PADETES, the Participatory Demonstration and Training Extension System, but its practice is often far from voluntary.

Every agricultural extension officer in the region is required to enlist 20 farmers in his or her area and is expected to find the most productive sites. This is mandated from above. Many farmers, however, are reluctant to be involved. Near Dessie, farmers are hesitant because:

- They can harvest only two crops a year instead of the usual three which they obtain through local varieties of seeds.
- Inputs come through big loans which must be repaid over many years.
- Farmers are completely dependent upon the timely deliveries of seed and fertilizer, which experience has repeatedly shown to be an unreliable arrangement.

Yet few farmers dare to refuse enrollment in the program when a DA designates their plots for the program. If they opt out, there is the fear, if not the actual threat, of having their land taken away and given to others based on accusations of mismanagement.

This, of course, is not the intended approach found in the program's training manuals, but is what occurs within the legacy of a top-down heritage built upon the supremacy of the expert's opinion and the traditional etiquette of peasant deference. Sasakawa Global 2000 and a host of other programs employ participatory approaches susceptible to contradictory interpretations and practices because of the traditional roles and relationships people automatically assume.

Development activities across the region typically continue to be *initiated* by outside experts — extension officers, donors, and bureaucrats — while village residents are expected to make a *response*. Consistent with current rhetoric about the need for local participation, this approach is increasingly employed in a more sensitive, consultative manner. For example, extension officers are encouraged to play more of a salesman role to convince rather than being a harsh taskmaster, though even this may not be put in practice. Still, the central relationship of "experts initiate, communities respond" is basically unchanged. For many people in Ethiopia, "community participation" is a euphemism for the more efficient and palatable solicitation of local involvement in projects that are conceptualized, planned, and funded by external authorities.

Challenges to Participatory Approaches

Such an interpretation is apt to reinforce passive tendencies among the rural population. People often wait for an outsider (who is well supplied with expertise, food aid, political power, or money) to tell them what to do. Dependency reigns. This does not mean people are incapable of assuming responsibility for development, but it does imply the need for a change in attitude and self-perception if they are to become primary actors in the development process. It also requires a change in attitude among outside development agents about the way they conduct their work in the rural areas.

The basic issue becomes one of matching appropriate practices of promoting participation to desired concepts and understandings. Many people say that participation should encourage self-confidence and local responsibility. This is certainly consistent with much of the international discourse about civil society. If this is the interpretation about popular participation one desires, then there is a need to turn the conventional relationship between development agents and the people upside down. Yet the subtleties and complexities of doing so in Ethiopia are enormous.

The issue of relief distributions is an example. More than a decade has passed since the world renowned famine of the early 1980s, yet food relief remains a dominant feature across much of Ethiopia. A simple idea is to use relief food as an incentive for encouraging development work. This is at the heart of "food for work" programs, often misleadingly referred to as "employment generation schemes." Determination of the development projects may be done in various ways; usually, they are decided and organized by PA leaders. Whatever the planning process, food for work undermines local responsibility. The link between the initiation by an external benefactor and the response of rural residents is reinforced, not broken. Passive waiting by the community for the outsider's arrival and initiative, replete with resources and guidance, is the logical result.

It often goes beyond passive waiting. Communities have become conditioned to actively *demand* assistance as a prerequisite for assuming direct responsibility in solving their own problems. The UN World Food Program (WFP) is a primary sponsor of "food for work" in South Wollo Zone, along with other programs for food security. The zonal WFP representative tells a story about distributing free fertilizer to farmers in one area. Weeks later he returned to this area only to learn that the fertilizer was still in storage and had not yet been used. When he asked why, he was told that people were insisting that a work day be organized with "food for work" payments before they would apply the fertilizer. Some might argue that this is a positive sign of peasants negotiating with the system, but it does little to promote local ownership or responsibility for development.

Throughout Ethiopia's history, both ancient and modern, people have become conditioned to depend on outside agencies or the powers above for the basic means of life and have come to expect reprisals if they fall out of line. Previous systems have fostered strong traditions rooted in obedience and paternalistic care. Self-reliance, self-sufficiency, personal initiative, and local responsibility are all concepts often referred to in theory but have been extremely difficult to realize in practice. In this historical perspective, the success of small community development projects, like those in Atare Genda, planned and implemented by the people themselves, is extremely significant.

THE COMMUNITY EMPOWERMENT PROGRAM (CEP)

The Community Empowerment Program was launched as part of Swedish development assistance to the Amhara National Regional State in north central Ethiopia. Pilot activities for the program took place in four districts (Legehida, Legambo, Debre Sina, and Saint) west of Dessie in the South Wollo Zone from mid-1994 through the end of 1996. Over 60 field facilitators were seconded or specially hired to work full-time on the program, which was funded by the Swedish International Development Cooperation Agency (Sida).

CEP as a Learning Laboratory

The primary objective of CEP, stated in the Plan of Operations, was to assist rural people to become agents of their own development. The program was not designed nor launched as a total package with a detailed blueprint; in contrast, it evolved as a process-oriented program. Conducting CPWs and planning small-scale projects was the key implementation strategy. This was for the sake of catalyzing local development initiatives by people in the *kires*. No external resources would be provided to assist the *kires* in the implementation of their projects. All work would be completed with locally-available resources and local know-how, or it would not be done at all.

This approach challenged many conventional assumptions about external support to local communities. The overriding issue during the pilot work of CEP was to find ways of supporting local initiatives by rural communities without undermining their journey toward self-reliance. Premature support often aborts that journey. Time was needed to demonstrate and establish a fragile bottom-up approach within an existing environment strongly dominated by top-down practices.

The program was designed with a strong bias on self-reliance and specially constituted teams of full-time facilitators in order to create a learning laboratory. As a pilot program, CEP was given permission to experiment with an alternative approach without prematurely being swamped by the prevailing context. It was thought that if participatory techniques were simply employed within an old top-down system, then a more human face might be presented, but very little of substance would likely change. Passive attitudes would only be addressed slightly and rural people would continue to lack an enduring sense of local ownership for sustainable development work.

The pilot phase of the program was, however, set within a larger strategic framework. CEP was not based on some simplistic idea of merely replacing a top-down approach with a bottom-up one. Rather, it was understood that a healthy dynamic relationship needs to exist between the bottom and the top so the two might complement each another. Since Ethiopia's unique history has resulted in a situation where top-down approaches have totally overwhelmed the bottom-up perspective, local empowerment is essential to establish a basis for a creative two-way dialogue.

The combination of local initiative and the nurture of community capacity for management of self-reliant projects is a fundamental first step for this. In addition, five issues were identified during the conceptualization of CEP as crucial for program support at later stages:

- Provision of technical expertise to enable communities to successfully complete local action plans.
- Eventual community access to external resources for activities too large to be accomplished with local resources.
- Effective collaboration of governmental, non-governmental, and business sectors in support of community initiatives.
- Adaptation of the extension service to support a bottom-up, process approach to development.
- The formation of institutional linkages to continue empowering local people to be agents of their own development.

The process orientation of the program implied that the best means of resolving issues like these was to allow various solutions to evolve over time rather than to impose specific pre-determined directives from the beginning.

Two-Year Pilot Activities

The experiences of Wuditu and her facilitation team in Atare Genda have served as an example of CEP interventions at the community level. Wuditu and her team, however, were only one of 12 facilitation teams working during the two and a half years of the pilot program. Similar experiences were repeated time and again across the four pilot districts of South Wollo during 1994-96. Community participation workshops were held in a total of 309 *kires,* over half of which completed the entire cycle of activities — three follow-up meetings in the year following the CPW.

During the two years of work, community self-help development projects were carefully monitored and documented in the *kires* where CPWs had taken place. All this work was completed solely on the basis of local community resources; no external capital assistance was provided. This was a shocking revelation to many government officials who had previously believed that significant development could only take place through officially planned and managed activities.

As a pilot program, CEP was designed to apply new concepts about popular participation and empowerment at the most grassroots level. Emphasis was put on gaining insights based on practical field experience. Though officials at the PA, district, and zonal levels of government were continually briefed about the purpose, design, and progress of CEP during the entire first year of implementation, this had only a superficial effect; theoretical concepts were not easily grasped through office presentations.

During the second year of implementation, several workshops were scheduled with extension officers, PA leaders, and district officials. These were crucial to enable institutional learning during the pilot phase of the program. The workshops were designed by CEP lead facilitators with the assistance of two external consultants; the lead facilitators were then responsible for organizing and conducting the workshops. Except for the workshops with the extension officers explained below, participants from the *kires* also attended. Though these workshops were tailored for each audience and varied in duration, they all shared common elements.

First, each workshop began with an introduction and general discussion about different development approaches. Drawing on their past experience, participants were asked to consider the benefits of and reasons for bottom-up and top-down development, self-reliance and dependency, and sustainable development.

Second, results from *kire* action plans were reported and discussed. This step in the workshops served as a practical link between the quantitative and qualitative monitoring activities of the program. Relevant statistics were presented about the number of CPWs and follow-up meetings; participation by men, women, and youth; the types and numbers of projects planned; and the implementation results. The *kire* representatives at the workshops told stories about the changes and accomplishments that had occurred in their community since their participation in the CEP workshops.

Third, discussion moved to the role and function of the focal audience for supporting local development initiatives. This was accomplished by having representatives from the lower levels meeting in one group while officials from the higher level (the focal group of the workshop) were meeting in another. For example, at PA workshops, representatives from *kires* met in one group and PA leaders in the other while at the district workshops, PA and *kire* leaders met in one group and district officials in another. The opinions of the two groups often varied at the beginning and were the source of several "hot" conversations between the different parties. This is not surprising in an environment in which, during the early days of CEP, there were numerous reports of PA leaders uprooting tree seedlings planted by *kires* because they had not first obtained permission from the PA committee.

Finally, after the dialogue about the benefits, desirability, and potential of self-reliance and bottom-up planning, participants created action plans for ways that the focal group of the workshop could begin to provide practical support to initiatives occurring at lower levels.

The workshops for extension officers were dramatically expanded in time and subject matter from the generic format described above. The program design included classroom training in participation techniques, followed by an opportunity to apply these techniques in the field. Though *kire* members did not attend the classroom sessions, the extension officers obviously met with *kire* members when they went to assist CEP facilitators conduct CPWs. They also participated in monitoring visits to nearby *kires* to observe progress on projects planned during previous *kire* workshops.

Step by step, this entire series of workshops from the *kire* to the PA to the district slowly began to give form to a growing consensus, from the bottom upwards, about the actual potential of grassroots communities to decide and act upon their perceptions of development needs. Beyond the mere granting of permission for this to occur, which in itself is a significant concession in much of Ethiopia,[2] officials at these intermediate levels began to develop practical ways to actively encourage and support community initiatives.

Several extension officers, for example, made arrangements with PA leaders to excuse some *kires* who had planned their own development projects from mobilization work days. Others experimented with facilitating their own community planning events through the use of the participatory techniques they had learned during the workshops. These reflect significantly new ways of working. Such behavioral changes were a reflection of emerging new attitudes, both of which were a product of the institutional learning taking place within the program.

One of the major problems identified repeatedly in the workshops was the apparent conflict of a bottom-up planning approach like CEP with the prevailing quota system in which numerous development targets are allocated to districts and PAs. Though many extension officers expressed their deep appreciation for the participatory methodology and experimental activities of the CEP facilitators, and their desire to do the same themselves, they thought it impossible to operate in such a manner as long as their supervisors required them to mobilize the community to meet specified development targets. The problem, as they saw it, was systemic. This problem also reveals the vast distances which are yet to be traveled if the small, though important, signs of local initiative generated within CEP are to be transformed into a civic movement.

FUTURE PROSPECTS

This chapter has been written just as the two years of the pilot program in South Wollo has come to an end. Insights from the CEP experience have been integrated into a draft program document for long-term region-wide support to the Amhara Region which will be financed by Sida. CEP has awakened considerable interest in the possibility of rural residents becoming agents of their own development, using their traditional structures of association as a foundation upon which to build. Most importantly, this has been accomplished through practical demonstrations instead of theoretical discussion.

Still, Ethiopia remains an extremely conservative society with deeply instilled traditions of top-down management. For two brief years, a unique configuration of conditions allowed CEP to function as a learning laboratory. During this time significant signs of hope for the emergence of a new civil society began to flower. The immense challenges for its future development, however, should not be underestimated. Long-established political structures and practices are very difficult to change, but once awakened, the power of new self-images among ordinary citizens cannot be underestimated. As one *kire* member said when asked about the prospects of his community continuing to do development work on its own once the facilitators stopped returning to his village, "We have come too far and learned too much to turn back now. We know what we are capable of doing and are ready to do it!"

NOTES

1. Many societies have traditional structures of voluntary association on which contemporary civil society can be built. For a description of pre-modern Arab associations, see Saad Eddin Ibrahim's chapter, "Populism, Islam, and Civil Society in the Arab World." pp. 53-66.

2. Even today, peasant farmers must obtain permission from the Department of Agriculture before they can harvest their own crops.

5. The Recovery of Civic Engagement in America

James P. Troxel

A quiet revolution is taking place between Americans working in small groups and with their government. This revolution has several different names and forms — community building, civic revival, national renewal. It is slow to build the connective tissue that would make it a national phenomenon. Born of neither the left nor the right, this mosaic of community efforts is not led by charismatic leaders or political parties so much as it is shaped by partners — from neighborhoods, from city hall, and from business.

— Curtis Johnson

Although neither the concept nor the reality of civil society is a recent phenomenon, a renewed interest in the subject emerged in Eastern Europe after communism crumbled. Leaders such as Vaclav Havel, the president of the Czech Republic, wanted to go beyond establishing new governments and create a culture that could sustain political and economic liberalism. They looked for help to those private groups beyond the reach of the state that had nourished dissident life, ranging from citizens' associations to churches, from human rights groups to jazz clubs. Around the same time, the Western democracies, which saw themselves as models for the rest of the world, were confronted by sagging economies, a fraying social fabric, and the loss of national purpose. Here too, experts and statesmen agreed, revitalizing civil society would overcome the malaise.

The challenge for civil society in the United States is to capture a spirit of responsible citizenship and public service. It will take a radical renewal of citizenship for the transformation of government to be fulfilled. Both are needed to realize a truly "civil society."

In this chapter, "public service" refers to both the work of government and citizen volunteers.[1] The voluntary domain in the United States includes a vast network of non-profit organizations. Sometimes observers refer to this domain as the "third sector" with business and government forming the other two. I invite the reader to view the voluntary and government arenas not as opposites, but as woven together in symbiotic connection. Civil society is found when both the voluntary and government domains are fully enlivened and functioning well together. While many use "civil society" to refer to those social activities which fall between the individual and the state, civil society and the public sector together are the focus of this chapter. I will examine what is taking place in the United States today in both the voluntary and governmental domains, suggest where they are blocked in recovering civil society, and point to some possible ways out of the dilemma.

THE RESURGENCE
OF ASSOCIATIONAL LIFE IN AMERICA

Our Nation's "Social Capital"

One hundred and fifty years ago, the great nineteenth century French commentator on America, Alexis de Tocqueville, marveled at our eagerness to form associations and called it perhaps our most distinctive characteristic as a nation. He called these associations "great, free schools of democracy."[2] In that sense, they play the most vital role in crafting civil society.

Recent history in America suggests it might be incorrect to say that civil society is being recovered. There are so many loud voices that seek to divide us. When black churches are burned, or synagogues and mosques are desecrated, America knows it is not immune to forces that have brought heartache and ruin to so many people all over the world.

In 1995, in a tremendously influential commentary, Harvard University social scientist Robert D. Putnam asserted that the voluntary social institutions that keep America's communities together are fading.[3] The article provided such evidence as the decrease in number of parent teacher associations in local schools and the decrease in the influence of civic-minded organizations. It humorously noted that even one of America's favorite pastimes, league bowling, is on the decline while at the same time the number of people bowling is on the increase. People seem to be "bowling alone" and foregoing the opportunity for vibrant civic discourse that takes place among teams of people on the bowling lanes.

Putnam refers to the capacity of communities to enjoy a vital civic life as its "social capital," comprised of such things as its norms regarding trust, reciprocity, and civic engagement that are indispensable to collective existence. According to Putnam, it is not that certain communities enjoy a more vital civic life because they are prosperous; they are prosperous because they have a vital civic life. To make democracy work better is to strengthen its degree of social capital.

Putnam's article produced wide discussion of his data as well as his conclusion. Much of it included attempts to refute his premise.[4] If, in fact, it takes voluntary associations to keep American democracy together, and if these associations are eroding, is democracy in America eroding as well? Not everyone thinks so. Indeed, some observers have suggested the nature of voluntary associations has simply shifted, particularly with the advent of electronic communication. Public discourse is now taking place not in the bowling league but on the Internet in the numerous "chat rooms." Richard Stengel, writing in *Time* magazine, cites social movements for women, minorities, and the environment, and voluntary organizations they have spawned, as evidence of associational resurgence.[5]

The elements of social capital are not always as visible as one might imagine. In their work on community assets, John McKnight and John Kretzmann of Northwestern University found that "communities that have initiated an 'Associational Inventory' have regularly uncovered a much more varied and numerous set of local associations than expected. One very low-income neighborhood in Chicago, for example, recently 'mapped' 249 local associations."[6]

These associations have often indicated a willingness to enhance their contributions to mutual care activities, such as reaching out to help teenagers or older people, and join with others to work on pressing community issues.

Civic Engagement

Civil society is strengthened when there is increased citizen involvement in the political process. Creative experiments in citizen participation have taken place over the last several years all across America. For example, Old Fort, North Carolina, a community of 700 in the foothills of the Blue Ridge Mountains, held its first town meeting and 10 months later, listed 13 major civic accomplishments including a new housing subdivision, fire station, park, community theater, drug store, and a car wash. Said one resident: "It's like getting a new chair for your living room. Once you put the new chair into the room, you start to look at the whole room in a different way. You see the curtains need to be changed or the couch is a bit tacky."

On a larger scale, St. Paul, Minnesota, a city of 270,000, has developed one of the most comprehensive participation systems anywhere in the country. Its 17 district councils, elected by neighborhoods, have specific responsibilities for zoning, housing, development oversight, and the capacity to hire and fire their own staff. One of these councils has organized 500 block clubs within its boundaries.

These stories are being played out in thousands of communities across the country. The theme that brings these stories together is basic social responsibility, the recovery of citizenship, or the citizen spirit, another key component of social capital. In his book, *Between Hope and History*, American President Bill Clinton remarked:

> I believe our sense of community is growing again. Indeed, wherever I go in this country, I see Americans joining groups, working together, seeking common ground, searching out joint solutions to make this a better country. Look around our communities. We see people working together toward common purposes everywhere: in efforts to strengthen schools, in neighborhood revitalization programs, in block watches, in campaigns to create performing arts centers, and in a thousand other ways every day. Especially when it comes to taking more community responsibility for saving our children from violence, gangs, and drugs, for helping our families to be strong, and reinforcing the sense of our fundamental values, there is a growing tide of effective community action all across America.[7]

The Yearning for Community

The search for community is an old theme in American history. It began with the pilgrims and other religious sects who brought a tightly knit, often oppressive social organization with them across the ocean. The founders stressed the need for "civic virtue," a tradition stretching back to Athens and the Roman Republic, by which individuals achieved their highest personal excellence through selfless service to the public realm.

In a commentary that serves as a good introduction to the civil society discussion, *Seattle Weekly* editor David Brewster describes a yearning for community that is rooted in something larger than self-reliance. It is free of the stoic retreat to individual self-reliance that is our modern mood and — without community — our only recourse in times of trouble. The idea of civil society is appealing, he says, because it provides a basis for a new synthesis, a new center, to American politics.[8]

What is community, and how did we come to lose it? Brewster helps answer this when he cites from *The Lost City*, a recent book by *Governing* magazine executive editor Alan Ehrenhalt about Chicago in the 1950s:

> Ehrenhalt wants us to understand all we lost in our sense of community … was a life with fewer choices. One stayed loyal to the [neighborhood bar and the] neighborhood butcher, who was known by name and was almost an extension of the family … plants almost never closed … life was lived public. We had communities that were familiar and secure; stable jobs and relationships whose survival we did not need to worry about … rules that we could live by.[9]

In a new edition of their book, *Habits of the Heart*, first published in 1985, Robert Bellah and his colleagues add their response to the same question:

> In *Habits* we spoke of commitment, of community, and of citizenship as useful terms to contrast to an alienating individualism .... But today we think the phrase "civic membership" brings out something not quite captured by those other terms ... the confident sense of selfhood that comes from membership in a society in which we believe ...[10]

The work of voluntary, non-profit organizations across the country has convinced many that the associational spirit is alive and well and that it is a key to the recovery of civil society in America. Still, it cannot complete the job alone.

GOVERNMENT ALONE IS NOT THE SOLUTION

Plight of Government

Since the 1930s, public welfare activities in the United States have been shared by the government and the voluntary sectors. With the passage of anti-poverty legislation in the 1960s as part of President Johnson's "Great Society," public funds poured into distressed neighborhoods all across America. Social service agencies came to the public trough and funding professionalized social services became an expected part of government's role.

Syndicated columnist William Raspberry summed up this situation when he wrote:

> Professionalization of the war on poverty had one disastrous consequence: It undercut the indigenous community leaders who had been toiling away for years, unpaid and largely unknown outside their neighborhoods. Local institutions ... were displaced by certified experts who had been trained in everything from professional social work to grief counseling .... Much of the pathology of the inner cities stems from the loss of gainful employment, as businesses either folded or moved to more attractive environs. Young men who couldn't find work were unattractive husband material, even for the mothers of their babies. Welfare became the father-substitute, with dismaying consequences. But part of the damage was done by those who only meant to help.[11]

During the 1980s, communities witnessed decreasing support of social programs by the federal government. As government programs retrenched and public-spiritedness shrank, the public sector was confronted by declining public participation in governance. A popular tax revolt limited government revenues in many local jurisdictions just as the public began to escalate its demands for public services and accountability. A related phenomenon was an uncertain consensus on how and whether to care for the poor.

Often reductions in funding were accompanied by an increase in the complexity of administering the funds. Sometimes it seemed the number of program administrators increased in inverse proportion to the number of program beneficiaries. Disgusted, the public increasingly demanded that the public sector meet certain, sometimes irrational, demands. Leaders must quickly produce clear value-added results. There should be less regulation and more leadership which must meet high ethical standards of public and personal conduct. Government services should emulate private-sector standards of efficiency and courtesy. New approaches should be "sold" to the public in which citizens should be viewed as "customers." Everything must contribute to a "seamless government" — and one that does not intrude upon people.

As Amitai Etzioni, a leading spokesperson for the communitarian movement observed, the remark that "the taxpayers shouldn't pay for [the Savings and Loan debacle], the government should!" reflects a major theme of entitlement in American civic culture.[12] As one citizen told his mayor, "Solve our problems, but stay out of our lives." In general, we are confused about what role government should play in American life, but we agree it should be different from the one it has played for the last 60 years.

Reinventing Government

At one time, public service was the most noble of professions, second only to the priesthood. Plato said the only ones capable of running government were the philosopher kings. Now, in the eyes of many, there is nothing less noble. A malaise has afflicted the 19 million Americans who are professional public servants of the federal, state, and local governments. We ask our public servants to stop crime, care for the indigent, ensure equitable access by all, feed the hungry, and care for the dying — all tasks that demand genuine personal engagement of the public servant. Yet many public servants have themselves become institutionalized by the institutions meant to care for others. They've become hardened trying to carry the weight of society's problems while filling out numberless reports. They've become mere functionaries.

In response, a trend has arisen to renew or reinvent the bureaucracy of government itself. "Reinventing government," as defined in Osborne and Gaebler's book,[13] is not as trying to fix something antiquated, but revolutionizing the whole governmental system and structure to "work better and cost less."[14] Complementing this effort is "total quality management," an approach to enhancing performance which is drawn from customer-oriented businesses. There are hundreds of "quality managers" at work at all levels of government, fine-tuning the microprocesses of governance, modernizing technology, and looking for regulatory flexibility.

The results of this reinvention process can be dramatic. For example, the New York City Sanitation Department transformed its equipment maintenance shop from a demoralized and inefficient mess into a national model and now advises private-sector trash haulers on how to handle maintenance. At one time, half the city's trucks were out of service each day and one-third of those that left the garage broke down on the road. Today, 100 percent of the trucks are ready to go each day, with a one percent breakdown rate.

Current efforts to reinvent government are only partially effective and appear to some as weak-kneed. The most dramatic success stories, including those documented in the book, *Government Works*, indicate that reinvention of government will not be complete without a radical renewal of citizenship.[15]

Indeed, the heavy emphasis placed in some government agencies on a customer service approach may be inadvertently undermining the cherished democratic principle of a people's government. Paul Light, a leading authority on government reorganization, believes the customer metaphor for public service might be useful as a first step in reinventing government, but will fail in the long run.[16] In government, a customer-oriented approach can produce simply more whining on the part of the citizens. People end up wanting more for themselves and cutbacks for everyone else.

"Right now you come to the federal government either for money or for permission," said John Dewitt, author of *Civic Environmentalism: Alternatives of Regulation in State and Communities*. "What you should come to the federal government for is information, for putting together partnerships, and for networking."[17] Another veteran of public life, John W. Gardner, former Chairman of the National Civic League, put it this way:

> Government still has a vital role to play in the effort to renew our communities, but the nature of that role is changing. We are coming to see that a society as complex as ours cannot function without greater collaboration between the sectors. Needless to say, if these efforts are to be truly effective, many government agencies and non-profit groups are going to have to give up some measure of autonomy in the interest of shared purpose.[18]

Reinventing Citizenship

The word "democracy" derives from the Greek words for people and power. It means more than simply people voting in elections as the only way to exercise power. Rather, it implies shared values that stress a balance between rights and responsibilities of citizens. American philosopher and educator John Dewey saw democracy as a shared way of life in which citizens are understood to be responsible members of a morally interdependent community. Or, as Abraham Lincoln stated, a democracy is "of the people, by the people, for the people."

Henry Boyte, of the Humphrey Institute of Public Affairs at the University of Minnesota, says that the original meaning of democracy "was a citizen-government with citizen-politicians and civil servants where accountability was sustained by what is best called civic muscle."[19] Citizens serving one another in such settings as business groups, school unions, voluntary associations, and religious groups is building the kind of civic muscle through which people gain voice in the larger world of public affairs. Citing examples such as the Civilian Conservation Corps of the Roosevelt Administration and the national cooperative extension system, Boyte emphasizes the need for a recovery of such "public work" which is the "expenditure of visible efforts by ordinary citizens whose collective labors produce things or create processes of lasting civic value."[20]

A public work perspective of the civil society shifts the emphasis on government as problem-solver to the development of civic muscle. When addressing problems of crime prevention, for example, resources and the capacity to act are enormously multiplied when the question shifts from "how do we provide more police?" to "what can the diverse set of people and institutions in the community contribute to creating a safe environment?" This approach frees government from being the only resource provider and prob-

Figure 1. Rebalancing Civic Governance

lem-solver to being a catalyst and provider of tools with a unique capacity to broker a multitude of cross-sector resources.

Today, America is facing crises in health care, welfare, job training, education reform, immigration, and other critical issues. The resolutions to these issues are not at all clear. Yet these "gordian knots" form the stuff of the recovery of civil society in America. It is clear that they cannot be resolved in conventional terms and forms. The key to finding our way back to civil society is through the community and its citizens working together with their public officials.

CIVIC GOVERNANCE: THE NEW VENUE FOR PUBLIC SERVICE

Reinventing the inner workings of government is not enough. More voter turnout is not enough. Voting is not where citizenship begins. Professor Phil Nyden of Loyola University, Chicago, has observed that people first participate locally in their communities and neighborhoods on concerns and issues that effect them personally. They then see themselves closer to the political process though they never use those words. They "feel" more ownership and have a greater stake in the process of community building. From this, they can buy into the electoral part of the political process.

I have illustrated this progression with a triangle representing "civic governance" — the meshing of the voluntary and governmental sectors in service to the general public. [See Figure 1.]

Public Policy

Citizen involvement in public policy development is not a new idea. Citizen advisory committees, blue ribbon commissions, and public hearings are conventional means for discovering the common ground of citizen consent. However, they are largely inadequate vehicles, not suitable for the problems at hand, and often adversarial in nature. Too frequently, they are simply rubber-stamping forgone and outworn conclusions.

Over the last several years, new formats and processes have emerged to enable citizens to participate in shaping their thinking and designing new strategies of public service. One of these formats is the community workshop, comprised of a broad array of citizens, governmental agencies, and public institutions effected by an issue. For example, in the Uptown-Edgewater community in Chicago, in a series of 22 community workshops held over a three month period in 1993, hundreds of citizens and dozens of governmental officials addressed youth and family issues. In the course of the workshop, ordinary citizens invented ground-breaking public policy by joining existing community assets such as church basements with previously lackluster government programs. The result was exciting new community-based alternatives in child care, recreation, culture, education, and public safety.

Examples of this kind of activity at the local level abound. On a national level, a new group, America Speaks, is attempting to harness citizen input on issues of public policy through a series of open forums across America.

Service Delivery

A new body of thinking about how government should be organized has penetrated the crusty old way of government doing business. Enter the citizen servant. Perhaps the most visible example of this in America today is community policing. Local beat patrolmen have stepped out of their police cars and begun to meet with block clubs, merchant associations, and other citizen based groups. Their common purpose is to reduce crime in the area, alerting would-be criminals that everyone — not just the police — is actively observing behavior in their neighborhood. In the United States, violent crime has dropped each year of the last five as a result of this approach.

Related to citizen involvement in service delivery is the trend toward greater involvement of government employees in helping to shape the quality of service delivery. The worker empowerment movement has touched public servants across the United States, and unions such as the American Federation of State, County and Municipal Employees have embraced these concepts.

The Illinois Department of Mental Health and Developmental Disabilities, now a part of the new Department of Human Services, is an example. Here, an employee involvement program dramatically improved not only the quality of life of the department's citizen-residents and patients but department employees, too, found a new outlet for creative problem-solving and renewed appreciation for their dedication.

Electoral Politics

Not only are citizens assisting in the transformation of the systems that provide the goods and services of government. They are also finding ways to express a new public will about our collective vision of what electoral politics needs to be about in America.

While voter registration and turn-out seems to be eroding across America, nonetheless citizens are finding new ways to make an impact. The increased use of referenda is evidence of this. Citizens are tired of the political action committees which dominate the legislative process of government. Citizens are urging a new image of the political leader as steward of the public intent, not its owner. As third party candidate Ross Perot has reminded us, citizens own the government.

We have also seen the increased use of town meetings and community-building planning sessions to allow local people to express their common convictions about what they want from their government. While the technology of the electronic town meeting is yet to be perfected as a device inclusive of everyone, its increased use is an indication of a new way by which people will be able to express the public will. The idea — proposed by many — for an extended voting period to allow America's highly transitory society to have greater opportunity to participate in electoral process is another example.

In sum, the very nature of public service is changing. It is a new form of civic governance that involves people more in the process. However, more work is needed before these new forms can be realized.

WHAT IS NEEDED

Working Together

Effective communities make use of extended political capacities. This is reflected in the way they define their problems, how they talk about them, how people respond to challenges, and in the type of actions that flow from a resurgence of political will. For government entities as for block clubs, the experience of alternative dispute resolution and civic participation are that diverse groups, with conflicting views and agendas, can find common ground. In government, this involves making the transition from a command-and-control leadership pyramid to team management within the organization, use of a "working public" in all aspects of agency operations, and acquiring the technologies of public and employee participation.

When nothing else works, people begin to collaborate. However, collaboration is more complex and demanding than many people realize. According to David Chrislip and Carl Larson of the American Leadership Forum, a national training institute of public leaders, collaboration goes beyond communication, cooperation, and coordination. As its Latin roots indicate, collaboration means "to work together." From 46 case studies in collaborative efforts to solve social issues, they learned that collaboration "is a mutually beneficial relationship between two or more parties who work toward common goals by sharing responsibility, authority and accountability for achieving results . . . . The purpose of collaboration is to create a shared vision and joint strategies to address concerns that go beyond the purview of any particular party."[21]

Collaborations between citizens and government are favored by many, but because collaboration is a human endeavor, it can be messy. It is not always efficient, it does not always save money, and it is not always the best choice. Nevertheless, many feel collaborative efforts hold special promise in dealing with social problems. In Chicago, another study of 14 citywide and 17 neighborhood collaborations found characteristics that were consistent across all collaborators: they were active and inclusively democratic, consensus-driven, had achievable action plans, and demonstrated capacity for community development and policy impact.[22]

Regaining Trust

In his recent popular book, *Trust*, Francis Fukuyama suggests that voluntary groups provide society with a laboratory to create the kind of social capital that makes democracy and capitalism flourish.[23] The ability to form groups such as Rotary Clubs and bowling leagues that will help smooth the frictions of democracy depends on trust. If a society has a culture of trust, and particularly if its members have the capacity to trust people outside their families, it generates social capital which is as useful as financial capital to its economic well-being. Social capital creates prosperity, not the other way around.

Re-engaging the trust of the broad public in civic life requires at least three major shifts by governmental leaders:

• Responding to the citizenry and in its diverse formations.

• Finding and publicizing new examples of public stewardship.

• Collaborating across traditional boundaries, whether of party, class, geography, or perceived interests.

Seattle-based community consultant Ron Thomas says, "How to do this is easy — respect and trust"[24] but, he notes, that requires reinventing our whole public apparatus. Trust is not easy to come by. When a labor union clings to a set of hard-won but obsolete work rules that are ultimately risking jobs, that is a lack of trust. The proprietary rights they have won are seen as all it has, since management can't be trusted. Indeed, notes Brewster, "in low-trust societies, workers are too suspicious to be flexible."[25] When patients who test HIV-positive refuse to authorize possibly life-saving tracing of their sexual partners, that is a lack of trust. When employers unduly monitor employees, that is a lack of trust. People often react to this lack of trust by claiming a violation of privacy. Weapons searches of school children or drug-testing of pilots, for example, draw fire as an invasion of liberties. Clearly, the challenge to regain trust in our society is immense.

Generating Ownership

Writing in *The Atlantic Monthly*, Harvard University professor Michael Sandel notes that sharing in self-rule requires knowledge of public affairs and a sense of belonging.[26] Such a sense is needed in one's workplace and community. Belonging is a minimum requisite of ownership and civic pride. Without belonging, any contribution is a form of "taxation without representation."

Experience has shown the best way to gain a sense of ownership is through direct participation. When people are directly involved in solving problems, they are more likely to take responsibility for implementing the solutions than if someone else tries to tell them what to do. This truth is so self-evident it hardly needs stating, but all too often it is overlooked or ignored. It is partially why the old attitude of "I'm here from the government and I'm here to help you" is so ludicrous.

Within the private sector worldwide, it has been documented that companies which engage their work force in creative problem-solving achieve better results than those that do not.[27] Why not capitalize on this same reality within the public realm as well?

In fact, there are growing indications this is happening in the public realm. In his chapter in this volume, Monte Roulier documents examples of communities working together to generate solutions to community problems and, in the process, staking their claim to "owning" those solutions.[28]

CONCLUSION

A recovery of civil society is taking place in America. It begins with the resurgence of local voluntary efforts of citizens banding together to solve their common problems. When conditions are right, it goes on to bring new life to the structures of government by creating an expanded arena of "civic governance."

Government is not a bad public service vehicle; it's just an incomplete one. It can't do the job by itself. It can't do it alone because it does not, and is not, able to deal with the subtle level of interpersonal relationships that go on between neighbor and neighbor. It is not able to deal in the arena of intimacy, a key ingredient of civil society.

Addressing the 1996 Democratic National Convention, Tipper Gore, the wife of American Vice President Al Gore, said, "A civil society is built by the smallest, simplest gestures. Things that we do every day without thinking twice about them." She told the story of a mother writing to her son in 1920. Like thousands of other mothers all over the country, she wrote the familiar words, "be a good boy and do the right thing." The son, 24-year-old Representative Harry Burn in the Tennessee legislature, took her advice to heart. He changed his mind and voted for women's suffrage. The measure passed in Tennessee and the 19th Amendment to the United States Constitution was ratified by one vote. It was one of the numberless victories that build civil society through small, simple gestures of "doing the right thing."

NOTES

1. This might also be called "public work."

2. Alexis de Tocqueville. *Democracy in America*. Reprint. New York: Harper & Row, 1988.

3. Robert D. Putnam. "Bowling Alone: America's Declining Social Capital." *Journal of Democracy.* Volume 6, Number 1, January 1995. p. 65. See also Putnam's other essays on the same subject: "What Makes Democracy Work?" *National Civic Review.* Volume 82, Number 2, Spring 1993. p. 101; "The Prosperous Community Social Capital and Public Life." *The American Prospect.* Volume 13, Spring 1993. p. 35; "Bowling Alone, Revisited." *The Responsive Community.* Volume 5, Number 2, Spring 1995. p. 18; "Tuning In, Tuning Out: The Strange Disappearance of Social Capital in America." *Political Science and Politics.* Volume 28, Number 4, December 1, 1995. p. 664; "The Strange Disappearance of Civic America." *Policy: A Journal of Public Policy and Ideas.* Volume 12, Number 1, Fall 1996. p. 3. Putnam's essays grew out of his longitudinal study of government effectiveness in Italy, described in *Making Democracy Work: Civic Traditions in Modern Italy.* Princeton: Princeton University Press, 1993. In this study of 20 powerful regional governments, Putnam found that such factors as ideology, social stability, prosperity made no difference for a region's acceptance of democratic institutions. Only "traditions of civic engagement" mattered.

4. See, for example, (a) Robert J. Samuelson. "Join the Club." *The Washington Post National Weekly Edition.* 15-21 April 1996. p. 5. (b) Richard Morin. "So Much for the 'Bowling Alone' Thesis." *The Washington Post National Weekly Edition.* 17-23 June, 1996. p. 37.

5. "Bowling Together: Civic engagement in America isn't disappearing but reinventing itself." *Time.* 22 July 1996. p. 35.

6. John P. Kretzmann. "Building Communities From the Inside Out." *Shelterforce.* September/October 1995. p. 8. See also John P. Kretzmann and John L. McKnight. *Building Communities from the Inside Out: A Path Toward Finding and Mobilizing a Community's Assets.* Center for Urban Affairs and Policy Research, Evanston: Northwestern University, 1993.

7. William J. Clinton. *Between Hope and History: Meeting America's Challenge for the 21st Century.* New York: Times Books, 1996. p. 116.

8. David Brewster. "The Encumbered Self." *Seattle Weekly.* 20 March 1996. p. 17.

9. *Ibid.*, citing from Alan Ehrenhalt's *The Lost City: Discovering the Forgotten Virtues of Community in the Chicago of the 1950s.* New York: Basic Books, 1995.

10. Robert N. Bellah et. al. "Introduction to the Updated Edition. *"Habits of the Heart: Individualism and Commitment in American Life.* Berkeley: University of California, 1996.

11. William Raspberry. *USA Today.* 10 February 1994. p. 11A.

12. Amitai Etzioni quoted in *Toward a Global Society.* Michael Walzer. (ed.) Providence: Berghahn Books, 1995. p. 99.

13. David Osborne and Ted Gaebler. *Reinventing Government.* Reading: Addison-Wesley, 1992.

14. This is the theme of Vice President Al Gore's National Performance Review, an effort to reinvent the federal government.

15. James P. Troxel. *Government Works: Profiles of People Making a Difference.* Alexandria: Miles River Press, 1995.

16. Paul Light is the author of a recent Brookings Institute study on the proliferation of layers of management between top administrators and front line workers. He was also the main staff writer for the Volcker Commission report on federal public service and the Winter Commission report on state and local public service.

17. John Dewitt quoted in *Governing.* July 1995.

18. John W. Gardner. *Governing.* July 1995. p. 53.

19. Henry C. Boyte and Nancy N. Kari. "Democracy of the People: Expanding Citizen Capacity." in *Capacity for Change: The Non-profit World in the Age of Devolution.* Indiana University Center on Philanthropy, 1996. p. 12.

20. Boyte and Kari. "Young People and Public Work." *Wingspread Journal* Number 18, Issue 4, Autumn 1996. p. 4.

21. David D. Chrislip and Carl E. Larson. *Collaborative Leadership: How Citizens and Civic Leaders Can Make a Difference.* An American Leadership Forum Book. San Francisco: Jossey-Bass, 1994. p. 5.

22. *Collaborating for Change in Chicago: A Progress Report on The Collaboration Project.* Chicago: MacArthur Foundation, December 1993.

23. Franics Fukuyama. *Trust: The Social Virtues and the Creation of Prosperity.* New York: The Free Press, 1995. p. 150.

24. Ron Thomas. "Civic Hopscotch: What Are the New Games in Your Town*?"* *Community Design Exchange.* Number 1, Fall 1994. p. 2.

25. Brewster. *op. cit.* p. 21.

26. Michael J. Sandel. "America's Search for a New Public Philosophy." *Atlantic Monthly.* March 1995. p. 57. Look for Sandel's latest book, *Democracy's Discontent: America in Search of a Public Philosophy.* Cambridge: Belknap Press of Harvard University Press, 1996.

27. See, for example, James P. Troxel. (ed.) *Participation Works: Business Cases from Around the World,.* Alexandria: Miles River Press, 1993.

28. Monte Roulier. "Local Community: Seedbed of Civil Society." pp. 183-196.

6. Consulting Egypt's Local Experts

Marlene Kanawati

> *There are nine things of which a Great Man [or Woman]*
> *must be mindful: to see when he looks, to hear when he lis-*
> *tens, to have a facial expression of gentleness, to have an*
> *attitude of humility, to be loyal in speech, to be respectful in*
> *service, to inquire when in doubt, to think of the difficulties*
> *when angry, to think of justice when he sees an advantage.*
>
> — Confucius

S uch qualities of the heart and mind, idealistic as they may sound, are necessary to empower people to participate fully as citizens in society. They lie at the root of Participatory Rapid Appraisal (PRA), a methodology which allows people to have a greater say and control over the direction of their lives, and which ensures that no one institution overpowers others, thereby making for balanced and shared social responsibility.

This chapter describes the impact of PRA on the community and its contribution to civil society. The PRA methodology and the attitudes it encourages and engenders are of the essence of the spirit of civil society. The examples are drawn from the experiences of the Center for Development Services (CDS) in Cairo, Egypt.[1]

CIVIL SOCIETY EAST AND WEST

In his opening chapter of this book, Goran Hyden says "Civil society is that part of society that connects individual citizens with the public realm and the state, i.e., civil society is the political side of society."[2] Hyden claims that Europeans see civil society as useful for "its ability to reform the state," while Americans see it as "good in and of itself because it is in civil society that democratic norms are lodged."[3]

Egyptian political sociologist Moheb Zaki maintains that civil society has been taken to mean "that aspect of social life that is distinct and removed from the realm of the state." It is the "public realm for the voluntary activities of autonomous individuals. As such, it is a realm of rights — political, social, as well as economic." Civil society "rests on the premise of the community of free individuals, free from the controlling power of the state, yet regulated by law in their activities."[4] He sees a development of the bargaining power of citizens vis-à-vis the state, with the latter accepting compromise and a lesser use of its power.[5] But the freedom of people to think and express their ideas requires that they be organized; hence the importance of associations, unions, professional syndicates, and the like. Some kind of strategy and method have to operate to educate people how to become citizens. The process is neither simple nor quick.

PRA is such a method that has been used successfully for the past 15 years all over the world, especially among poor and illiterate people. Though it began as a way to assess needs, make evaluations, and help in feasibility studies, it has proven its capacity to enable grassroots people to express their ideas and opinions freely, to define their own reality and problems, and to devise their own solutions. In other words, people become decision-makers in their communities, a responsibility they then share with their leaders, funders, or helpers.

With PRA, the researcher becomes a facilitator who helps the community go back to the root causes of their problems. Thus, when solutions are devised, the community, the facilitator, the development agency, and the funders are all able to tackle the problem at various levels, to respond to immediate consequences with a short-term plan, and to deal with root causes with a long-term plan.

In this joint work, people have a say in the kind of development that takes place. They gain self-confidence as individuals and become more responsible as a group or community. They begin to realize that organizing themselves as a group may give them more weight and more power to negotiate than acting as individuals. They begin to feel they are in control of their life and destiny, rather than drifting and being led. This is what empowerment is all about. The projects they help plan are their projects, which creates the sense of responsibility to follow through. They contribute their time, effort, and money if they can afford it. This is the best way to obtain sustainability in development.

Most of all, people acquire the habit of thinking, deciding, and working together, and overcoming their differences and conflicts. This is the first step to creating civil society where it does not exist, because participation in this manner creates "the forum in which habits of the heart and mind are nurtured and developed."[6] This power to control decision-making is the essence of politics and political rights. Once political leaders, both formal or informal, become conscious of that power, they begin to feel the need to gain the support of these citizen-based groups.

Non-governmental organizations (NGOs)[7] are at the heart of this kind of organized power. They know who are the poorest and the most powerless and where to find them. When they organize a PRA to make a community needs assessment to determine their priorities, NGOs become the mechanisms that elicit citizen participation. It is critical to train these associations in PRA to ensure the views of those at "the bottom of the society" are included.[8]

In Egypt, as well as in Morocco, Tunisia, and Algeria, governments encourage NGOs to complement public spending on social services such as education, health, and social welfare.[9] However, they fail to allow these organizations to freely empower people for fear things may get out of hand. Yet many associations lack the know-how of empowerment. Some continue to dictate their projects without bothering to ask their beneficiaries about their needs. They even make a point of not letting them participate because they see the poor and illiterate as ignorant and unaware of their own interests. Thus, a first step in upgrading any institution is to engage its board and employees in PRA training to explain its principles, to induce a change of attitude, and to let them practice PRA within the community they serve, in order to discover the community's needs and realize how basic participation is to human development. They then become aware of PRA as a methodology that can help create civil society and empower people.

If NGOs go to these groups and rally them through a PRA, they can then say "this is the will of the community" and not just that of its leaders. Politicians will be more likely to take their views into consideration as "the voice of the people." By using PRA in the communities they serve, NGOs will contribute to the creation of a civil society with a voice that reaches the state and participates in decision-making *with* the state. This creates a balance of power between the state and civil society. Such a balance benefits both parties since, as Zaki puts it, "No strong and vibrant society can exist in the absence of an equally strong state."[10]

Indeed, a nation where civil society has a strong voice which is heard by the state or even democratically contested is one in which the state gains legitimacy because it has the support of civil society — a point often overlooked by authoritarian states. A strong civil society does not imply lawlessness. On the contrary, it places an emphasis on law, legality, and human rights, and an agreed understanding of an organized social life in which everyone's rights are respected, including the state's. Authoritarian states that reject these notions do not understand the concepts or processes involved.

Zaki maintains that disorder is out of the question when he says that civil society refers to a "community of free individuals, free not only from state control but of communally imposed ideological or religious doctrines, yet law-regulated activities."[11] He rejects recent disorders in Egypt and the Middle East caused by fundamentalists trying to impose their ideological and religious doctrines by violence and threat, not only on the state but also on their own communities. As Egyptian scholar and activist, Saad Eddin Ibrahim, reminds us, "Though they limit state authority, yet these organizations [of civil society] help protect the state against extremists that seek organized violence."[12]

ORIGINS OF PRA

According to British scholar and development consultant Robert Chambers, PRA evolved from various sources as far back as 1977. Each source has contributed ideas, techniques, or experiences that have helped develop PRA to its present state. As Chambers puts it, PRA is a "family of methodologies" which have evolved in different directions.[13]

Chambers identifies five sources. One is a Brazilian, Paulo Freire, who wrote "Pedagogy of the Oppressed" in 1968. Here he spelled out his theory of "conscientization," that poor and exploited people can and should be enabled to conduct their own analysis of their own reality."[14] This idea is at the heart of PRA and its derived methodologies, and has become an integral part of participatory research. Out of this grew "Activist Participatory Research" from which PRA took the idea of dialogue (rather than a scheduled interview) and participation to "enhance people's awareness and confidence and to empower their action."[15]

In India, Rajesh Tandon and colleagues established a "Society for Participatory Research" which adopted this idea as its main philosophy, spreading the practice of participatory research to Bangladesh and other countries. The discipline of applied anthropology also contributed techniques of conversation, information interviews, and focus groups, as well as the importance of attitudes, behavior, rapport, and acknowledging the "native's point of view."[16]

Another early source of PRA was the University of Thailand where, in 1978, "agro-ecosystems analysis" contributed to PRA some of its fundamental techniques, particularly visual ones such as informal maps and diagrams.[17] These maps allow groups to draw a visual image of their community as they see it, locating social groupings, social services, roads, and problem locations. As a result of dissatisfaction with surveys, their costs, and biases, researchers in Thailand created Rapid Rural Appraisal (RRA) which spread to 27 countries. In 1985, the term "participatory" began to be used in RRA, becoming "Participatory Rural Appraisal," of which seven types were identified. The idea was to involve the community using the outsider as catalyst.[18]

In 1988, Indian and Kenyan NGOs began to use PRA in rural areas. India became the innovator in that field and developed the idea of the practitioner as "facilitator" and trained many government organizations (GOs) and NGOs to use it. The London-based International Institute for Environment and Development helped spread PRA to 15 countries.[19]

PRA has been adopted by the World Bank, the Food and Agricultural Organization, the United Nations Development Programme, the United Nations Children's Fund (UNICEF), the United States Agency for International Development (USAID), Britain's Overseas Development Administration, and governments through the influence of these organizations that fund GOs. Recently, USAID funded PRA training for a major GO working with the development of Egyptian villages to promote the wider use of this technique in Egypt. In the Maghreb region, the World Bank, with the agreement of the Ministry of Development, organized PRA training for professors, teachers, and administrators, which culminated in undertaking PRA throughout the Maghreb and caused the Ministry to change its development policy. Many large institutions have realized the vast potential of PRA as a first step towards development and as a methodology for involving grassroots organizations.[20]

ESSENTIALS OF PRA

PRA is a way of learning from and with community members about their life and community as an integrated system. It aims to investigate, analyze, and evaluate constraints and opportunities, or assess a topic, problem or question, in order to understand it, and to make informed and timely decisions regarding development projects.[21] It is most often used to assess community needs, priorities, opinions and attitudes, beliefs, and behaviors.

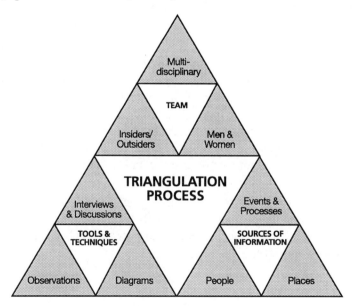

Figure 1. Triangulation Process

PRA is an intensive and systematic method which includes a form of cross-checking known as triangulation. [See Figure 1.] To provide a comprehensive picture of a situation, PRA is carried out by a multidisciplinary team of men and women with different skills and viewpoints. The team must include community members who help the team gain access to, and trust of, the community in a minimal time.[22]

Researchers become facilitators. Once they explain their purpose, they offer the community tools that encourage people to speak. They listen rather than lecture, they are patient and do not interrupt, they show humility in an attempt to learn rather than teach, and they show interest in what members know, say, and do. Facilitators make a special effort to involve all community members — men and women, young and old, wealthy and poor, powerful and powerless, as well as members of different ethnic and religious groups, with special emphasis on the disadvantaged. The more knowledgeable people on certain topics are called key informants, who may include school teachers, old men and women known to have a good memory of the history of the community, or informal leaders known to resolve disputes. One must have a variety of information sources, including people, places, and observation.[23]

Underlying these practices are key values or premises:

• Community members know and have something to give.
• Community members, not facilitators, are the experts on the community.
• Community members are important partners and the project beneficiaries.
• Community members must take decisions for their own future.
• Appropriate attitudes are critical.
• Facilitators do not patronize community members but treat them as equals.

Since facilitators eventually depart, local NGO members are encouraged to become facilitators, in order to learn the method for ongoing use. They can continue the process by analyzing on the spot all information obtained daily, focus on what still needs to be investigated, and come to conclusions about the total picture of the community's assets, liabilities, and needs as defined by its members. Through this joint process, the community learns how to think and act collectively for its common good, to cooperate, and to gain confidence — basic elements of civil society.

In most research methods, researchers bring a "top down" attitude. They are the experts and the people are informants from whom they extract information, then go away, leaving the community without any benefit. With PRA, the community changes.

PRA IN AN ARAB RURAL COMMUNITY

One example of PRA in action involves an Arab rural community in which CDS had been asked to do a needs assessment by a United Nations organization which wanted to help this community but needed to assess its needs.[24] The UN team requested to be trained in PRA and helped in its application in two villages so they could continue doing PRAs in other villages they had chosen for an integrated rural development project.

We requested four young people from this community — two men and two women — to be included in the training. During the training, the communities asked their youth about us to satisfy their curiosity about our intentions. As a result, we were not refused entry into their homes and places of work. We trained 24 persons, who were divided into two groups, one for each of the two villages.

The first day, we asked a group of men and women to draw a map of their village which indicated boundaries, main roads, and residential and agricultural areas. Then we asked them to draw the main services such as schools, health centers, churches and mosques, the marketplace, and neighborhoods of different socio-economic groups. After this, we took a walk through the village to draw a cross-section of it, which we call a *transect*.

The next day, we used semi-structured interviews to understand the prevailing conditions — social, economic, environmental, and political. The area was suffering from drought, lack of water sources, and youth unemployment. We began in the poor quarters of the village. As we entered the one room houses, we saw unemployed men sleeping while women rushed about doing housework. When the women woke up the men, they looked depressed. We told them we wanted to understand the prevailing conditions, and what they saw as possible solutions and priorities. At first, we obtained half answers and a lack of interest. We interviewed individuals or groups, depending on whether we were seeking personal opinions or shared views, or more technical information which required key informants or focus groups.

As we sat with a group of farmers, they identified their agricultural outputs, resources, and problems. We asked them to prioritize the problems according to their importance, using a tool called preference ranking. Then, using a matrix, we asked them to name the criteria they had used for prioritizing. Part of the analysis involved drawing a causal diagram which goes backwards from effect to cause to root causes of problems. Finally, we asked them how they usually solved their problems and if they could think of alternative solutions.

Since most problems related to a lack of water, they spoke of devices they used to deal with this and of alternatives. We asked them to estimate costs and identify the contribution the village could make in voluntary labor and know-how, and their readiness to contribute these. While farmers were clear about their problems, they had never considered alternatives nor thought of calculating costs. This group held two other meetings during the week in which they called other farmers to join them.

A group of non-agricultural laborers were less articulate. When we asked them about their resources, they first said they had no idea. Since chances of employment were few, they only thought of emigration. When we asked them for alternative solutions, they spoke of using local raw materials to manufacture products to sell to the city. We also had meetings in which women expressed their concerns about the men. We asked what they could do to help the men within cultural constraints and they began to think of solutions. We had started a general discussion on issues they had given up discussing because they thought it led nowhere.

Through this process of participation, people realized they were not alone but could come together and create joint work. Previously, they had thought of each other as competitors, but now they realized that through cooperation, they could complement one another. The mayor said we had created a movement in the village. Fear of the future had been replaced by an atmosphere of hope and excitement. People were visiting one another in the evening despite cold winter weather. Even better, people were engaging in heated discussions about possible alternatives. These discussions spread to include an uncompleted school. Villagers spoke of seeking funders' help and unemployed workers contributing their services at half price to get it done. A wealthy farmer offered his vehicle to transport chickens for poorer farmers to raise, and then transport them to the city for sale when fully grown.

When the assessment was completed and the report written, we invited the UN officials and asked the mayor and others to arrange a village meeting to present the results. So many people came that we had to move the meeting to the school courtyard. In PRA, public reporting is essential to obtain majority approval that the findings represent community opinion and are valid. This is one of the democratic principles, cultivated by PRA, which allows development projects to be developed with the community, facilitators, and funders working together. Community members had already thought of several projects and asked the UN representatives when they could start. The UN officials asked them to prepare a written plan and organize a committee with whom they could discuss design and implementation. The UN officials declared they had never seen anything like this during their long experience in development work.

The PRA had created a unity among community members so they could negotiate with UN officials as one body. It was not the project, but the PRA process itself that had helped this community become conscious of its potential and resources, gain the courage to face a depressing situation, and find the ability to define its needs and take decisions concerning possible solutions and prioritized projects. In PRA, the assessment phase itself becomes a development method as community members become aware of their potential and power as a group. This is how civil society is built.

PRA WITH CAIRO STREET CHILDREN

In 1988, the late Richard Helmsley from Britain joined a group of business and professional men and women to establish an association called Hope Village.[25] The purpose of the association is to develop informed strategies to help street children reintegrate into society, as well as to raise society's awareness of this problem.

At first, services consisted of providing children with a place to have a hot bath, eat a hot meal, rest, talk about their problems, and eventually rejoin their families. Although the association closed at night, many children would sleep during the day because they had sleepless nights. The majority were boys aged between 9 and 14. Though a number of children came regularly, they continued their life on the street almost unchanged. They still needed income and undertook activities the association staff suspected were illegal, or at least harmful to themselves. Life in the street had taught the children not to trust anyone.

CDS was asked by UNICEF to provide the association with technical assistance. The main goal was institutional development, while the secondary goal was the development of their program, namely, devising strategies to reach the children, develop individual and family counseling and case management toward reintegrating children into their families, and managing internal residence in the home.

The PRA approach and method were seen as the best way to deal with both the staff and the children. The philosophy behind it would ensure their cooperation, respect their autonomy, and allow an assessment of the whole situation, including both service providers and children. Both groups would analyze and identify their problems, suggest possible solutions, and select those they were ready to adopt. Guiding them through this process would help them do it on their own in the future. CDS staff began the process of discovering the roots of the problem by adopting the attitudes and behavior basic to PRA discussed in the previous example. As a result, the children soon began to chat with them and trust them.

First, it was important to understand the staff's viewpoint. The two PRA techniques used were discussions and priority ranking. Once staff had spoken of the problems that caused children to run away to the street, they were asked individually to prioritize them, using the preferential ranking matrix. The results indicated that the most important causes were family neglect, physical abuse by family and teachers, child labor in unsafe jobs, and school drop-out for economic reasons, in that order. Staff then identified and prioritized street children's health and social problems, including sexual abuse, glue sniffing, smoking, and skin diseases.

Next, CDS facilitators investigated the children's viewpoint. To begin, they gave the children paper and colored pencils and asked them to draw four or five problems they face. They then asked them to present each problem and comment on it. PRA's use of visual media helps everyone focus attention on the drawing and topic rather than on the discussants, which helps them become more involved in the discussion and reduces shyness or inhibition.

As the children explained their drawings, they revealed the causes that led them to the streets. Some left when their parents divorced; some were sent away by parents, others were sent by parents to become apprentices, but were abused and beaten by the boss and given a small wage for long work hours, a wage on which the parents lived. Whenever a child attempted to leave a cruel boss, his parents would beat him and force him to return, so he would run away to the street. In other cases, parental neglect led the child to drop out of school and live on the street. The ultimate abuse was sexual exploitation by families or teachers.

Once the problems were out, the children were asked to prioritize them. Using the preference ranking technique, the children ranked their problems thus:

1. Police pursuit and arrest
2. Cruelty and dismissal by employers
3. Physical aggression and social problems
4. Family breakdown and ensuing problems
5. Cigarette smoking and glue sniffing
6. Society's rejection of street children.[26]

As the problem of glue sniffing surfaced, children were asked to draw the dangers resulting from this activity. Using role playing, the children were encouraged to act out the different stages from obtaining money to buying the glue to loss of consciousness. All this was documented by photographs.

Two other PRA tools were used in the next phase — recounting one's daily routine from waking to sleeping, and drawing a map of the place where this routine takes place. The map was most revealing. The children drew the whole quarter of the city, including their sleeping place, the police station, the association, where they played video games, the shops where they bought the glue, and where they hid it between the railway lines. They chose this hiding place because it was close to public water closets and where they washed clients' cars. Their sleeping-place was close to a tall tree where they could hide from police. From there they could also see their scout who stood at the street corner to warn them of police raids. They were careful to sniff glue far from other street children, as police would undertake raids in areas where they noticed children sniffing glue. They also put on the map the pharmacy where they bought medicine whenever one of them fell ill. They would collect money from the whole group to do this — a self-support mechanism in the absence of any other.

These two tools revealed the two-edged pattern of their daily life — children stole from and beat one another yet also supported one another at times of illness or police threat. Whereas conversation had resulted in bits and pieces of information, this technique gave a comprehensive account which enabled both association staff and CDS professionals to clearly understand the situation, the actors in it, and how to deal with it. CDS staff decided to explain to the children the effects of these drugs on the brain and body. They made a child-size maquette of a boy and showed the relationship between the brain, arms, and legs through the nerves represented by transparent tubes. The children loved the maquette and called it "Sayid Glue." A physician explained the effect of glue sniffing. She put a soft drink through the plastic tubes, showed it reaching the brain and causing numbness, thus preventing children from picking up things from the floor, falling if they tried to walk, or becoming semi-conscious. She then asked who could explain or repeat the effects of drugs on nerves. A couple of children did, then all of them wanted to. When the physician asked if they could explain the effect to other street-children they said they could. At the children's suggestion, photographs of the doctor's explanations were copied and made into a booklet which the children used to explain to others the dangers of glue sniffing. While some street-children reacted angrily by tearing the booklets, others stopped sniffing glue or taking drugs, and still others wanted to join the association.

The children were then asked if they were ready to take up an honest job. Yes, they replied. Through PRA, an assessment of the kinds of income-generating activities children practice in the streets was made, and a savings plan devised to create a capital base for small commercial enterprises. The children had a good sense of marketing and a knowledge of what people wished to buy, so they designed the project and chose the items to sell.

PRA has been a key method for creating in them the feeling that they were important, respected persons in their own right, and helped them analyze their condition and understand what had happened to them. They found listeners who believed in them, supported them, provided protection rather than denounced them, and offered information about drugs they could use to teach their peers. They had not been forced at any point. It was always up to them to take a decision. A program of reintegrating the children within their original families is now being designed. Where the child has expressed the wish to recontact his family, the association is doing this.

Respect for personal autonomy and the ability to understand one's condition and analyze one's problems re-establishes people's faith in themselves and others. It gives them the feeling they can manage situations and decide about their own problems. For the poor, illiterate, powerless, and disadvantaged, this is doubly so.

IMPACT OF PRA ON FACILITATORS

In the preceding examples showing the effects of PRA on the community, it has been assumed that facilitators have the appropriate attitude. What happens if they do not? Can working with PRA have an effect on the facilitator, as it does on others? It would seem logical that without the proper attitude, PRA lacks one of its most important bases, and cannot be called PRA at all. How can someone who lacks the proper attitude be affected by a method that assumes it as a necessary condition?

The answers to these questions are to be found in another example from the Near East Foundation (NEF), the parent body of CDS.[27] No project is established by NEF without a PRA in the community. In late 1995, NEF undertook a PRA in an area of Cairo called Sayedah Zeinab. Staff began by identifying community members for the PRA team. An architectural firm

Contributing to Civil Society

Institution Development	Community Development
WHERE WE BEGAN	
1. Top-down approach	1. Failure to accept collective responsibility
2. Assume knowledge of the needs of the community	2. Inadequate positive incentives
3. Failure to create initiatives	3. Low self-confidence
4. Failure to encourage participation	4. Low achievement/motivation
5. Provide physical/material resources	5. Weak social ties at community level
6. Technological solutions	6. Acceptance of status quo
	7. Dependence on outsiders
WHERE WE ARE	
1. Interaction with community	1. Proactive/show initiative
2. Associations become a channel for articulating community needs	2. Show concern for community welfare
3. Increased trust	3. Willingness to be involved
4. Success in experimentation	4. Coming together for purposeful activity
5. Belief in taking a closer look	5. Sense of community
6. Openness to the community	

Figure 2. Attitudinal shifts resulting from PRA

headed by a dynamic and renowned architect joined the half dozen NEF staff to help upgrade the area. Three architects were convinced by NEF to participate in the PRA to discover how the community saw their own reality and needs.

There were also several NGOs in the area, only a few of which were active. One of the project's objectives was to activate local NGOs, let them find out for themselves their own communities' needs, and to strengthen them through an institution-building process. Therefore, it was decided that the NGO board members and staff had to be included in the PRA team.

After training this heterogeneous group of architects, NGO members, and community residents in the attitudes and techniques of PRA, the group was ready to take up the role of facilitators in the assessment. As usual, the PRA had a catalytic effect on the community but the effect of the PRA on the research team was unexpected. As the team leader noted, "It is those who do the PRA who change because they become aware of the real problems within the society. Their eyes are opened."[28] He presented a chart of the results of PRA [See Figure 2], including how the architects and the NGO board members and staff changed their attitudes towards the community.

Before, they had assumed they knew the needs of the community. Now, they realized they did not know their needs and interacted with the community to discuss matters of concern to them. Previously, NGOs were doing traditional programs such as a vocational training center, a nursery, and a clinic, but now they became a channel for articulating community needs and began to experiment with new ideas. This led to increased trust between the community and NGOs. Earlier, NGOs had not encouraged community participation because they believed people did not know what was good for them. Now they became open to them. Formerly, NGOs had tried to provide technological solutions, but now they were ready to discuss solutions with the community.

In the same vein, another PRA was carried out by a team in Darassah, a huge slum containing deteriorating archaeological sites. According to the team leader, the greatest impact of this PRA was on those from the local government and other institutions who had became facilitators. It was as if they had worked in this community with closed eyes. They were so shocked by what they heard and saw that their attitudes changed completely. Their skepticism about the inhabitants changed to understanding and concern, even remorse, and a desire to do something about the situation. Because the area had been infamous for its drug trade, they had thought of all its inhabitants as "a bad lot." The police had raided the area two years ago and all the drug dealers were now in prison. The facilitators visited many families who were completely ruined as a result of this action. They discovered a community in despair, yet one filled with many skilled craftsmen who kept alive their cultural heritage.

After the PRA, there was a change of attitudes and strengthening of social ties. As with the rural village experience, persons who had never spoken together began to communicate; archaeology officials spoke with the craftsmen and local government personnel explained to the community the reasons for enlarging streets. An atmosphere of common understanding and of coming together to discuss issues of concern began to take place.[29]

PRA does change all parties, because it brings people together in an informal encounter that assumes an attitude of equality, humility, and understanding. The tools used require the researcher to listen, wait, and learn from the community. It is a method which decision-makers at higher levels should be encouraged to use to enter the world of the poor, powerless, and disadvantaged. When rulers and ruled listen to each other, powerless and powerful connect democratically, and civil society comes into being. As Goran Hyden reminds us, "Civil society is that part of society that connects individual citizens with the public realm and the state."[30] Only by such a connection can civil society reform the state, for the state is formed of individuals, and is not just a moral entity.

PRA enables such connections to occur, because it creates a situation in which the facilitator and community members are striving for the same goal — the well-being of the community. Community members open their hearts and homes to these outsiders who show concern for their well-being, who are ready to listen, to share their problems, and to encourage them to take responsibility for their own lives. As a result, facilitators feel they are appreciated and have become more understanding persons. As subjective a judgment as this may be, it is a valuable and not inconsequential by-product of PRA.

CONCLUSION

PRA contains enormous possibilities that seem hopeful given the long and recurring attempt to find a methodology to encourage effective participation, particularly among the poor, women, and disadvantaged. In order to achieve democracy and civil society, all strata of society need to have a voice. PRA provides a way for that to happen. From there, the next step is for people to claim their rights, vote, and formulate opinions on public policy.

Tocqueville reminds us associations are necessary for the education of citizenry, regardless of their socio-economic condition. As one of the key groups in civil society, it is appropriate they practice techniques like PRA in order to provide the voiceless with a channel through which they can express their needs and opinions, as the example of Sayedah Zeinab shows. Moreover, encouraging local government to participate in PRAs, as happened in Darassah, creates a connection that flows from state to individual citizens and vice versa.

This example showed the beginning of a movement to reform the state. If repeated more broadly, this activity could catalyze a reformation movement.

This is not an expression of political rights only, but of social and economic rights, as Zaki points out.[31] Powerless people are not only powerless in a political sense but even more so in a socio-economic sense. The poor are often badly treated even by others like them or those slightly better off. In Egypt, the poor often meet with more sympathy than elsewhere because it is thought they are born poor by divine design. Still, efforts to help them are not always well designed. Their lack of education and skills makes it more difficult to help them out of their poverty and much effort and creative thinking is still needed.

PRA is a method that helps people realize they themselves are a resource. It creates in people a consciousness of their potential and their power as a group over the power holders. As such, they have a responsibility to make sure their decisions are fair and well thought out. This kind of responsibility is accompanied by an awareness that they have an important role to play in the life of their country. In this sense, they become fully participating citizens and not merely statistics.

The qualities of a Great Man or Woman described in the Confucian quote at the beginning of this chapter appear in many religious or cultural value systems. It is as though the wise ones of all ages have come to the realization that such values are necessary for societal well-being. Many people think of them skeptically, for they seem too idealistic. Yet, around the world, PRA has become an accepted mechanism to restore this idealism in practical, down-to-earth terms.

Since ideas of democracy and civil society are appearing throughout the world today, it is not pure chance that PRA should also be taking hold. Maybe it is in part a reaction to the many disappointments and failures in systems of governance that so much effort is going into finding ways to realize this idealism. The challenge today is to unite communities and to create a connection between the state and citizens to reconstitute civil society. PRA is a vital and creative way of doing that.

NOTES

1. Founded in Cairo in 1990, the Center for Development Services (CDS) is a semi-autonomous organization sponsored by the Near East Foundation. Through CDS, qualified Arabic-speaking and bilingual professionals are available to serve the development community throughout the Middle East and Africa. CDS staff have extensive practical experience in community development, adult education, training, research, technical assistance provision, small and micro enterprise, management, organization development, agricultural extension, health, and social science applications.

2. Goran Hyden. "Building Civil Society at the Turn of the Millennium." pp. 17-46.

3. *Ibid.* p. 5.

4. Moheb Zaki. *Civil Society and Democracy.* Cairo, Egypt: The Ibn Khaldoun Center. Dar El Kutob Publication. 1995. p. 4.

5. *Ibid.* p. 6.

6. Hyden. *op. cit.* p. 17.

7. In Egypt, the term NGO is used to cover a wide range of non-governmental organizations. It might be helpful to make the distinction between NGOs as professional or semi-professional service organizations, and community-based organizations (CBOs), which are grassroots, citizens groups. Some of the "local NGOs" referred to in this chapter might be more accurately described as CBOs.

8. CDS/NEF have been doing this kind of training which has resulted in significant individual and institutional change.

9. Kandil Amani. *Civil Society in the Arab World.* Cairo: CIVICUS, 1995. p. 11. Also Shahera Youssef. "Education and Civil Society." in *Civil Society.* October 1996. p. 9.

10. Zaki. *op. cit.* p. 6.

11. *Ibid.* p. 4.

12. Saad Eddin Ibrahim (ed.) *Civil Society and Democratic Transformation in the Arab Nation* (in Arabic). The Yearly Report 1992. Cairo: Ibn Khaldoun Center. Soad El-Sabbah Publication, 1992. p. 14.

13. Robert Chambers. "Appraisal: Rapid, Relaxed and Participatory." Institute of Development Studies, Discussion Paper 311, 1992. Chambers is a key member of the Institute of Development Studies of the University of Sussex who helped develop, spread, and document the various tools and attitudes in PRA. The information in the section, "Origins of PRA," is taken from this document. p. 1-13.

14. *Ibid.* p. 2.

15. *Ibid.* p. 3.

16. *Ibid.* pp. 4-5.

17. *Ibid.* p. 4.

18. *Ibid.* pp. 8-9.

19. *Ibid.* p. 10.

20. This is based on the author's personal experience in CDS technical assistance work. She was part of the PRA Training Team.

21. Joachim Theis and Heather M. Grady. *Participatory Rapid Appraisal for Community Development: A Training Manual Based on Experiences in the Middle East and North Africa.* London: IIED. Save The Children Publication, 1991. p. 22.

22. *Ibid.* p. 27.

23. See Appendix entitled "Participatory Rapid Appraisal," from Theis and Grady, 1991. p. 27.

24. This account comes from the author's experience in an Arab country that was passing through difficult socio-economic and political conditions. For this reason, it is best to leave it anonymous.

25. CDS Report on "Activities of Hope Village" presented to UNICEF (in Arabic). Cairo: Unpublished Technical Assistance Report, 1997. The Report comprises four sections. The account is taken mostly from Section Two, with the introduction from Section One. Unfortunately, the report has no pagination to refer to.

26. *Ibid.* Section Two. This ranking result is the only part which is translated word for word from the original; the rest has been paraphrased with comments. In addition, specific information was obtained from interviews with two persons working on the team, Dr. Soliman Farah, the team leader, and Dr. Tindiar Adel, a physician team member.

27. Interview with the team leader of this project, Mohamed Abdel-Hafiz. Moreover, the author has attended at least four presentations of the project to the public and to CDS staff, and has been following up the project out of professional interest, in addition to reading one of the reports on the project quoted below.

28. *Ibid.*

29. Interview with the team leader, Samer El-Karanshawy, on the Darassah PRA.

30. Hyden. *op. cit.* p. 18.

31. See first part of this chapter, p. 114.

7. Reforming Indian Education from the Inside Out

Bhimrao Tupe

In reforming education, civil society must complement the government by performing functions governments cannot do, redefine the purpose and nature of education, and present it as an investment in human capital with a high rate of return.

— Mona Makram Ebeid

E ducational reform concerns everybody directly or indirectly. In many parts of the world, ineffective and obsolescent education systems fail to realize the purpose and objectives of education. People blame governments for this state of affairs since, in most countries, education falls into the lap of governments to fund, organize, and deliver. Yet, increasing numbers of people are realizing that governments cannot and should not bear total responsibility for education. The private sector, through corporations and foundations, can play a key, catalytic role in seeding new educational ventures, as well as upgrading institutions and curricula.

However, it is the third sector — civil society — where much attention is being focused today in education. The role of non-governmental organizations (NGOs) and other civil society organizations in reforming state-run education systems is increasingly important. This was highlighted at the ICA conference on civil society in Cairo, Egypt, in September 1996, by Dr. Mona Makram Ebeid, a former member of the Egyptian Parliament, acting President of the Association for the Advancement of Education, and Professor at the American University in Cairo.

In her presentation, Ebeid called on civil society organizations to pressure legislators to adopt new policies and to complement government by performing functions governments cannot do, such as teaching tolerance and self-initiative, promoting human rights, and creating a "culture of democracy." She also stressed the need for civil society organizations to work on curriculum reform. Schools in Egypt, as in many countries, are noted for fact memorization rather than creative analysis and problem solving. "An educational system needs to raise responsible citizens who can take part in the future of society. Child development and personality development are crucial parts of the educational process," she said.[1]

In addition, Ebeid underscored the need for teachers to be better trained and motivated. "Teachers need a sense of belonging to the problems of Egypt. They must know that they, and not the government, are responsible for helping to solve the problems of today and tomorrow."[2] She pointed to the advantage private schools have over public schools in that they can carefully choose their teachers, train them, and remove them when necessary.

Much of what Ebeid was advocating has already happened in the project from India highlighted in this chapter. However, it didn't happen in a vacuum and didn't result from some outside consultant's advice. The project grew as a response to the urgent need for change experienced by teachers and administrators working in grassroots educational institutions. Their sense of malaise was serious enough to make them want to do something about it, to the point of going way beyond the course of duty to achieve their ends.

ROOT CAUSES OF THE EDUCATIONAL MALAISE

Society's frustration over education comes from all sides. Its purpose, curricula, focus, and methods are isolated from community life, it suffers from a disproportionate emphasis on acquiring information, and its institutions are more and more prone to commercial influences.

While most people are preoccupied with these surface problems, there are others who have decided to deal with root causes of the malaise. They are seeking long-term, sustainable solutions in response to the fundamental crises affecting education today. Four such crises stand out.

The first crisis is philosophical. When only four per cent of Indian primary school students graduate from college and when the state of Maharashtra has eight million educated unemployed, the benefits of education are not as clear as they once were. People ask, "Why education?" This question has become vital for everybody. Why learn, why be educated, why teach, why send our children to school? These questions come up again and again. A common answer is short-sighted and shallow: "Whether it works or not, we have to continue with it because we don't have a better alternative."

The second crisis involves curriculum. It shows up in many forms, most commonly in the question: What is education in today's context? What knowledge, information, skills, and attitudinal development should be the focus of the curriculum? What is taught in schools invariably falls short of achieving educational goals because day-to-day education is geared to achieving higher marks in examinations, not to the growth of the total person.

A particular concern in India is that the curriculum is becoming too heavy. Some preschool students are faced with as many as seven books to digest in one year even though, in principle, preschools are not mandated to teach a formal academic curriculum. Nowadays, children are expected to know the three "Rs" — reading, writing, and arithmetic — before they come to first standard. Teachers, too, say the new curriculum is so difficult they cannot teach it unless they study it in depth. The curriculum is moving away from hands-on skills and character building to a focus on examinations and job procurement.

As a result, academically successful students rarely receive a "life education." The preoccupation with studying books to attain higher marks in an examination does not allow for students' psychological or social development. The result is that when many students enter the world of employment, they do not achieve the same degree of success as they did in school. Thus, we are left with the question: What is an appropriate curriculum for the total development of the student?

The third crisis is one experienced by educators, both as individuals and institutions. It is a vocational crisis. Increasing frustration makes people wonder, "Why should I continue with this job?" No longer is teaching associated with a sense of innovation, nor is it respected as a profession the way it once was. Teachers are considered employees like everybody else in the work force. Teaching has become "just another job." Moreover, it is another job which is grossly underpaid compared to other professions demanding equivalent qualifications.

The hardships of teaching — overcrowded classes, extra hours of tuition, lack of motivated students or parents, meager pay — might seem bearable if they bore fruit in the lives of students or teachers, but rarely does this seem to be the case. Teachers are overburdened with work yet they feel they are not doing what they should be doing. In order to survive, they often end up playing the same games as other government employees, adopting a "9 to 5" attitude to their work. As one teacher said, "I only have seven years left to retirement. What more is there to do now?"

Finally, teachers daily experience a pedagogical crisis. What were once regarded as effective teaching techniques are losing their magic. Teachers are aware that traditional methods such as delivering lectures or rote learning are ineffective in light of today's ever-expanding array of technology and multimedia devices. These methods can help students pass exams but do not make them independent learners and thinkers.

One senior teacher expressed her concern about this when she said: "Why is it, that no matter how hard we try to make teaching fun, students seem to he more attracted to outside activities and play? There is something basically wrong in our teaching approach." Teachers have come to see they cannot depend on their educational degrees to get them through. They have to be creative and continually update their knowledge and skills.

EDUCATIONAL REFORM

Some people become paralyzed by the immensity of these crises, but for others, they provide a challenge and inspire new responses. They all have a role to play in the total process of transformation but some are more limited than others, seeking only quick fixes or applying Band-Aids® to deep wounds.

What is required to reform education is a leap in thinking or a paradigm shift. The place of examinations and evaluation needs to be looked at from a new perspective. Reform efforts must go beyond immediacy and surface-level thinking and seek fundamental change. They must happen at different levels and in different ways. Several ways they are happening in Indian education today are through:

Policy Initiatives

In the midst of its struggles, the Indian education system has taken some significant steps to reform itself. The number of schools and educational institutes, the ratio of girls to boys, school facilities, and educational standards all have increased substantially. For instance, in three districts of the Pune Division of Maharashtra state, from 1985 to 1995 the number of high schools increased from 934 to 1,687 and the number of students appearing for the Secondary School Certificate examinations conducted at the end of tenth standard more than doubled.

Even more impressive than these figures are two major policy initiatives which have taken place over the past few decades. In 1970, the Government of India appointed the Kothari Commission to design an educational reform policy for the whole country. The commission recommended that the existing "7+4+4" pattern — seven years of primary education, four years of secondary, and four years for post-secondary degrees — be replaced by "10+2+3" — ten years of primary and high school education, two years of junior college, and three years of college education. Education up to high school was to provide basic knowledge and competency development while the +2 education was more vocationally oriented.

The proposal was good but achieved limited results. This is a common experience in bureaucratic systems. As one teacher said, "The general purpose of any reform policy is usually well studied, thoughtfully considered, and created by experienced experts, but falls short in the implementation stage. Rarely, are the system and the people who administer it prepared and equipped to change themselves in order to bring about change."

The second initiative, the National Education Policy, was adopted by the administration of the central government's newly formed Ministry for Human Resource Development in 1986. This policy promoted a more comprehensive approach to educational reform, setting different objectives for each level : for pre-primary, its objective is child care; for primary, it is education for all; for high school, it is quality of education; for junior college, it is vocational programs; and for college education, it is to provide complete education. Like other plans and policies, this too is experiencing hardship due to a lack of participation and motivation on the part of those implementing it. The need for local participation and initiative has become an established fact today. It is the missing link in the chain of reform. It is the key to making change happen.

Innovative Parallel Experiments

In contrast to these "top down" policy changes, there is a ground swell for change in education arising out of voluntary efforts at the grassroots. These bold and future-oriented experiments being undertaken by individuals or groups are proposing alternatives to current education practices. Some have a particular focus such as teaching methods, curriculum building, and environmental awareness, whereas others are more general. Certain schools, such as Mirambika in Delhi, Aditi in Bangalore or Hasant High School in Bombay, have become known for their innovative approaches, open nature, and future orientation.

Unfortunately, Indian society as a whole is not yet ready to take the insights of such schools and move in a new direction. Only large metropolitan centers such as Delhi, Bombay, Madras, and Calcutta, or fast-growing cities such as Pune and Bangalore, have allowed some openness for these innovative experiments to grow. But no matter how good the education is in these schools, students must still face the harsh reality of Board of Education examinations which force them to return to the formal education system in order to obtain accreditation.

However, after a number of years, the education system gradually has come around to absorbing some of these new models and approaches. The Environmental Studies (EVS) focus of the Parisar Asha Project from Bombay is a case in point. This project is based on the premise that to learn students must interact with their environment. It encourages students to question and think creatively while developing an environmental awareness. Developed in 1972 by Gloria d'Souza at her experimental school in Bombay, it was finally adopted in 1986 by 35 municipal schools in the city and by a further 175 schools in the neighboring state of Gujarat. Now it has become part of the Maharashtra state education system.

Voluntary Innovation Within the System

While some have chosen to forge educational experiments through their own pilot projects, others have been able to develop new models for reform while remaining in the educational system. Recognizing the need for systemic change, this proactive approach demonstrates the possibility of change by creating examples of it. These efforts are more localized, usually limited to particular schools or institutes.

The Srujan Anand School in Kolhapur in southwest Maharashtra is a good example. Under the auspices of the Antar Bharati Shikshan Mandal educational institute, it was launched in 1985 by Lila Patel. Although it follows the syllabus and text books prescribed by the state education authorities, it does not limit itself to those. The school has developed an integrated, holistic, and multimodal approach to education which places a high value on creativity, enjoyment, and commitment to learning, and involves students, teachers, and parents in the process.

Slowly, the Indian educational system is developing openness to receive the insights of these experiments and is organizing training programs to incorporate them into its ongoing operations.

Networks of Local Innovators

A fourth approach to educational change is new but becoming more widespread. It involves individuals transforming education by networking together and catalyzing innovation. Those who have the vision and the will to bring about change are collaborating and networking across the boundaries of schools, institutes, and educational levels. This approach is adding an important dimension to the change process. It has a greater potential for sustainable, long-range change because it has arisen from the local level and has access to more people and resources.

The Eklavya Project in Hoshingabad, Madhya Pradesh, is a good example of teachers networking for innovation. It aims to optimize self-directed learning by working with students, teachers, and the education system itself. Another is the ICA India's educational project where lessons learned from successful, innovative approaches are shared and tested to equip and motivate teachers for change.

A JOURNEY OF LOCAL INITIATIVE

While hundreds of tourists flocked to the famous Lonavala hill station to enjoy their 1995 Christmas weekend, about 80 teachers from three districts of Maharashtra state came together for a rather more serious activity. The gathering was totally voluntary, without any government directive or incentives such as traveling allowances. Teachers from Lonavala organized and financed it with local contributions, as well as from their own pockets.

Participants gave up their holidays to attend. One teacher was to be married in a few days but he was there. They represented different educational institutes, academic levels, administrative systems, educational backgrounds, and teaching positions. Yet they came with one thing in mind — to work to break open the vicious cycle of despair and perennial complaining about education in India. S. Y. Kulkarni, former principal of Bombay's[3] vocational training college, the Industrial Training Institute (ITI), summed up the feeling of many present: "Why must we be trapped in narrow thinking of primary school, high school, college, or ITI? We are all responsible for the same thing — to educate the younger generation. If we want education to change in totality, we must all work together."

These teachers were inspired by a vision of transforming education by transforming individuals, including themselves. B. B. Savant, an assistant headmaster, typified this attitude. "I used to feel I was a teacher by chance because, like many others, I needed a job, saw an opening in this field, and became a teacher. I faithfully did what I was paid to do but it was just another job and my work reflected it. When I came into contact with the ICA, I realized how a job can become a life vocation. This changed my whole relationship to my work."

This group of teachers evolved out of a six-year action research project conducted by The Institute of Cultural Affairs India (ICA India). A non-governmental organization involved in community and organizational development, the ICA has been working in India since 1976. Its Maharashtra Village Development Project and work with organizational transformation in the private sector has earned it a reputation as a social innovator.

The project, which covered Raigad, Thane, and Pune districts of Maharashtra state, was funded by the Canadian International Development Agency. Entitled "Innovative Approaches to Formal Education," it was designed to effect change in education through introducing state-of-the-art concepts, research findings, new teaching and learning processes, and most important of all, the ICA's Human Development approach. This approach assists people to become self-confident, self-reliant, and self-sustaining by awakening them to their hidden potential and how to actualize it. It builds on the work of leading thinkers in the human capacities and education fields including Kenneth Boulding, Barbara Clark, Edward deBono, Howard Gardner, Jean Houston, Bernice McCarthy, Paul MacLean, Roger Sperry, and Alvin Toffler.

Foundational Principles

The ICA India's education project is built on the following foundations:

- *Educators themselves must be motivated and equipped to take an active part in educational transformation.* Unless they are part of the change process, transformation is not possible. Through carefully designed training inputs, educators participate in a vocational journey.

- *Educators must be made aware of the untapped potential within each person and be given practical methods and skills to activate that potential.* Scientists have shown that human beings typically develop only 7% to 12% of their human capacities. Tapping the other 88-93% is the challenge teachers face. This human development task involves balancing textbook teaching with activities which effect attitudinal and behavioral change.

- *A comprehensive, whole systems approach to development, incorporating physical, environmental, mental, psychological, social, and spiritual growth.* Such an approach addresses the curriculum, equipment, environment, school management, and staff development. One educational institution which embraced this holistic approach to education is the Bombay ITI.

- *Networking and collaboration of locally initiated innovative approaches.* People from various schools, institutions, and educational levels come together regularly to share, plan, think, and learn. This practice has led to a strong sense of being a team or social movement, as described by S. S. Apte, a retired headmistress: "We used the word 'we' so many times [at a weekend gathering] that teachers started to become 'we.' Since then, there was no going back to 'I' thinking."

Project Phases

From 1985 to 1988, the ICA India worked closely with many high schools and other parts of the education system in Raigad District of Maharashtra as part of its village development programs. Through regular interaction with the ICA, headmasters and teachers became more interested in the ICA's Human Development approach and asked the ICA to offer its training to teachers and students. Since the ICA was looking for an appropriate way to work with education, it welcomed the invitation. The project developed in several phases.

Research

During 1989 and 1990, the Institute began its work in education with a pilot project, working with teachers and students in 12 high schools in Panvel Taluka (sub-district) of Raigad district. Before finalizing the curriculum for this experiment, the ICA conducted and evaluated pilot training programs with seven schools using human capacity exercises, image change activities, and personality profiles.

Feedback from the schools was mixed. Some teachers were fascinated by the newness and benefits of Human Development and began using it in the classroom. Others found it difficult to accept because it was not directly related to the textbook type of teaching with which they were familiar. Their preoccupation with examinations was so great that they regarded anything else as an unnecessary interference. Overall, however, the ICA was encouraged by the initial response and decided to expand the program to more schools.

Impact

Having worked with educators for two years, the Institute's reputation and credibility spread through the regional educational networks and it started to receive requests from a growing number of schools, some quite distant from its office. In response to these requests, the ICA conducted Human Development training in distant corners of Pune and Thane districts. This led the ICA to design a second phase of the project for mass impact on the system by saturating three districts and all educational levels within those districts with training activities. Over 1,200 teachers from pre-primary, primary and high schools attended three-day or six-day introductory training programs.

This training helped create a supportive environment for the project in the education system. The impact of the program was visible in Gurukul High school in Lonavala when the training was conducted during the Diwali vacation. In the beginning, teachers were unhappy about losing their valuable vacation time. As the training unfolded, they became so involved that by the end they said they would not have minded if the program were twice as long. As the project's impact grew, the need for a visible demonstration of its methods and advanced training for teachers became more urgent. This led to the next phase.

Intensive Training and Demonstration

In order to demonstrate how the Human Development approach can be used in schools, the ICA India conducted a three-year action research project with different parts of the education system in the three districts. The project included a comprehensive approach to bring about change in all aspects of education including curriculum design, teaching, learning, school environment, staff development, and institutional improvement. It was intended to train people in new concepts as well as to create examples of visible changes in schools.

Over 1,000 teachers from primary schools, high schools, teacher training colleges, ITIs, and educational authorities participated in a three-week curriculum. Topics ranged from teaching with seven intelligences and accommodating different learning styles to memory development and left brain/right brain exercises. Teachers who showed particular openness and initiative were selected for advanced training in a residential training program which explored issues such as the school as a learning community and strategies for educational transformation.

Talking about the effect of this training, H. N. Thigale, a senior teacher from Sahyadri, said, "It is difficult to pinpoint changes in teachers who went through this training because our whole lives have been affected by it. Whether at school, in the classroom, or at home, we think and act differently now. No matter what hardships we face, we maintain a positive vision and determination."

These heartfelt words of Thigale were put to the test one day when he was a member of a coordinating team of in-service training programs. At the last minute, the resource person wasn't able to come so they were faced with an immediate problem of engaging the participants. When all other replacement options had been tried, Thigale volunteered to lead the session. He used the participatory discussion and workshop methods he had learned from his ICA training. To his surprise, and everyone else's, this session became the highlight of the program. Many present had heard about these new methods, but for the first time they actually experienced them being used by a trained facilitator.

The most important outcome of this program was the activities which individuals or teams of teachers initiated in their schools. Each school created a strategic plan which included a mission statement and culture-building activities. Individual projects included yoga classes for students and teachers, a children's library, subject-related question banks, group singing, writing and poetry competitions, and activities for handicapped and slow-learning students. Team or school projects included end-of-day meditation, school environment beautification, a geophysical study of riverbeds, vocational guidance, a science exhibition, and the formation of Parent-Teacher Associations.

The benefits of these projects were widespread. Schools experienced greater academic success, as well as other physical, human, and organizational improvements. The Sahyadri Vidhyalaya Sheel Phata school in Khopoli, midway between Bombay and Pune, reported the percentage of students passing 10th grade examinations increase every year from 34% in 1992 to 76% in 1995. Several secondary schools and the Bombay ITI received state or national awards for their work.

Networking Local Innovators

Buoyed up by the changes they experienced in their own schools, about 150 teachers wanted to meet to exchange ideas and experiences, as well as for personal and professional development. Some helped organize the Lonavala meeting in December 1995. They formed an Education Motivation Committee of 24 people, a coordinating committee of five people, and ten program committees. All 150 teachers participate in at least one of the ten groups which coordinate activities in their schools.

The program committees include Publications and Documentation, Vocational Guidance, Music and Performance, Students' Training Programs, Outdoor Curricular Activities, Teacher and Facilitator Training, Yoga and Character Building, and Innovative Projects Research. The Publication Committee publishes a quarterly newsletter which includes articles on teachers' projects, experiences, creative writing, new educational ideas and information, and vocational guidance. The music committee created a teachers' singing group who write, publish, and perform songs with educational and motivational themes.

All committees are voluntary. Teachers contribute effort, time, and money out of a strong sense of commitment to and interest in revitalizing Indian education. Efforts that began as individual initiatives are now coming together and being offered to an ever-growing network of teachers and educational administrators.

CONCLUSION

From this grassroots movement and other similar ventures, a new vision is being forged of how Indian education can change. Neither planners in New Delhi nor researchers abroad can turn this vision into reality. While members of this particular movement draw on the insights, breakthroughs, and practical experience of experts in education and related fields, it is their own decisions and determination to create the new on a daily basis that provides the impetus for change. They are the vital connection between educational policy and the student, the missing link in the chain of social change that many top-down policy directives fail to take into account.

Granted, it was an NGO, in this case the ICA, that catalyzed this movement. Although the ICA continues to anchor its development and facilitate its evolution, this project has become much more than "an ICA program." It is another face of civil society making its presence felt through the public school system in western Maharashtra. It is a small beginning but one shouldn't underestimate its significance nor its potential to make a much needed contribution to India's vast education system.

This movement has shown, once again, that ordinary citizens — in this case, educators — can be a vital force for social change, given the chance to articulate their vision of the future, the tools to work towards that vision, and a supportive network to assist them in the process. In the language of civil society, it has shown that when citizens come together in free association, network together with trust and reciprocity, create mechanisms of exchange and communication, they can catalyze needed changes beyond the scope of the state but complementary to it.

NOTES

1. From her panel presentation on the role of education in civil society at the Cairo conference. See page 11 for further details of the conference.

2. *Ibid.*

3. The current government of Maharashtra has renamed Bombay "Mumbai," the traditional name for the city.

8. Civil Society in Romania: An Evolving Partnership

Alice K. Johnson & Barbara T. Wright

The challenge of the next century will be to build democracy on a more human scale and to expand the capacity of citizens for self-governance and public problem solving.

— Don Eberly

C ivil society is the network of free associations through which people care for one another, build community, exercise influence on government, and stimulate local commercial activity. Civil society is the foundation and context for supporting, critiquing, and reforming the private economic sector, the public governmental sector, and the social, non-profit/ non-governmental sector. It is the communal infrastructure that underlies strong public, private, and voluntary organization.

To support the development of civil society in Romania, the Mandel School of Applied Social Science (MSASS) at Case Western Reserve University in Cleveland, USA, developed a conceptual framework in 1996 for an Institute for Civil Society Development (ICSD).[1] The mission of the ICSD is to foster a vigorous civil sector through democratic government, a just, developing economy, and voluntary association. Its vision is a flourishing civil society consisting of interacting, caring communities which support the full human development of people through community health and social services, education, family support, citizenship, diverse cultures and traditions, and social and economic development.

The proposed Institute for Civil Society Development (ICSD) at MSASS will foster vigorous civil societies by linking Cleveland communities and institutions with communities and institutions in Romania. These partnering organizations include universities, corporations, foundations, non-governmental organizations (NGOs), and government agencies. In collaboration with ICSD, these organizations will provide opportunities for international exchange, educational programs, technical assistance and training, and evaluation activities. ICSD partnerships will also serve as field placement sites for students from the United States and other countries interested in international social work, the management of non-governmental organizations, and the development of civil society.

PRINCIPLES OF CIVIL SOCIETY DEVELOPMENT

The emerging new world order is one of interdependent nations with democratic forms of government in a global economy dominated by multinational corporations and information technology. The ability to participate effectively in this new order requires a process of evolution on the part of countries moving from centralized state economies and controlled politics to democratic markets and free association. The historical development of the United States, with its democratic tradition in social and economic development, suggests basic principles which are critical for the establishment of an emerging civil society. These principles are:

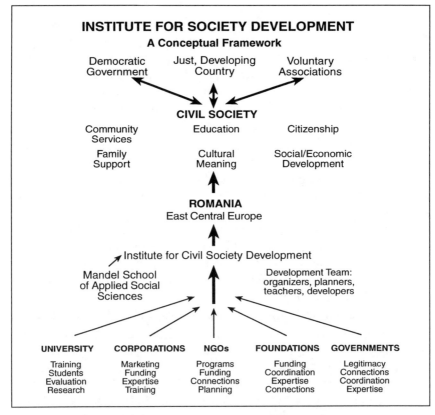

Figure 1. Institute for Civil Society Development

Participation. This implies a strategy of listening to and involving local citizenry and leadership. It means organizing society so there is access to and influence in decision-making by persons at all levels of society, in contrast to programs set up and run only by professional elites.

Inclusion. This means that no group or minority is excluded or left out. It requires democratic processes, equal treatment, and social justice.

Reciprocity. This focuses on strengthening relationships to develop mutual support systems. It contrasts with the approach that identifies people in terms of their problems or deficiencies and then establishes programs to meet those deficiencies. This key principle differentiates a strategy of community building from one of social welfare.

Structural change. This affirms that change is more than motivating individuals. It means recognizing and dealing with the social structures or habits within which personal behavior and consciousness are reinforced and assume meaning.

Cultural appropriateness. This affirms the integrity and importance of diverse cultural traditions and expressions as well as a commonality at the root of all cultures. It implies a strategy in which diverse cultural expressions are celebrated, renewed, and unified within communities.

Holism. This supports strategies that link economic, political, cultural, and spiritual dimensions of local communities. It is based on the premise that values and affiliation move people and that a sense of belonging and meaning are as important as financial well-being.

Learning. This calls for constant learning through critical inquiry. It implies a strategy that is self-reflective, evaluative, self-correcting, and based on actual results.

Action. All the above principles are rooted in this one. It is the principle of human power — the ability of a community to act in concert. It is through this principle that humankind accepts tradition, develops initiative, forms a community, connects to the world, and projects a future. Freedom, social justice, and distributive power are defined by, and rooted in, this principle. This is the principle that uses civil society development as a strategy for human development.

These principles provide the foundational support for the development of strong community affiliations. By integrating them into practices and programs, the foundational tenants of civil society are communicated. Together they distinguish the proposed Institute from other efforts in international social development or civil society work. This uniqueness focuses on existing strengths, principles of diversity, regional linkages, and the resourcefulness of the collective community.

These principles and the strategies they imply will guide the ICSD as it develops. In partnership with communities in Romania, the ICSD will help plan projects, organize programs, develop resources, and staff local community-based ventures. In its partnering and supportive role in the formation of civil society in Romania, the ICSD plans to:

- Organize community-based leadership
- Link universities with the emerging non-profit sector
- Facilitate community-centered approaches
- Develop regional capacity for social and economic development
- Support self-sustaining and self-sufficient networks of associations
- Promote collaboration between government, NGOs, and corporations
- Support the interaction and international exchange of leaders, students, and scholars

HISTORICAL PERSPECTIVE

Romanian history is documented back to the seventh century BC when trading routes were established between Greece and the area known as Transylvania. The people of this area, known as Dacians to the Romans and Getae to the Greeks, attempted to form a state to stop expansion of the powerful Roman Empire. Although they failed, the eventual mixture of Roman-Dacian people formed the foundation of the Latin-based language used today in Romania.

The invasion of Transylvania by the Hungarians in the 10th century marked the beginning of a contentious struggle for control of this region. By the 13th century, all of Transylvania was under Hungarian rule. In the 16th century, Transylvania came under Turkish dominion during the Ottoman Empire's conquest of Hungry and, in the 17th century, it was governed by the Hapsburg Empire. Following the defeat of Austria-Hungary in 1918, Transylvania was joined with the neighboring principalities of Wallachia, Moldavia, Banat, and Dobrudja to form the nation-state of Romania. In spite of the influences of its many invaders, Romania maintained its unique culture and language.

In 1940, northern Transylvania was torn from Romania by Nazi Germany. German troops entered Romania and General Antonescu joined Germany's battle against the Soviet Union. The Romanian people, however, resented the Nazi invasion and dissension spread throughout the country. Unexpectedly, when Romanian allegiance changed in 1944, Germans found in the country were taken captive and Romania announced its affiliation with the Allies. Soviet and Romanian troops drove the Hungarians and Germans from Romania and retook control of Transylvania. After World War II, when the government of General Nicolae Radescu was less than accommodating to the Soviet presence, the Soviets dissolved the Romanian system and installed the pro-Soviet Petru Groza.

On 8 November 1945, the Romanian people expressed their dissatisfaction with Communist rule in a collective celebration of their exiled king, King Michael. According to Wingrove, over 15,000 political leaders, students, workers, and professionals rallied in Bucharest's Palace Square to say a decisive no to Soviet influence over Romania.[2] Before the day was over, Groze's Soviet-backed troops moved in to crush the demonstration, resulting in a blood bath remembered by Romanians to this day.

In 1965, Nicolae Ceausescu came into power as Secretary General of the Communist Party. Ceausescu ruled Romania with a deadly force that repressed and controlled the economic, political, social, and personal lives of his subjects. Dissidents were managed by the lethal *Securitate* or secret police. NGOs that existed before World War II were, for all democratic purposes, dismantled and replaced by communist youth organizations, trade unions, or other state-mandated membership associations.[3] The ban on democratic associations was attached to a ban on Western professional journals in 1977, when Romania suppressed all cultural and educational exchanges with the outside world.

Another Ceausescu policy known as "systematization" eliminated both historic city centers and rural villages and replaced them with high-rise commercial and apartment buildings.[4] Rural peasants and others were forced to abandon their private homes and move to crowded apartments. In order to meet state-mandated production schedules, these new apartments were often "finished" without heat, water, and electricity. The land acquired through systematization was hastily industrialized, and as a result, there was extensive rural-to-urban migration which disrupted the extended family networks that helped care for infants and small children and children with special needs. At the same time, policy required each woman of child-bearing age to produce a minimum number of children. State-run orphanages were flooded with these children who were abandoned by parents who bore them to meet the quota. Theoretically, these children were to be raised by the state creating a future collective of individuals with allegiance only to Ceausescu.

During more than 40 years of strict Communist rule, the Romanian economy was based almost entirely on government provision of goods and services. The legacy of Ceausescu's regime was food rationing, energy shortages,[5] and total state control of education, health, labor, and social protection.[6] Ceausescu's fall from power in December 1989 ended his dictatorial reign but not the influence of the Communist Party. Many leaders who took control of the government following the execution of Ceausescu and his wife were closely linked to the previous system of power.[7] Nonetheless, since 1989, the extreme economic policies of the Ceausescu regime have been reversed and strategies have been implemented to move the country towards a functioning market economy.[8] Private commerce is now encouraged and more than 100,000 for-profit enterprises, representing 10 percent of the GDP, have been established.[9]

During this transition period, unemployment has fluctuated around 10 percent, the standard of living has declined by nearly 30 percent, and inflation has been as high as 70 percent.[10]

Romania continues its struggle for independence and self-determination. The November 1996 elections resulted in the removal of incumbent Ion Illiescu, a former aide to Nicolae Ceausescu,[11] in favor of the first non-communist president since Ceausescu's demise. The new president, Emil Constantinescu of the Democratic Convention of Romania (CDR), has been assisted by more than a 30 percent increase of CDR representatives in the Senate and the Chamber of Deputies which comprise the Romanian parliament.[12]

President Constantinescu has many problems to overcome as he tries to move Romania into the 21st century. The infrastructure is in perilous condition from years of neglect; supporters of Communist ideology are still strong in some sectors; the economy continues to be ravaged by inflation; and many people and communities still live in fear and isolation due to the historic power of the *Securitate*. At the same time, in reaction to years of control by the central government, a ground swell of new for-profit, commercial enterprises and non-profit organizations has occurred. The emergence of these organizations has been commonly viewed as one of Romania's first steps toward democracy.[13] The rebirth of the non-profit sector in Romania was influenced by international voluntary organizations which arrived after the revolution to respond to the needs of thousands of institutionalized children. This outpouring of international relief has exposed the Romanian people for the first time in 40 years to humanitarianism, voluntarism, and the philosophy and operation of non-profit organizations.[14] Romania's new government is hoping to move the country towards greater foreign involvement by focusing on possible membership in NATO and the European Union, as it attempts to address problems at home.

THE ICSD PROCESS

Romania is strategically located in East-Central Europe. With a population of 23 million, the country can be neatly divided into four regions which have differences in culture and religion, number and type of NGOs, and the presence of minorities — German, Hungarian, Jewish, and Serbian. Each region also shares similarities and, in part, a common history with the border regions of its adjacent states. These pre-existing linkages suggest that natural, cross-cultural, and cross-regional transfers of civil society activities can occur from Romania to its neighboring regions.[15]

These four regions provide a logical framework for civil society development in Romania. The ICSD plan to facilitate the development of civil society in Romania builds on this reality and is projected as a three-step process:[16]

- **Listening Phase.** Key people are interviewed from inviting institutions and other potential participating organizations. Teams of interviewers carry out an assessment of assets and opportunities in each region of Romania. This provides a profile of each region, identifies key leaders, highlights the assets and strengths of communities, discerns an emerging vision, and notes obstacles to social and economic development.

- **Educational Phase.** Based on the outcomes of the Listening Phase, key organizational people are convened to form a sponsoring group. A participative process is used to train these leaders in the theory and practice of community building and coalition development.

- **Organizational Phase.** Based on the outcomes of the Educational Phase, the organizational and management structures of a community-building process are identified. This stage refines the emerging vision of civil society, develops a strategic plan for the community, and plans for resource development and the organizational auspices through which future community-based initiatives will occur.

This three-phase development process also builds on the Mandel School's ongoing contact with community leaders in each region of Romania.[17] MSASS has conducted a variety of programs with social work departments in universities, government ministries and institutions, and non-profit organizations. For example, faculty have offered social work training seminars there since 1991 and were instrumental in convening the first Conference on Social Work and Social Policy at the University of Bucharest in 1992.[18] The School has used a development-oriented perspective to facilitate professional exchanges, develop training seminars, and provide graduate scholarships for Romanian students,[19] a contribution valued at more than $60,000. The School has also been involved in technical assistance and research on Romania's non-profit sector. With funds from the Rockefeller Brothers Fund, The Mandel Center for Nonprofit Organizations was the first US academic institution to provide training and technical assistance to non-profit managers working in the areas of human rights, social services, health, and environmental issues in Romania.[20] A grant from the AT&T company provided the first monies for research on Romania's non-profit sector.[21] In addition, MSASS has continued to provide in-kind support of nearly $100,000 per year to Romania through its voluntary activities.[22]

This six-year affiliation has produced an active network of potential contacts for the operationalization of ICSD initiatives, an understanding of Romanian culture, and an objective view of the changes that have occurred since the revolution. Moreover, as part of the development of the ICSD conceptual framework, numerous Cleveland institutions have been consulted to ascertain their willingness to participate in the Educational and Organizational

Phases of the project by providing consultation, training, and internships to persons in Romania.

LISTENING AND LEARNING IN ROMANIA (LLR) PROJECT

During the summer of 1996, 29 American professionals and students went to Romania to initiate the Listening Phase of the plan. LLR teams conducted interviews in five key cities: Iasi, Cluj-Napoca, Timisoara, Oradea, and Bucharest. Each team consisted of a professional from one of the participating universities, a graduate student or recent MSASS alumni, and a bilingual, cultural interpreter from Romania. Key persons from a cross-section of Romanian society were interviewed, including university faculty and students, heads of new NGOs, ethnic minority leaders, public administrators, religious leaders, business people, local government officials, and political leaders.

The interviewing teams carried out an assessment of regional assets, reviewed opportunities for the creation of social and economic development initiatives, and asked questions regarding ethnic collaboration and/or conflict in each region. Each team interviewed approximately 20 people in two weeks for a total of 220 interviews. Each participant maintained a personal log. Team leaders were designated as interviewers, while student team members recorded each interview. Summary sheets identifying key assets, community linkages, collaborative efforts, and potential barriers were provided for immediate perception reviews by the team following the interview.

In September 1996, the faculty/student teams met at MSASS for a two-day debriefing to develop a profile of each region of Romania based on the interviews. Prior to the debriefing, each team prepared a summary of the information they obtained during their interviews. Data was organized into the following categories:

- General profile of the region
- Opportunities for social and economic development
- Major obstacles to social and economic development
- Emerging vision of civil society.

The next section summarizes the content of 46 interviews in Iasi, Romania. The data shows the undeterred strength of the Romanian people to seek a national identity and correct the transgressions of past leaders. Struggles which began centuries ago are still evident. If civil society begins with individuals forming free associations through which they can influence their communities, the seeds of this process can be found in the following descriptions.

Profile of the Iasi Region

More than any other, this region in the northeast part of the country has experienced invasions, tumult, and oppression. Iasi is a major city of about 250,000 people located near the border with the former Soviet Union. This proximity to its historic foe and purveyor of communism is considered a handicap and potential threat. At the same time, its distance from Bucharest means it lacks the benefits the capital provides and contributes to a sense of marginalization. However, the distance from Bucharest also provides a sense of freedom from attention and scrutiny by the capital.

Iasi is a spiritual, cultural, educational, and county governmental center. It is the headquarters for the Romanian Orthodox Church. In contrast to the proliferation of apartment blocks are the numerous monasteries and churches from Iasi's heyday as the capital of Moldavia. These monasteries, churches, palaces, and theaters add an old-world charm. Many famous people, such as the poet Eminescu who helped shape Romania's national identity, came from Iasi, were educated in, or taught in this city. The city's patron, St. Parascheva, helped build solidarity within the community. There is significant local pride in Iasi. Many professors and students are associated with the university. Some described it as a safe place to live because of its low crime rate.

Iasi has some manufacturing industries, especially clothing, rugs, plastics, pharmaceuticals, heavy metal, and furniture. The surrounding area is agricultural and is one of the major wine-producing areas of Romania. Based on the 1992 census, Iasi County has a population of 806,778, comprising 795,691 Romanians, 6622 Gypsies, 2778 Russians, 598 Jews, 455 Hungarians, and 263 Germans, and 371 people of other ethnic origin.[23] There is a broad range of cultural groups represented, notably Middle East Arabs, Gypsies, Greeks, and Jews. Religious affiliation is primarily Romanian Orthodox, with smaller representations of Roman Catholic, Pentecostal, Evangelical, Mennonite, Seventh Day Adventist, and Bahai faith communities.

Opportunities for Development

One of the strongest assets identified in this region is its human resources. There is a high percentage of intellectuals, professors, and students who comprise a highly motivated, intelligent, and energetic pool of resources. Many are informed about current issues at the local, national, and international levels and are multilingual, non-materialistic, and demonstrate an interest in creating new systems to serve the community.

Connections with international resources have been established and some aid has been received. There has been an overwhelmingly positive response to international assistance.[24] Positive outcomes include cooperative funding of social and economic programs, technical exchanges, joint business ventures, student and professor exchanges, medical assistance, management training, social services, business economics, and consumer relations. Business leaders have expressed a desire for further international exchanges and collaborations.

Two strengths identified by many interviewees were the natural resources of this area and the ability of people to handle adversity. The natural beauty of the countryside and the historic monasteries offer great potential for tourism. People perceive Iasi as a cultural capital and are proud of their new academy and philharmonic theater. The rural area surrounding Iasi has agricultural potential, and traditional skills such as wool weaving and carpet making could be developed into cottage industries or community projects.

Iasi leaders showed insight about the personal and national challenges facing their country and region. The election of the mayor from the opposition party was seen as a positive step forward. Despite occasional religious conflicts, the area is tolerant of diversity and desires unity through cooperation. Many individuals reported volunteering to work with orphans, children, and for human rights.

Obstacles to Development

Overall, three obstacles to development emerged from the individual items — the lack of infrastructure to support reform measures, limited or non-existent financial resources to realize people's visions, and the misuse of scarce resources to meet immediate needs. Major obstacles to social and economic development identified in the interviews can be divided into six categories:

Political. Little public trust in elected officials and government in general, resulting from unevenly applied laws, a punitive redistribution of tax monies, and the denial of adequate funding for certain programs; limited local autonomy, coupled with poor administration; unemployment; lack of management skills; lack of a fair document to enter the European Union; minority rights; inaccurate images of Romania in the Western media; lack of knowledge about democracy.

Educational. Students' knowledge not integrated with public life; students lack skills to be activists; lack of books; absence of problem-resolution models; the perceived negative impact of the large number of foreign students whose enrollment makes university education less accessible for Romanians.

Economic. Public utilities, roads, sewers and equipment distribution insufficient to support growth and development; corruption in business and government and a lack of personal integrity impede growth; the NGO sponsorship law, which allows only 5% of annual profits to be given tax-free to NGOs, inhibits civic-mindedness; dearth of modern equipment, facilities, technology, and quality supplies to enable companies to develop; lack of training in financial planning, attracting international investment, competing in international markets, negotiating loans, and managing inflation; little appreciation of the importance of accountability for individuals and public and private enterprises; pervasive control of the former communist regime; lack of personal initiative; suspicion of working together in cooperative endeavors.

Agricultural. An inadequate national agricultural policy; lack of cooperative action in agricultural ventures; poor equipment; land distribution issues; the small size of land holdings prohibits efficient crop production; rapidly rising costs of produce and other food items; concern about the welfare of farmers — "If they die, we die."

Social and Health. Lack of stable care systems and unequal access to those systems. One respondent noted, "One has a choice to make when ill and needing medicine — either die, or learn to open the door with your head because your hands will be too full with tips to get the door open."

Ideological/Religious. Variations in values and cultural norms; subtle ethnic tensions regarding the effect of certain groups on the well-being of the community, e.g., references to Gypsies focused on child welfare and indiscriminate business practices; church arson; beatings related to religious conflicts.

In addition to the above concerns, many individuals raised issues regarding the transition Romania is in today. Statements indicated confusion over the number of choices available and which course would be best for the future of the country. There was concern that Romania would lose its identity in light of growing international influence. Trainees who had been given technical assistance abroad found the equipment to implement their learning was not always available. Others expressed a sense of inferiority after being exposed to the West. One individual stated, "We were told we were the best! With international exchange, we have learned this is not true, so now what do we do?" Others expressed frustration at the false hope often raised by international visitors. "We have experienced empty promises. It appears we are going to get help, then nothing happens."

Emerging Vision

Participants' visions for the future — personal, local, or national — can be described in the following five categories:

Political. Free expression; elimination of political extremes; democratic development without a violent response to ideological differences; an organized, non-secular, liberal system free of state guidance; collaboration between the church and the mayor via the efforts of the Orthodox archbishop of Iasi; development at a quicker pace.

Educational. A cultural renaissance for the region based on Iasi's role as an academic and cultural center for Romania; stronger organizations for supporting students, greater encouragement to open their minds through intellectual pursuits, and living conditions that provide greater dignity; modernization of education, science, and technology; the work of Romanian intellectuals represented at national and international levels; diagnostic skills, intervention strategies, specialized work in drug or alcohol programs, and family preservation services for social work students; incentives to keep children in school; improved public education for Gypsy children.

Economic. Iasi becomes another "Silicon Valley" through the development of research and technology; international investment through modern information systems, coordination between cultural and economic communities, and development of a regional, strategic business plan; community planning process; mentorship program for youth leadership development; concern for community development and a desire to cultivate this in tandem with economic development; revitalization of the Jewish community; development of tourism; Iasi becomes a strong economic center and "the capital of quality"; management training adapted to the Romanian situation; relationships with countries interested in what Iasi has to offer.

Social/Health. Expanded awareness of the region's cultural heritage, traditions, and park and recreational facilities; private health care services with better access and management of resources; public education about children with disabilities and an increase in resources for this; programs for alcoholics, battered women, elderly pensioners, and unemployed persons; NGOs and government collaborate in special social services, albeit with distinct and separate lines of authority and control.

Ideological/religious. A balance between a life with technology and a spiritual life; Christian principles interwoven into lifestyle choices; strong collaboration between the mayor and the Orthodox Bishop; increased religious and ethnic cooperation, especially in the development of social programs. As an example of the latter, the expansion of the Jewish community's elderly food program was seen as a way to contribute to the economic well-being of poor persons of other faiths.

Indications of Civil Society in Iasi

This section describes the interview data in light of the civil society principles enumerated earlier, that guide ICSD initiatives.

Participation. The majority of interviewees were impressed that the LLR Teams came to listen. One leader noted the uniqueness of the project was that it came with no money but offered a partnering approach by identifying Romanian leaders interested in mutual exchange, networking, and collaboration. Although respondents indicated a high level of interest in a community-building process, there was no avenue for such involvement in Iasi at the time.

Inclusion. Iasi was seen as a homogeneous society except for some religious and ethnic related incidents. Most interviewees, however, did not understand the issue of ethnic marginalization, particularly in reference to Gypsies and members of small evangelical denominations. However, there was movement in this area; for example, university students who were part of an interdisciplinary group for diversity had begun a project to integrate Gypsy children into regular schools. Some faculty were also involved in a program for gifted children.

Reciprocity. The LLR Teams met many people working by themselves or with one or two others. Most active people tend to be isolated and do not have large support networks. One unexpected outcome of the interview process was putting people in touch with other people whom they had never met before and who were involved in community-based projects.

Structural change. People in Iasi recognize their country and city are in the midst of a difficult transitional period and need structural change. While the lack of resources, coupled with the low quality of life, diminishes the motivation of some people, others are empowered by the opportunity to change. Some key leaders are promoting innovative programs and structural change through non-profit organizations, public-private partnerships, and alternative institutions for street children.

Cultural appropriateness. After many years of communism, Iasi is renewing itself as the cultural capital of Romania. Events include the St. Parascheva Fest in October, a summer music festival, monastery tours, and national ceramic fairs. English, French, German, and American libraries and cultural centers have opened.

Holism. Centuries of tradition are being broken by the Orthodox Church in Iasi through the establishment of a social service agency. The Church has started a new trend of supporting outreach in communities and promoting non-profits. It has also started a joint degree program in social work and theology. In one parish, a priest is starting a health clinic and an agricultural development program for improving the life of peasants.

Learning. Several interviewees were quite astute in their understanding of the benefits and pitfalls of international aid programs. They were able to contrast and compare the failure of government programs with failures in international aid. They understood their community and provided clear examples of how they envisioned their community in comparison to the events of the recent and more distant past.

Action. Coming without a defined and funded project impressed the leaders interviewed in Iasi. They were interested in the idea of acting together in a partnership approach, linking Cleveland institutions and individuals with institutions and individuals in Iasi in a collaborative learning and action-oriented process. They saw this as a way of training young people and learning both community process and management skills at the same time. They also saw a community approach as a way of mentoring quality people coming out of universities. Since there are few jobs for them, they could staff community development projects.

The LLR Teams also learned that some elected officials and media representatives had discussed trying to start a community development approach in the community. They noted a general climate of free exchange of information and that some individuals had become wealthy and could give back to the community. Romania's long history of central planning and budget allocation from the state and the political system had not given people any experience in participatory community building. This seemed an ideal time to remedy that situation.

CONCLUSION

The 220 interviews carried out in the Listening Phase of the ICSD process comprise a database of key people and institutions upon which the remaining phases will build. In assessing the value of the ICSD initiative, two questions come to mind: Why is the ICSD initiative unique? How is it related to other efforts to build civil society in Romania?

First, ICSD uses a community-based approach that builds upon other efforts that have supported the development of Romania's non-profit sector. For example, the Soros Foundation has financed programs for NGOs in electronic communication, education, and training. Funding from the Soros Foundation and the European Union has helped to create the Romanian Civil Society Development Foundation. The purpose of this foundation is to provide grants to NGOs and establish an NGO Resource Center in Bucharest. The US-based NGO, World Learning, in partnership with Support Centers International and the National Democratic Institute for International Affairs, has implemented the Democracy Network Program funded by the United States Agency for International Development. While these programs provide small grants to NGOs, they focus solely on the NGO sector with particular emphasis on technical assistance and training seminars for NGO leaders. However, these projects have nurtured an interest in the development of civil society as evidenced in interviews with many NGO leaders. In the Educational Phase, ICSD will work with these and other NGO leaders who have been nurtured in their infant stages by these aforementioned technical assistance and training projects.

Second, the ICSD approach does not limit its civil society work to the governmental sector as previous democracy assistance initiatives have done. Similar to initiatives focusing on NGOs, those that have targeted the governmental sector have focused mainly on technical assistance and training seminars provided by outside consultants. As a result, this assistance is often provided without the benefit of any integration into Romanian practice or any process for implementation and evaluation. In his book *Assessing Democracy Assistance: The Case of Romania*, Carothers addresses the limitations of this method, which transplants Western European ideas and processes rather than developing a culturally appropriate model for Romania.[25] The Educational Phase of the proposed ICSD framework takes civil society development in Romania one step further. It operationalizes an inclusive process which engages local Romanian leaders from all sectors — government, business, non-profit organizations, religious institutions, and universities — in a participative, community-based planning approach. The outcome of this phase will be the development of a culturally specific planning and implementation process and evaluation plan.

Third, the proposed ICSD framework uses a regional approach to support the development of civil society. Building upon the existing strengths of each region, universities, private industry, non-profit organizations, government, and key leaders are drawn together and supported based upon the defining principles of civil society. Each region develops its capacity to act as a conduit for resources to local ventures which, in turn, provide local expertise and technical exchange to participating members. It is expected that organizations and leaders in Romania participating in the ICSD process will identify social and economic development initiatives for their local communities which will be supported by the ICSD process, but will be built upon existing leadership capacity.

Fourth, the ICSD uses a social development approach concerned with both economic and social development at the same time. According to Midgley,[26] social development theory is largely untested and there has been no rigorous or consistent effort at international social development from a university base. The Organizational Phase of the proposed ICSD process will involve major universities in the USA and other Cleveland institutions in partnership with Romania. This approach pulls community leaders together in an interactive and collaborative process that is mutually beneficial to the development of civil society in Romania and in the USA. This process features two-way learning about the organization and management of local development in both countries. The formation of a community-based networking approach to social and economic development responds to a major problem in the development of civil society in Romania — the lack of information and cooperation among organizations.[27]

In summary, the plan for civil society development envisioned by ICSD is innovative. It acknowledges the need to bolster local entities comprised of indigenous staff and the importance of building upon existing programs. It incorporates the concepts of networking and collaboration among government, business, NGOs, universities, and religious institutions. At the same time, it sets up a mechanism through which additional international assistance can be provided and monitored. Most importantly, the ICSD process serves as an umbrella for community-based planning and an incubator for the maturation of civil society.

NOTES

1. The funds for establishing this Institute in the United States are being sought from a variety of foundations and international business corporations.

2. D. Wingrove. *Romanian Press Review*. 6 November 1995. Available on-line: http://www.halcyon.com/rompr/33cdavid.html

3. A. K. Johnson, L. Ourvan and D. Young. "The emergence of non-governmental organizations in Romania: International support and the third sector role." *Social Development Issues*. Volume 17, Number 2/3, 1995. pp. 38-56.

4. J. P. Telgarsky and R. J. Struyk. *Toward a Market-Oriented Housing Sector in Eastern Europe*. Washington, DC: The Urban Institute Press, 1990.

5. J. F. Brown. *Eastern Europe and Communist Rule*. Durham: Duke University Press, 1988.

6. J. R. Himes, S. Kessler and C. Landers. *Children in Institutions in Central and Eastern Europe.* Innocenti Essays No. 3. Florence: UNICEF International Child Development Center, 1991.

7. T. Carothers. *Assessing Democracy Assistance: The Case of Romania*. Washington DC: Carnegie Endowment for International Peace, 1996. p. 11.

8. A. Ben-Ne and J.M. Montias. "The introduction of markets in a hypercentralized economy: The case of Romania." *Journal of Economic Perspectives*. Volume 5, Number 4, 1991. pp. 163-170.

9. KPMG. *Investment in Romania*. Toronto: KPMG and Bucharest: Romania Development Agency, 1992.

10. B. Deacon, M. Castle-Kanerova, N. Manning, F. Millard, E. Oroosz, J. Szalai and A. Vidinova. *The New Eastern Europe: Social Policy, Past, Present, and Future*. London: Sage, 1992.

11. "Romania turns a page." *The Wall Street Journal*. 23 November 1996. Available on-line: http://www.turkey.org/news/selected/112396se.html.

12. "Final election results are in." *Romanian Press Review*. 11 November 1996. Available on-line: http://ww.halcyon.com/rompr/211news.html.

13. A. K. Johnson and D. Young. (In press). "Building the nonprofit sector in Romania." *Voluntas.*

14. A. K. Johnson, R. L. Edwards and H. C. Puwak. "Foster care and adoption policy in Romania: Suggestions for international intervention." *Child Welfare*. Volume LXXII, Number 5, 1993. pp. 489-506.

15. O. Gavrilovici. "History, geography, and culture: A rationale for the regional development of civil society in Romania." Presentation made at the Seminar in International Social Work. Cleveland: Mandel School of Applied Social Sciences, Case Western Reserve University, January 1996.

16. While three distinct phases have been stipulated, in fact the listening, training, and structuring continue so that the process is dynamic and grows through interaction, networking, and social and economic development.

17. The four regions and their five main cities with which MSASS had previous contact are Muntenia (Bucharest), Moldova (Iasi), Transylvania (Cluj-Napoca and Oradea), and Banat (Timisoara).

18. A. K. Johnson and L. M. Ourvan. *The Development of Social Work Education in Romania (Dezvoltarea Invatamintului in Domenuil Muncii Sociale in Romania): A Report to the Ministry of Education in Bucharest, Romania.* Cleveland: Mandel School of Applied Social Sciences, Case Western Reserve University, November 1992.

19. See A. K. Johnson. "Social work education and social development in nations overcoming Soviet oppression: Romania." Paper presented at the APM Council on Social Work Education. Washington, DC, February 1996; V. Groze and A. K. Johnson. "The development of an empowerment-based approach: Solving child welfare problems in Romania." Paper presented at the APM Council on Social Work Education. San Diego, March 1995.

20. A. K. Johnson and D. R. Young. *Executive Education Program for Non-governmental Organizations in Romania.* Final Report to Rockefeller Brothers Fund. Cleveland: Mandel Center for Non-profit Organizations, Case Western Reserve University, December 1993.

21. (a) A. K. Johnson, L. Ourvan and D. Young. "The emergence of non-governmental organizations in Romania: International support and the third sector role." *Social Development Issues*. Volume 17, Number 2/3, 1995. pp. 38-56. (b) A. K. Johnson and D. Young. (In press). "Building the nonprofit sector in Romania." *Voluntas.*

22. "MSASS Contributions to Romanian Projects: 1990 to 1995." Cleveland: Mandel School of Applied Social Sciences, Case Western Reserve University. Unpublished report.

23. Source: National Commission for Statistics, Romania.

24. Compare this to the situation described by Susan Fertig-Dykes in her chapter on the former Yugoslavia, "Sparks of Hope In the Embers of War: Civil Society in The Balkans." pp. 67-82.

25. For a comprehensive discussion of US democracy assistance to the governmental sector, see T. Carothers. *Assessing Democracy Assistance: The Case of Romania*. Washington DC: Carnegie Endowment for International Peace, 1996.

26. J. Midgley. *Social Development: The Developmental Perspective in Social Welfare*. London: Sage Publications, 1995.

28. L. Constantinescu. "The Romanian non-governmental organization position." Paper presented at the Romanian Information Center Meeting, York, United Kingdom. Information reported in INFOSOROS. Buletin Informativ al Fundatiei Soros pentru o Societate Deschisa din Romania, October 1995, p. 3.

Section III

NEW FRONTIERS OF CIVIL SOCIETY

Introduction

Civil society is the incubator of new ideas. It thrives on risk, creativity, novelty, and invention, and offers the best of what it finds to the institutions of society, as a gift.

— Alan AtKisson

In aviation language, civil society has taken off and is fast gaining altitude. The number and types of voluntary associations at the core of civil society are countless and growing rapidly. The networking that forms the nervous system of civil society grows exponentially, especially among those who have access to such communication channels as the Internet and electronic mail. Collaborations and exchanges between organizations and across all kinds of boundaries continue to multiply. In the midst of this explosion of citizen engagement, particular dimensions of civil society stand out as critical and deserving attention. The second half of this book draws attention to some of these.

To set the stage, Brian Stanfield presents the collective work of citizens from Canada and other countries who have identified key economic, political, and cultural trends in today's society. Given that this is a "work in progress" and that it needs input from beyond North America, nevertheless it is a good example of citizens coming together outside the framework of government or the marketplace to do their own social analysis as a basis for determining societal directions and forming public policy. This type of participatory, grassroots research is grist for civil society's mill. Significantly, one of the 17 named trends is "Bracketed Civic Sector Finding Its Voice."

One trend evident in many countries today is the desire to revitalize community life as the place where we learn the skills of citizen engagement. Monte Roulier refers to this as the need to strengthen civic infrastructure — that complex interaction of people and groups through which decisions are made and problems resolved.[1] Drawing on his experience with the US-based National Civic League, he describes five of ten components of the Civic Index, a tool used by communities in several countries to assess and upgrade their community-building capacities. A useful part of this chapter is the list of seven "success factors" which help determine how effectively communities are building communal infrastructure or social capital.

Paul Watson reminds us that one of the critical and often overlooked factors in creating civil society is the role of youth. In a powerful testimony borne from his own experience growing up in the streets of Harlem, New York, he calls for the full and equal participation of youth in community development, from planning through implementation. We exclude youth from these processes or give them only peripheral roles to play, at our peril. What's more, he maintains, the traditional individual counseling approach will no longer heal the wounds and damage to society that such exclusion brings. Instead, Watson points to a growing global movement committed to making a more strategic approach, which he calls Community Youth Development, an integral part of civil society worldwide.

In similar fashion, Janice Jiggins underscores the need for inclusive participation of all people in the development of civil society by highlighting the role of women, still deemed to have minority status in many parts of the world. She points to the powerful role of women's voluntary associations and organizational networks in remaking civil society, despite strong opposing cultural norms in two different societies. In Nigeria, for example, women health workers are not only coming together to respond to local health issues, they also are directly impacting government policy through intense collaboration and personal courage. The example of South Indian farmers shows how people gain confidence and power when they have access to knowledge based on their own experience and values — a confidence and power that can even challenge the vested interests of a powerful private sector.

Another way grassroots people have been awakened to their own potential has been through microenterprise development. Ten years ago, providing seed capital to the poorest of the poor was a fairly new concept in international development. Today, it is an accepted keystone of economic development and is becoming recognized as a vital component in forming civil society. Mildred Leet documents the experience of Trickle Up, one of the pioneers of the microenterprise movement. Her examples show clearly that microfinancing does much more than provide capital to the economically disenfranchised. It also enhances self-esteem, provides organizational skills, and increases the social capital which builds civil society.

Mirja Hanson introduces another basic prerequisite of civil society — the need for effective methods to elicit the inclusive participation so often referred to in the literature on civil society but so often lacking in practice. In her many years as a professional facilitator in communities, government agencies, and private businesses, she has accumulated a wealth of practical skills and insights into what works and what doesn't work in participation. Techniques aside, perhaps the most valuable insight of Hanson's chapter is her call for a new kind of shared leadership which embodies civil society's values of inclusion, trust, reciprocity, and tolerance rather than those of control, direction, elitism, and established interests.

Working to create civil society is one thing; knowing if and to what extent you are achieving it is something else. Robert Bothwell, reporting on another "work in progress," shares his efforts to establish indicators to measure a healthy civil society. While much work on indicators of sustainability is happening around the world, indices of civil society are not receiving quite the same attention. Although in an early phase, Bothwell's work is a valuable addition to the dialogue on civil society. When measures of civil society's strength and effectiveness can be substantiated, both governments and the private sector might be more ready to acknowledge civil society as an equal third party. At the same time, civil society itself can benefit significantly from the knowledge of the impact and deficiencies of its presence.

Defining who is and who isn't part of civil society is a matter of considerable disagreement, as Bothwell points out. Many argue that fundamental religious sects and extremist political factions are, by definition, outside the realm of civil society.[2] Most admit mainstream religious organizations as an integral part of civil society. Koenraad Verhagen asserts that religious organizations have a unique role to play in society, both in terms of the value systems they furnish and the catalyst for social transformation they often become. He proposes that organized religion be considered a distinct fourth sector, alongside government, the market, and the civic sector. Certainly, the moral, ethical, and spiritual basis of society is a critical issue that demands further attention and is one to which civil society can make a significant contribution.

Finally, John Epps begins to move in this direction in his presentation on core values of civil society. While he departs from the sectoral understanding of civil society and defines it as a society in which the economic, political, and cultural dimensions are in balance, he makes a strong case for defining core values of civil society and offers a participatory process whereby citizens can come together to redefine those values. A valuable contribution of his chapter is the question he raises of cultural relativism — are there universal values of civil society applicable to all socio-cultural situations and if so, who determines them and how? In his opening chapter to this book, Goran Hyden raises the same issue as the struggle between the "universal" and "particular." His call for empathy, tolerance, and the readiness to dialogue with others, especially "those not yet convinced,"[3] is a helpful reminder to all of us involved in building a global civil society.

NOTES

1. Monte Roulier. "Local Community: Seedbed of Civil Society." pp. 188.

2. For a discussion of the role of Islamic activism in Egypt and the Middle East, see Saad Eddin Ibrahim. "Populism, Islam, and Civil Society in the Arab World." pp. 53-66.

3. Goran Hyden. "Building Civil Society at the Turn of the Millennium." p. 42.

9. Citizen Analysis: Discerning the Signs of the Times

Brian Stanfield

Trends tell you the direction a country is moving in. The decisions are up to you.

— John Naisbitt

T rend analysis has been going on for a long time. Even in the Bible, readers are advised to "interpret the signs of the times."[1] In our time, business has shown a keen interest in John Naisbitt's *Megatrends*[2] and other works. Much of the trend analysis happening in 1990s is market-oriented, such as that of Popcorn and Marigold in their latest popular trends analysis book, *Clicking.*[3] The idea is to "braille" the culture to see which way people are moving, to determine the relationship to needs and wants, and to position your company to hop on the trend and bleed it for a quick profit.

There are other reasons for being alert to trends, however. In the first place, a trend analysis involving wide-reaching public participation can be invaluable for guiding policy formation. So much policy guidance derives from partisan think tanks or special-interest lobbying. More policy guidance is needed from the civil sector in the form of independent, grassroots trends analysis.

In the second place, such analysis can provide a way for organizations to integrate business and social prosperity, so economics can be viewed as a servant of society rather than the dominator.

In the third place, social analysis can be a tool for identifying the real breakthroughs needed for civil society to prosper.

This is a status report on a social research program in process. As the millennium approaches, the Institute of Cultural Affairs (ICA) is working with local citizens to investigate positive and negative trends emerging in our times. The purpose of this research is to identify the critical social changes and the most urgent social needs in society, as well as the key actions required to bring about a humane future for the next century.

A small group from ICA Canada planned and catalyzed this trend-gathering process, with participation from others in Canada, the United States, and people from several other countries who attended the conference, "The Rise of Civil Society in the 21st Century," organized by ICA International in Cairo, Egypt, in September 1996. This chapter pulls together over 1,000 pieces of data generated by these participants in response to the question: What are indicators of social change in our times? This data was plotted on the Social Process Triangles [See Appendix], clustered into common themes, and named as trends. As part of the data gathering process, we consulted numerous books and articles on social trends. A selected listing of these is at the end of this chapter.

The trends are divided into economic, political, and cultural, according to those areas of the social process that are most affected. While the bulk of the trends data came from North America, readers in other parts of the world may discover them resonating in their own milieu. Since this is only the beginning of an ongoing process, we welcome your comments and input.

ECONOMIC INDICATORS OF SOCIAL CHANGE

In the economic arena, the data pointed to five main areas of social change — environmentalism, the world of work, the runaway economy, technology, and community-based economics. Care for the Earth and equitable distribution of resources are not only necessary to ensure everyone has access to an adequate livelihood but they are the foundation on which civil society is built.

1. Structural Environmentalism

There are two overriding insights in this arena: natural resources are being used up faster than they can regenerate; and limiting growth is now acceptable economic policy. These insights are giving rise to policies that will promote better stewardship of the natural environment and shifts at the structural level. In other words, the environmental movement has moved beyond its "evangelical" days of waking up people to the crisis toward getting its message written into the structures of society.

This is a trend the forces of civil society championed a long time ago. They sounded the alarm of caring for the Earth. Now environmental innovation is commonplace: chlorofluorocarbons are being phased out; recycling is becoming more comprehensive and intensive; what used to be called "garbage" is a valued part of the resource stream. Garbage trucks are often called "Environmental Resource Services." The movement for sustainable agriculture gathers strength and there are many creative experiments in clean fuel production for automobiles, from electricity to canola oil. There is interest in resource-conserving buildings with insulation, solar panels, halogen lights, or special bulbs. People are looking to alternative forms of fuel-saving transportation, such as public transport, bicycling, or walking. Some business firms have developed comprehensive environmental policies for purchasing and have institutionalized waste management.

Voluntary movements still play a major role in bringing such matters to the attention of the public, but environmentalism has shifted from being a purely volunteer concern to being a business. Witness the growth of the ecorestoration and bioremediation industries which restore prairies and river valleys and use toxin-digesting bugs to clean up oil and chemical spills.

Social change in this area has a long way to go before it is thoroughly institutionalized in organizations, businesses, communities, and households. For example, while more and more office buildings have recycling programs, many do not employ the "source-separation" method. They simply separate out garbage when it's picked up and sort it then. So while organizations may be complying with new municipal ordinances, they have not come to terms with what is really needed. Those which have are making structural changes and creating a much deeper wave of environmental change.

2. The Throwaway Job

As globalization strides across national economies like a colossus, jobs migrate to countries where labor is cheapest; workers easily become pawns in the globalization power play. Companies are streamlining, downsizing, re-engineering, and right-sizing for global competition, which means increasing profits through decreasing employment, but at the expense of employees and communities. Massive layoffs and cutbacks send the message that human resources are expendable. We are in the era of the throwaway job and the throwaway worker. Middle managers are among those who have suffered most. Time after time, middle managers have been given the ax, resulting in a tragic loss of stored-up wisdom and information.

The key insight here is that the "job" or "secure position" in the firm as we have known it is giving way to the concept of employability. Work is no longer a synonym for "job." For many, work now consists of a series of short-term projects or contracts with firms that outsource work orders. Natural ability and the right attitude may be more important to employability than a postgraduate education. In addition, more people are finding the courage to start their own businesses.

Where jobs are plentiful, such as computer programming and software design, highly skilled people find work wherever they want it, but they may also find they have to work up to 80 hours a week at a rapid clip. In these situations there is a high degree of employee burnout. At the same time, technology is allowing more people to work at home on their small business or work projects — a return to cottage industries. However, working at home can often be just as demanding as office-based work. Whatever its location, work is becoming increasingly stressful as the future of work seems to lie in multiskilling and multitasking. The faithful repetition of the same task from nine to five is giving way to the human as whirling dervish.

In his public talks, social critic and author Jeremy Rifkin questions how society will provide a livelihood for the millions who will not be able to "get a job" because those jobs will have been absorbed by smart technologies that do not need humans. Rifkin comments that one way nations are dealing with the jobless is to put them in prison. In the United States, where two per cent of the male population is in jail, this costs $30,000 per year per person. This is not shrewd economics. Civil society is going to have to take up some of this slack by inventing structures that act as outlets for people's energy and creativity. Governments and wealthy corporations will need to support these structures, if they do not want a social cataclysm.

3. The Runaway Economy

The globalization of the economy, the increase in free trade zones, and the internationalization of exchange mechanisms are key factors affecting the distribution of wealth in the 1990s as global corporations replace nation states as arbiters of the economy. Wealth and power is increasingly concentrated in large financial conglomerates and global corporations. Nothing new in this. What is new is the logarithmic increase in these multinationals over the past ten years, from 7,000 in 1986 to 40,000 with over a quarter of a million affiliates in 1996. Of the top 100 economies on this planet, 50 are now transnational corporations (TNCs). Over 70 per cent of global trade in goods and services is controlled by just 500 TNCs, 350 of which, in turn, control over half of the world's direct foreign investment today. The upshot is that wealth is distributed unevenly. The economy of the 1990s rewards capital more than labor. As profit is increasingly privatized, costs are socialized and passed on to the taxpayer. We have a runaway economy with nothing in control.

This becomes more apparent every day. Resources in the financial sector outweigh the production sector by 70 to one. A rise in the stock market is no longer an indication of a rise in employment. Rather the opposite. While banks make huge profits, the North American consumer has gone on a massive spending spree that totals half a trillion dollars in credit card debt. With little or nothing in reserve, citizens are more and more at the mercy of banks.

World financial markets are susceptible to chronic manipulation. More money can be made from trading in money than from investing in technological and social innovation. As trillions of dollars hurtle round the world in nanoseconds, the economy becomes more and more detached from the real world. And as the wealth of global corporations multiplies, governments are expected to become fiscally responsible in order to create a positive environment for business. To wipe out past deficits, governments engage in massive budget cuts to community services at the same time as they privatize public assets.

There is a sense of a rapidly growing underclass. As more and more people stand in food bank lines or live on the street, financiers and "symbolic analysts" live in their wealthy fortified enclaves, isolated from the consequences of their actions. Governments, whose job it is to regulate the runaway economy, are in league with the runaway. The global economy is still in its Wild West stage, but the sheriffs have all headed out of town.

4. Technology-Driven Values

One results of the information and communication revolution is unlimited information exchange and a globalized communication system. The information explosion has yielded a glut of information, creating the cliché "information overload." The Internet links users across the globe, enabling them to converse in cyberspace, network, create "virtual communities," and participate in on-line self-help groups. Similarly, the 500-channel universe of television makes available a vast array of entertainment and information, much of it at the lowest common denominator of artistic achievement. Television and the Internet have become symbols of a society whose information technology is more powerful than people's readiness to reflect on, digest, and package that information into manageable and relevant pieces. These media are replacing religion and community organizations as the source of values.

The success of technology has devalued human and natural resources through devaluing human work, it has resulted in the rise of "technobabble," and has promoted a form of communication that is information-rich and wisdom-poor. The greater the undigested information, the less the wisdom. There is a growing perception that technology is a tyrant taking whatever it wants at whatever cost from nature and undervaluing the human dimension. Society sorely needs what Canadian author and engineer Ursula Franklin has called "redemptive technologies"— those that give back to people the opportunity to make a contribution to the technology dialogue, that monitor health and environment-related parameters, and that help in the study and sharing of successful approaches.

5. Community-Based Economics

While some feel woefully victimized by the loss of jobs and the runaway economy, others are challenged by them. Witness the tremendous increase in local economic activity, much of it community based. We hear of new community-based economic and service systems, of native people's organizations running profitable businesses, including casinos. There is the rise of local alternative money systems and local economic trading systems, such as LETS with its green-dollar approach, as well as the promotion of local cooperatives and alternative businesses such as Coop America. There are local loan programs for new business and peoples' banks and cooperatives. After government cutbacks, agencies are learning fast how to pool resources for greater effectiveness. Home-based businesses and cottage industries, and home-based employment, such as telemarketing, are booming as people find ways to survive layoffs and downsizing. There is considerable growth in the craft economy, and people are finding that part-time work has an up side: it means time for other interests, such as crafts and hobbies.

Gradually, a new economy is emerging based on new attitudes. With less money for material acquisitions, and more environmental concerns, people are — voluntarily or involuntarily — restricting growth lifestyles and learning how to do more with less. The conserving ethic is becoming fashionable; second-hand clothing stores and discount stores abound. It is no longer considered unacceptable in genteel society to share an order in a restaurant. Hand in hand with this is a rise in consumer sensitivity to social issues, and a corresponding increase in consumer advocacy.

POLITICAL INDICATORS OF SOCIAL CHANGE

Several political indicators point to a major obstacle to the formation of civil society — the alienation between people and their governments and its services. However, other indicators point to a resurgence in social responsibility and local engagement, themselves a manifestation of the rise of civil society today.

6. Disappearing Government

The increasing alignment of government with big business and narrowly-defined economic concerns is leading many governments to shrink government functions and privatize government jobs and public services. Governments find themselves supporting unenlightened self-interest rather than the concerns of the wider public. Such developments have led to a radical re-interpretation of the role and responsibilities of governments in democratic society.[4] Intervention by governments in the market to regulate the operations of corporations on behalf of the public interest is now largely a thing of the past. Governments are retreating from meeting the basic needs of their people through universal social programs and quality public services. The United States is witnessing not only a rolling back of Johnson's "Great Society" of the 1960s, but even of

Roosevelt's "New Deal" of the 1930s. Canada, which has prided itself on its social safety net for unemployment and health care is fast whittling it all away. A similar trend is occurring in Europe with the Maastricht Agreement's reduction of social benefits and insistence in individual self-sufficiency.

Now, the prime role and responsibility of governments is to secure a favorable climate for profitable transnational investment and competition. Democratic governance, imperfect though it may be, is being supplanted corporate governance. People see their governments, from local to national, withdrawing from their role of governing by shrugging off the regulatory function, and even the legislative function, as more decisions are made by cabinet or the supreme court, rather than the legislature. The initial response is voter apathy, increased public skepticism of government and industry, and a distrust of "politicians' politics." While governments search for ways to be fiscally responsible, often through massive budget cuts, the public demands from the government participation in decisions, as well as honesty and accountability to the community.

7. Systemic Poverty and Insecurity

One casualty of these campaigns for fiscal responsibility is governmental withdrawal from the provision of services. Social security systems — welfare, pensions, child support — are becoming bankrupt. Government is turning its back on social assistance. People who have relied on the social safety net for generations are watching with great insecurity as that net unravels fast. The result is a growing underclass of people who are undereducated, underpowered, and underprovided. As resources for the poor shrink, the poor see government cuts aimed at themselves, the most vulnerable members of society.

The result is that more people are using food banks, including children who are becoming a large percentage of the poor. The homeless have become far more visible, begging for money and work on the street and even door-to-door. Dramatic retrenchment in social programs also means that communities are being squeezed for dollars and losing basic services, and the human face of those services, in particular; for example, in Canada, the government employment agency has many computerized kiosks which offer no interpersonal communication for those seeking work.

As a result, there is growing fear and insecurity in society: fear of economic instability, shrinking personal income, and a leveling off of financial aspirations. Add this to the growing fear of crime and violence, partly engineered by the media, and society is perceived as unsafe and stressful. Increased fear and stress are making people burrow in at home, a response which writer Faith Popcorn has called "cocooning." People also cite a declining respect for authority, a loss of consensus on social rules, and increasing alienation from society.

8. Civic Sector Finding Its Voice

While many people blame "the government" for all their problems, they nevertheless feel they must appeal to the government to solve the problems. This mindset results in a proliferation of advocacy groups, a zealous preoccupation with "my rights," often without a parallel concern for "my responsibilities." One result of this is that millions of dollars are poured into appeals for litigation; it is easier to sue your neighbor than to take responsibility for him. Those who use channels provided to put pressure on governments for needed social change are marginalized by governments' reference to them as "special interest groups." Often the whole civil society is referred to as a special interest group, which results in an impoverished vision of citizenship. People are regarded as consumers rather than citizens; their main function is to borrow and buy and keep the economy going while their civic function has become reduced or forgotten.

However, being ignored by the government has been a boon for many citizen groups. Eventually, they come to see the need to move beyond a dependency or entitlement mindset, assume responsibility for their own problems, and become participants rather than observers. The self-help movement is providing a way for people with similar challenges to tap their own creativity in solving their problems. At the municipal level, there is much citizen input on issues. More social action groups are not only dealing with social problems but working together and sharing resources, especially when government funding cuts make this necessary. Simultaneously, government agencies and local jurisdictions are seeing themselves as part of a system in which inter-agency cooperation is essential.

9. Taking Personal Responsibility for Health

Health and wellness is another social domain in transition. To stay healthy, we now have to deal with more than just germs and infections. Over-stressed ecosystems are taking their toll on human health, as well as on animal and plants which we depend on for food. Air quality, affected by carbon dioxide emissions and other contaminants such as dioxins, is exacerbating lung diseases. The increase in chronic disease of all kinds eats up health dollars. AIDS keeps striking down more individuals, especially those in the prime of life. Mental disease is on the increase; the number with dementia are expected to triple by 2031. The right-to-die movement is questioning many health care standards for terminally ill patients.

Just at the time when the need for health care has never been greater, governments have started cutting into the health safety net. Faced with cutbacks, hospitals are doing more with less, combining with other hospitals, or closing. The move is to a managed health care system, or community-based health care where the kind of care is decided by an administrator, not a physician.

While the medical health care system is more stretched, and as emergency health measures become less affordable, alternative health care systems are thriving. On the one hand, we are witnessing a deterioration of the monopoly of the medical profession over health care as other non-medical health-care practitioners have gained credibility and become more popular. On the other hand, we see the erosion of mechanistic models of the body and the emergence of a way of caring for people that goes beyond the physical, bridging Eastern and Western therapies and acknowledging inclusive and multifaceted body-mind-spirit-environment relationships.

While the medical establishment is suspicious of alternative health measures, the public keeps voting for it with their check books. People are acquiring the know-how and technologies to promote their own health with a whole panoply of measures: vegetarian and other diets; exercise; alternative drugs; special vitamins, tonics, homeopathic remedies, herbal restoratives, weight-loss measures; and meditation and other body-mind-spirit practices. The future seems to be demanding an alliance between the medical establishment and alternative therapies that would offer people the best of both worlds.

10. The Regional Response

One response to the dramatic globalization of the economy is the localization of polity and a growing attachment to one's cultural traditions. One aspect of this is the rise of the region as a political and cultural force, with pressures for political decentralization and movements for regional separatism. In Canada, Quebec separatism periodically boils over then returns to simmer. There are similarly strong separatist movements in Spanish Catalonia, in Lombardy in northern Italy, and in the former Soviet Union. A second but related aspect of this trend is the tribal instinct for "hiving off," illustrated by those ethnic areas demanding the right to be different; for example, the Basque country of Spain, Armenia, Kashmir, and Chechenya. A third aspect of this drive toward regionalization is that more federal functions in nations are being devolved to states or provinces, where policy making and services distribution are closer to people.

CULTURAL INDICATORS OF SOCIAL CHANGE

The ICA's social research over the last 25 years has indicated that the cultural arena of the society is the key to restoring imbalances in the political and economic arenas. Seven cultural indicators of social change were identified, relating to public education, lifelong learning, the search for meaning, changing family patterns, the senior boom, local community, and multiculturalism.

11. Collapsing Public Education

Like the economy, education is in transition from an industrial second-wave model to a third-wave model where learning, knowledge processing, and the development of personal and social wisdom is the order of the day. Previously, the purpose of education was tied to job readiness. Education even borrowed its technologies from the factory floor. This model grouped learners by grade and class while the teacher made curriculum decisions for the learners. Now, jobs are disappearing, as is the factory floor, and public education is all at sea. Schools clutch at the computer to solve all their problems, but computers continue to access the enormous glut of undigested information from the information revolution to no great purpose. Schools have given up teaching students how to think, feel, and make decisions. Universities express disgust that schools are graduating illiterates.

The decline of public education is well documented. It has to do with the shift from education by bureaucracy to education by choice; the development of parallel education structures, such as charter schools, private schools, home schooling, and the privatization of public schools. Many parents are paying extra to place their children in private or special schools. Thus, public schools have become holding centers for those who can't afford to pay for customized education. The alternatives do little, if anything, to deal with the urgent needs of mainstream public education.

12. Lifelong Learning

Major change is going on in education, but not necessarily in public schools. One change is the shift from school-bound, child-bound, time-bound education to lifelong learning. One result of this is that the "three boxes of life" approach — school, work, retirement/leisure — is obsolete. As we move into a learning rather than an education mode, learning of every kind — practical, professional, civic, and spiritual — will be coterminous with life and enhance every aspect of living from prenatal stimulation of senses to old age.

IQ, a measure of logical-mathematical intelligence, once prevailed in education and determined learning capacity. Now, multiple kinds of intelligence are recognized and learners group themselves according to interests. The facilitator helps learners to diagnose learning needs from an understanding and application of different learning styles. The teacher of old is becoming a facilitator, while in business, the boss is becoming more of a coach and a mentor. At the same time, isolated, competitive learning is being overshadowed by collaborative mutual learning, as in brainstorming or problem-solving task forces. In the past, no one taught us how to learn and how we learn. This great gap is now being filled.

One consequence of this is that work, learning, and living can all be carried on in the same space. The monopoly of schools and colleges over learning is being broken. The "shadow education" system of business and industry already enrolls as many students and spends as much money as all of higher education. Companies have started playing a university role, such as the Bank of Montreal's Institute for Learning at one end of the scale and McDonald's "Hamburger University" at the other. The concept of learning as something confined to a school and for one portion of life is disappearing. Partnerships between schools and business are becoming more common while the centuries-long dominance of the curriculum by academics is almost over. The challenges of living in a world of permanent future shock are becoming the real-life curriculum for learning.

13. The Search for Meaning

Accompanying the economic and political trends discussed earlier is widespread despair and a growing spiritual vacuum, especially among the young and the urban underclass. Symptoms include increasing stress, health problems, depression, a chronic sense of frustration, and ultimately suicide.

In the midst of this void is a crisis in values. Leadership is without guidelines. Ethics often mean situational ethics where each decision is made in a different context; there is no overarching ethical system. For youth and adults, the language of individualism seems more potent than religious language. Whether in families or corporations, financial values overrun and dominate cultural values. This has produced a widespread search for meaning at all levels of society. Individuals are undertaking personal searches for wisdom; they are going to mystery schools, participating in sweat lodges and retreats, and joining groups dedicated to personal development. They are engaged in a quest for values that will place their daily lives in a more inclusive context. An upshot of these quests for meaning is the decision to see work as a vocation rather than a job, and a radical re-examination of career choices based on personal wisdom rather than what is available in the job market.

There appears to be a great hunger in many people for something profound in which to anchor their lives. Those on a spiritual quest can choose from a planetary menu of readings, practices, and methods. They are adopting practices from Eastern religions, such as Zen, tai chi, yoga, and other forms of meditation. Many people are fascinated by native spirituality; they participate in sweat lodges or pow-wows and seek native understandings of life. Thousands attend retreats, workshops, and rituals with people like Jean Houston, Robert Bly, Marion Woodman, James Hillman, and many others for healing and spiritual development. Another quite different manifestation of this search for meaning is the resurgence of evangelical and fundamentalist Christian churches and religious sects. Enhanced by the use of television and computers to convey their messages, these groups are attracting followers in increasing numbers.

These initiatives are another face of civil society, with a focus on the inner life, personal salvation, spiritual well-being and the spiritual transformation of the planet. While mainstream Christian denominations decline in numbers and influence as a source of inspiration and guidance in people's lives, alternative forms are taking their place.

14. Reweaving Family Patterns

One of the most visible cultural shifts is the dispersion, if not disappearance, of the nuclear family — mother, father, and children. Nuclear families are in the minority as multiple forms of the family take their place. Interest in traditional marriage is declining while there is growing legal recognition of marriages beyond man-woman partnerships, and a new definition of close, continuing, caring relationships. The expanding commercial trade in embryos, the number of couples opting for *in vitro* fertilization, and the rise of the surrogate father and make it possible to have children without being married. There is a growing acceptance of homosexuals and bisexuals; corporations such as Levi-Strauss and Hewlett-Packard, as well as many local government authorities, are granting spousal rights and benefits to gay employees, while there are increasing attempts to have same-sex partnerships legally recognized.

Amid uncertainty about the future for the next generation, some children are moving back home or staying longer with their parents. Working mothers are teaching their children to be more independent and resourceful. A number of young people are becoming more aware of their responsibilities, are ready to be risk-takers, and have a strong concern for the future.

Women are gradually being liberated from typecast roles and expectations. Families are adapting to this in various ways; fathers involve themselves in parenting and choose to stay home to raise their children, while mothers go to work. The family breadwinner role has become interchangeable. Women are moving into occupations traditionally the domain of men — management, the armed forces, police and fire departments, and a range of professions. Though relatively few, more women are playing key leadership roles in society. The male backlash at the women's revolution is still real, but when women are allowed to lead, they are running things their way.

15. The Senior Boom

In 1996, people born under the sign of the mushroom cloud turned 50. As the millennium turns, millions of post-war baby boomers will be entering their fifties. Their numbers are swelling what is already a senior boom. As health science and financial means help elders sustain health and live longer, the number of seniors living active lives increases. Centenarians are no longer the wonder of the world. Seniors continue to empower themselves physically by taking charge of their health through diet, exercise, and continued engagement in society, while such organizations as the Gray Panthers and the Canadian (or American) Association for Retired Persons enable elders to wield social and political muscle.

More seniors are staying at home, maintaining their independence. Many others join retirement communities where their independence is enhanced by a variety of social activities, security, and guaranteed lifetime care. Also, later life is becoming a time when elders do not retire completely but shift gears to part-time or seasonal work mixed with volunteering and productive leisure activities. Increasingly, senior citizens need work income to survive. In European companies, phased retirements blur the lines between work and leisure to take the stress out of life changes. Some seniors are beginning new careers after retirement. The retired are being increasingly re-hired by companies who value their experience. Some serve as mentors to newer employees.

These increasing numbers of seniors and retirees will put great pressure on pension and health care systems in the near future. However, as a bank of energy, wisdom, and experience, they have the opportunity to dramatically increase the social capital of civil society.

16. Longing for Community

As people continue to learn how to handle diversity in multicultural communities, they are also seeking to balance individual and community roles. One of the by-products of the self-help movement is that participants are restoring the idea of community and rediscovering what it is like for neighbors to care for one another. Such "safe" communities are becoming privileged places for those who can't find friendship anywhere else. This kind of clanning is allowing people to work together with others on the basis of commonality or personal need.

In more tangible ways, this is also happening with the development of co-housing and eco-communities, such as those pioneered in Denmark, where the commitment is not only to the community but to creating ecological wholeness and caring for the environment. Establishment of heterogeneous and diverse communities is proving difficult, although the need may be more urgent.

In local geographical communities, government cutbacks are forcing people to become more active politically. Grassroots people are encouraging greater community involvement and interdependence using new-found collaborative approaches to revitalize neighborhoods and cities.

17. Juggling Cultures

The increase in regionalism mentioned above goes hand in hand with an increase in pluralism with its bewildering variety of languages, nationalities, races, religions, cultures, and lifestyles. While ethnic conflict continues, pluralism proliferates and any sense of "the universal" flies out the window. Juggling cultures becomes one of the most needed skills of the late 20th century, as more sub-groups demand special sensitivity in meeting their needs, as minorities demand their rights, and as people of all races and ethnicity flock to large cities. This involves the need to understand, tolerate, adjust, and celebrate radically different people of many cultures. The capacity to welcome and cherish diversity is critical if there is to be a new global understanding and interaction.

For many people, this is happening through experimenting with the cuisine and music of a variety of sub-cultures and sub-groups. In many cities, one can sample Sephardic, Amish, or Cajun cuisine, or listen to reggae, ska, calypso, Tapa, and even Gregorian chants, or a blending of folk, rock, and rap to create a "world music." A similar phenomenon is the growing fascination with art of indigenous peoples, from the Inuit to Australian Aboriginals. At the same time, the voices of these people are being heard, especially in the struggle for treaty rights, and many are rediscovering their cultural heritage. Coupled with this is a renewed fascination with native culture that goes beyond anthropological interest to a spiritual quest.

CONCLUSION

Like the Chinese character for crisis, many trends identified here contain both danger and opportunity, negative and positive potential, within them. The greater the danger, the greater the possibility of change. The challenge for society is to minimize the dangers while maximizing the opportunities to create the new in a humane, sustainable way.

What are the implications of these trends for civil society? Economically and politically, more pressure is being put on civil society to reclaim its responsibility, whether for recreating local economies or picking up the slack left by governments as they retreat from their role of service provider. Culturally, civil society is being called upon to fill the gap left by religious and public education institutions, by providing opportunities for life-long learning and vehicles for peoples' search for values, myths, and rituals for profound living. The degree to which citizens take on these roles will radically affect life in the 21st century.

SUGGESTED READING LIST

Economic Trends

John Dalla Costa. *Working Wisdom*. Toronto: Stoddart Books, 1995.

Ursula Franklin. *The Real World of Technology*. Toronto: Anansi Press, 1990.

Paul Hawken. *The Ecology of Commerce*. New York: HarperBusiness, 1993.

Hazel Henderson. *Paradigms in Progress*. Indianapolis: Knowledge Systems, Inc., 1991.

Brian P. Itall. *Values Shift: A Guide to Personal and Organization Transformation*. Rockport: Twin Lights Publishers, Inc., 1994.

David Korten. *When Corporations Rule the World*. San Francisco: Kumarian Press, Inc. and Berrett-Koehler Publishers Inc., 1995.

Jeremy Rifkin. *The End of Work*. New York: Tarcher/Putnam, 1996.

Political Trends

Tom Athanasi. *Divided Planet: Ecology of Rich and Poor*. New York: Little, Brown and Company, 1996.

Peter Drucker. *Post-Capitalist Society*. New York: HarperBusiness, 1993.

James Gordon. *Manifesto for a New Medicine: Your Guide to Healing Partnerships and the Wise Use of Alternative Therapies*. Don Mills: Addison-Wesley, 1996.

Michael Lerner. *The Politics of Meaning*. Don Mills: Addison-Wesley Publishing Company, 1996.

James P. Troxel. *Government Works: Profiles of People Making a Difference*. Alexandria: Miles River Press, 1995.

Cultural Trends

Dee Dickinson. (ed.) *Creating the Future*. Aston Clinton: Accelerated Learning Systems Limited, 1991.

Ken Dychtwald and Joe Flower. *The Age Wave: The Challenges and Opportunities of an Aging America*. Los Angeles: Tarcher, Inc., 1985.

Howard Gardner. *Frames of Mind: The Theory of Multiple Intelligences*. New York: Basic Books, Inc., 1985.

Jean Houston. *A Mythic Life: Learning to Live Our Greater Story*. San Francisco: Harper, 1996.

Malcolm Knowles. *Self-Directed Learning: A Guide for Learners and Teachers*. Chicago: Follet Publishing Company, 1973.

John Ralston Saul. *The Unconscious Civilization*. Concord, Ontario: House of Anansi Press, 1996.

NOTES

1. St. Matthew's Gospel 16:3.

2. John Naisbitt and Patricia Aburdene. *Megatrends 2000: Ten New Directions for the 1990s.* New York: William Morrow and Company Inc., 1990.

3. Faith Popcorn and Lys Marigold. *Clicking: 16 Trends to Future Fit Your Life, Your Work, and Your Business.* New York: HarperCollins Publishers, 1996.

4. See James Troxel. "The Recovery of Civic Engagement in America." pp. 97-111.

10. Local Community: Seedbed of Civil Society

Monte Roulier

> *Civilizations come to birth and proceed to grow by success-*
> *fully responding to successive challenges. They break down*
> *and go to pieces if and when a challenge confronts them which*
> *they fail to meet.*
>
> — Arnold Toynbee

Toynbee's quote, written in 1948, aptly describes the experience of numerous communities around the world as they enter the 21st century. Too many communities seem to be "breaking down and going to pieces" because of an inability to meet their challenges. Citizens are losing faith in their collective ability to shape or control their futures. Any sense of community, of connectedness, of personal responsibility, or ownership toward the community is quickly slipping away.

Unprecedented change in the last two decades has brought about an impotence that pervades communities worldwide. This impotence can be attributed in part to the rapid globalization of markets which has helped precipitate ecological crises, international organized crime groups, urbanization, and a booming global underclass. The mega-corporations have effectively dominated international and national policies in order to fulfill their charge to maximize profit in the short-term, while absolving themselves of responsibility for lingering, complex social problems. As a result, there is a diminished sense of community identity and of personal security. Human interests and the interest of the "common good," once the jurisdiction of community, seem to be no match for corporate interests. The full promise of an increasingly technologically advanced and globalized society has not been realized by communities. Writer and social commentator Peter Drucker underscores this point:

> We are learning very fast that the belief that a free market is all it takes
> to have a functioning society — or even a functioning economy — is

pure delusion. Unless there's first a functioning civil society, the market can only produce *economic* results for a very short time — maybe three to five years. For anything beyond a few years, a functioning civil society — based on community organizations like churches, independent universities, or peasant cooperatives — is needed for the market to function in its economic role, let alone its social role.[1]

Concomitantly, government, too, has largely failed to serve the needs and aspirations of its people and their communities. The greatest portion of every developed country's budget is devoted to entitlements or social services, while all of these countries' social problems seem to be quickly rising.[2] The endless debates between national and global policy makers about the right balance between, or formula for, government intervention and market autonomy are missing the point. Society's most pressing problems have not been resolved by the welfare state or consumerist capitalism; instead, both have played a major role in eroding the vital middle ground that exists between the poles of government and the market — civil society and its institutions, the places where we take ownership and responsibility for one another and our communities.

The numbing daily reminders of the social pathology that has gripped communities on every continent leaves many searching for answers. Perhaps this accounts for so much renewed interest in "civil society." This growing sense of community helplessness should motivate us to re-examine the substance behind this concept that recently seemed only relevant to academics and philosophers. The sense of community, of belonging, of common bonds and trust which appeared effortless in past generations is difficult to imagine in most communities today. The decrepit state of civil society is self-evident. However, it is within that same civil society — revitalized — that we can find solutions. This chapter points to some of those solutions and provides a framework that may be instructive in thinking about strengthening civic capacity and civil society.

POCKETS OF HOPE

Although countless communities have "given up," there are many others that give cause for hope. The local level — cities, villages, towns, and city-regions — is the leverage point for civil society. As Daniel Kemmis, author and former mayor of Missoula, Montana, USA, states, "It's only in cities [local levels] that we will form basic human ties to create the sense of wholeness, of intimate association, of social health, needed to offset a politics of universal anger and mistrust, to recreate a democratic order in our time."[3] "Civility" and "citizenship" derive their meaning in the context of local community, and often in the most unlikely places.

Karelia, Russia

The northwestern Russian republic of Karelia faced many of the seemingly insurmountable challenges of other former Soviet regions after the break-up of the world power. The collapse of the Soviet Union, its economy, and its institutions produced rampant inflation, extraordinary unemployment or employment without pay, and tremendous social distress. The centralized government that had taken care of almost every basic need of the Russian people from "cradle to grave" was now absent. Suddenly, local and regional Russian communities with little or no prior experience were struggling to create new governance structures.

The resource-rich Karelian republic had long been known for mining iron, copper and coal to maintain the military-industrial complex of the Soviet Union. Forestry was another source of employment and revenue. By 1991, a handful of opportunistic government officials and regional Mafia groups were preparing to exploit insufficient laws and sell plentiful natural resources to foreign countries at rock-bottom rates for short-term gain. Meanwhile, collective farms were quickly folding; the capital city of Petrozavodsk was unable to provide basic needs for young and elderly residents; prostitution, drug use, and crime were increasing; and the self-esteem of residents was declining. In stunning contrast, some citizens of Karelia decided to view their precarious circumstances as an opportunity.

Thirty year-old Oleg Vasilievich Chervyakov was one of the those who saw more favorable possibilities. Oleg had a vision for creating the largest national park in Russia, and for saving other pristine areas of this remarkable region. He and an unlikely group of idealists, people who had never enjoyed real decision-making power in the past, were able to bring together government leaders, heads of collective farms and fisheries, newly emerging businessmen, and educators to dialogue about the most desirable future for the region. They developed alternative solutions that met the interests of the greater community, rather than playing "zero-sum" politics over extremist positions to retain the old system which was not working or to sell off the bulk of their resources to foreigners.

One outcome was the designation of the half-million hectare Vodlozero National Park. The new park includes a significant tributary of the largest watershed in Europe, and provides protection to the dense, coniferous forest with a wide variety of berries, mushrooms, and medicinal plants, as well as extensive wildlife, including many endangered species. The park authorities agreed to take responsibility for providing jobs to unemployed people, to assist many collective farms develop better management practices, and to provide needed financial support to surrounding communities.

Also contained and preserved within the park are the remains of early Russian settlements — old village structures, peasant houses, and spectacular ancient churches. Students in Karelia now have opportunities to learn about their proud history which had been lost during the Soviet period, their unique natural environment, and to appreciate the natural and historical heritage they are now able to inherit.

Using a concept which is new to their region — dialogue between various sectors and interests — has proven effective in achieving mutually acceptable approaches to balance employment and financial needs along with protecting a cherished environment. In the process, they are involving people and giving skills to their youth for the future. Karelia is still a long way from overcoming its Soviet legacy; however, it is a markedly different region from the one that complacently sat back and waited for answers from Moscow.

Senegal and Zaire

The worldwide microcredit movement has focused renewed attention on the role of microenterprise development in bringing hope to some of the world's most desperate communities. The movement has been extraordinarily success-ful in fulfilling its mission to support human and economic development of families mired in severe poverty, while creating healthier, more sustainable communities. It is a truly community-driven approach. Microcredit systems vary from community to community but share these similarities:

• Provide working capital loans to finance self-employment opportunities
• Promote family and community savings
• Develop skills
• Encourage mutual support and self-worth

The purpose of giving credit to the world's impoverished people is to help poor communities achieve long-term solutions to pressing challenges that re-flect the fundamental interrelationship between prosperity, social equity, and a healthy environment. In the process, it is having a major impact on indi-vidual lives.

Khady Ding of Senegal survived day by day while trying to find food for her four children. Her only long-term hope was that aid from relief agencies would keep coming. In 1990, members of Khady's community established a village bank. Khady received her first loan of $US 40 which she used to pur-chase livestock. Joining the village bank significantly improved Khady's life. She now raises healthy cows, chickens, and sheep. Selling her livestock pro-vides Khady and her family with a steady income, and her ability to repay early loans allows her to assume larger loans, repaid in monthly installments. Khady's family has become self-reliant. In addition, she is learning to read in the village bank literacy program. People in Khady's village now perceive her as a leader in community affairs.[4]

Ali Alibirighi of Zaire has also benefited from microcredit. After spending several years organizing women into farming collectives, Ali talks about the civic benefits of microcredit: "First the women would buy chickens and raise them together. Later they became active in village politics. They would attend meetings and talk about what they wanted to make their lives better. People began to respect them and listen to them." [5]

Microenterprise development is much more than providing capital to the impoverished. It is about building community, cultivating skills for collaboration, seeing human potential, and gaining control over the future. Communities whose economies are developed and controlled locally, where the impoverished have access to capital, are vibrant places looking inward for solutions rather than outside themselves. The predicament of the world's poor is not being solved by paternalistic mega-development organizations, no matter how noble their intentions. Microenterprise development is a reminder that a community's greatest asset is its people, regardless of educational attainment and social position.

Lawndale, USA

In recent years, the teen pregnancy rate of high school girls in the Chicago suburb of Lawndale has exceeded 30 percent. Some might assume this is to be expected from an impoverished community like Lawndale where over 50 percent of the population live below the national poverty line. These babies, born to unwed, welfare-dependent, teenage mothers, stood a statistically slim chance of breaking out of the crushing cycle of poverty in their community.

This story has taken a surprising turn, however. Leaders emerged from churches, schools, hospitals, civic organizations, and local government to reclaim responsibility for their young people and the future of their community. Lawndale neither waited for nor begged the federal government or foundations for money to solve their problem. Lawndale decided to tap into existing community assets rather than focus on its needs and deficits.

These assets and resources came in the form of volunteers — from retired seniors to local business people. The community developed a comprehensive mentoring program in which every teenage girl and boy in high school was teamed with an adult in the community. The program required few financial resources. It connected young people with their dreams, ideas, jobs, and as a result, a brighter future. The community began to re-establish a culture of embracing its young people. Within two years, Sinai Hospital, one of the partners in the mentoring program, confirmed that teenage pregnancy had been reduced nearly 100 percent. Lawndale's problem with teenage pregnancy has been solved through the time, talent, and energy of its citizens, not by outside relief.

Perhaps Arnold Toynbee's quote should be amended to say: Civilizations come to birth and proceed to grow by successfully responding to successive challenges. They break down and go to pieces if and when a challenge causes them to give up and quit taking ownership for their destiny.

Karelia, Lawndale, and the two communities in Senegal and Zaire are good examples of the many communities around the world that have chosen not to give up and are discovering ways to build healthier futures. These communities are taking action on immediate problems and strengthening their civic infrastructure at the same time.

CIVIC INFRASTRUCTURE

Entering the 21st century, every community will continue to meet successive challenges that will require repairing and strengthening its civic infrastructure. Civic infrastructure is the complex interaction of people and groups through which decisions are made and problems resolved — how the community as a whole works or does not work together to set priorities and confront challenges. The quality of this interaction determines the a community's health, both economic and social.

As such, civic infrastructure is similar to the term "social capital." Harvard political scientist Robert Putnam uses social capital to explain civic capacity when he defines it as networks of trust and reciprocity that facilitate coordination and cooperation for mutual benefit.[6] Social capital, then, is the currency of a healthy community. While civic infrastructure and social capital use different metaphors to convey meaning, the terms are interchangeable. Putnam would argue that the long-term success of a community is determined by the amount of social capital, a currency built up over time.

Communities have witnessed the onslaught of social change and the corresponding deterioration of their civic infrastructure. Like physical infrastructure, the civic infrastructure must be maintained, and sometimes rebuilt, if a community hopes to assert control over its future.

In addition, the quality of the civic infrastructure will determine if and when a community "breaks down and goes to pieces." The US-based National Civic League, an organization that assists communities to improve their governance by vigorously promoting citizen participation and collaborative problem-solving, has developed a theoretical framework called the *Civic Index* for communities to evaluate and improve their civic infrastructure.[7] The ten components of the Index describe the types of skills and capacities that must be present for a community to effectively confront a multitude of challenges, whether it be a village that has lost critical, arable land to a natural disaster or a metropolis that must find adequate low-income housing. Communities around the world — in the Czech Republic, the Republic of Georgia, Rwanda, the United Kingdom, and Uzbekistan — have used the index to evaluate and develop strategies to improve their civic infrastructure.

The following section contains excerpts and brief descriptions of five of the ten components of the Civic Index, along with some questions for communities to answer.

Citizen Participation

Citizen participation is required to create and maintain a healthy, vibrant community. Without regular interaction among citizens, community ceases; it becomes merely an area with a random collection of people. In many countries, citizen participation involves becoming active in local organizations and affairs, engaging in public forums, serving on community boards and commissions, belonging to social and religious organizations, and voting in local elections. Citizen participation is asking questions and involving oneself in working toward solutions.

Meaningful citizen participation has become more difficult than ever. Most of the world's population now lives in urban areas where participation is inhibited by the anonymity that leads to mistrust of fellow citizens, perceived enormity of problems leading to feelings of futility, and excessive work demands on families and their time.

While voting in local elections is an important act of citizen participation, it is only one measure and aspect of citizen participation. Low voter turnout around the world is often misconstrued as apathy or indifference toward community affairs. More typically, it represents cynicism and feelings of futility about individual action. Much evidence suggests that people are eager to participate in their community and to connect with their neighbors. The problem is there are few obvious and meaningful avenues for participation.

In the last decade of this century, citizens in a number of formerly nondemocratic countries from Russia to Nicaragua have been given the right to participate in relatively free elections. Voting in legitimate elections initially proved to be an important and symbolic act of citizenship. However, the people of Russia, Nicaragua, and other countries soon learned that the privilege to vote is seldom accompanied by the change for which they hope. Voting alone does not suffice for citizen participation. Communities need to find creative and meaningful ways for citizens to deliberate on important decisions and to be a part of building a stronger community.

Sample Civic Index questions on Citizen Participation:

• Is participation proactive or reactive?
• Are there formal (public hearings) and informal (town/village square dis-

cussions) mechanisms for dialoguing about pressing issues?

- How visible and active are local civic groups, associations, clubs, and churches?
- Do citizens know how local government works?

Community Leadership

Meeting challenges in the 21st century will require that communities develop leaders who are representative and results-oriented, who are willing to take risks, and who are willing to be self-critical. The skills and attitudes of effective leadership for the next century may be different from those often associated with effective leadership today.

Relying on a handful of key decision makers in a community to make all decisions and resolve all problems does not work well now and will become even more futile in the future. According to Paul Lorentzen:

> Leadership ... increasingly resides in the many rather than the few; in joint rather than individual endeavors; and in the empowerment rather than the control of others .... Improvement [in leadership] will occur as positions are attained by more persons who have a strong sense of self, a large philosophical value system, and the ability to empower others to learn and contribute individually and together as co-leaders.[8]

Leaders in communities that are moving in positive directions strive to create win/win solutions. These new-style leaders use their power to convene and bring people together. They listen as often as they talk. They set examples for others by behaving in ways consistent with their stated values.

Business is an important part of community leadership and will continue to be challenged to carve out a larger leadership role for itself. The private sector must find more inventive ways to work to improve community. Business has a huge bottom-line interest in healthy employees who are largely a by-product of healthy living conditions. Maximizing profit in the short-term as a leadership credo no longer works.

At the same time, local government is struggling to find an appropriate role. The devolution of problems and responsibilities from central government to local government places greater importance on the integrity and effectiveness of local government. Effective local government leadership will embrace and encourage citizen involvement and input rather than be threatened by it. The lack of faith in government at all levels underscores the importance of local governments holding themselves to the highest ethical standards and working in creative and entrepreneurial ways.

Community leadership, whether from non-profit, business, government or unaffiliated citizens, will be challenged to develop the trust of the broader community. Trust, a central element of a strong, robust civil society, is the lubricant that makes action possible. Trust implies accountability, predictability, and reliability.

Sample Civic Index questions on Community Leadership:

• Is there active leadership from all three sectors?
• Is government willing to share decision-making power?
• Are there effective traditions and programs for nurturing new leaders, especially for those segments of the population not traditionally involved in decision-making?
• Is leadership results-oriented?
• Do leaders take a long-term view?
• Do leaders consider the common good for the entire community?
• Do leaders from the three sectors work well together?
• Is there trust and respect for leadership in the three sectors?

Intergroup Relations

Perhaps the greatest challenge to communities and nations is intergroup relations. Most wars occurring in second half of this century have been waged within borders, not across borders. Extra effort will be needed to ensure that young people break the tendency of hatred toward neighbors of different color or religions.

Most communities are composed of organized ethnic, racial, or religious groups formed to express and protect their members' interests. The degree to which these solidarity groups co-exist in relative harmony and cooperate in resolving shared problems is an essential and key measure of civic health.

As communities continue to diversify ethnically, racially, socio-economically, and religiously, programs are needed to increase communication and appreciation among groups and within the community as a whole. Communities must provide all groups with the skills and opportunities to become actively involved in community affairs.

The value of community groups as a vehicle for peer modeling, self-esteem enhancement, and cultural pride cannot be overstated. Equally valuable is the group's capacity for peaceful conflict expression, mediation, and resolution. Healthy intergroup relations results from an openness to, and respect for, diversity.

Sample Civic Index Questions on Intergroup Relations:

• Is the community dealing with ethnic and racial diversity?
• Does the community promote communication among diverse populations?
• Do all groups have the skills to become involved in the community?
• Do groups cooperate in resolving broad disputes?
• Is the community dominated by narrow special-interest groups?

Community Vision and Pride

Communities deal successfully with the challenges they face when they develop a clear picture of where they want to go and when they take pride in their past. When citizens are brought into a community vision-creation process they become invested in that vision. It is theirs and they become stakeholders in their community's future.

Communities that take time to create and revisit their common vision develop a vastly different mindset than those without any sense of direction. A community with a meaningful, compelling vision spends more time deciding how to make things work than it does deciding who to blame. A vision enables a community to consider taking a longer-term approach to problem-solving which addresses root causes. Communities without vision become stuck in the rut of creating short-term "quick fixes" to problems. Communities need to spend more time focusing on the assets they have to build on and less time analyzing what is not working.

Articulating aspirations for the future is an empowering experience that raises a community's collective self-esteem. Greater community pride is a natural consequence of citizen participation in vision creation. The work of Robert Fritz, an expert on organizational and system change, provides evidence that communities and organizations that spend energy working toward shared visions are better able to catalyze and sustain action than those focusing on short-range problem-solving.[9]

Sample Civic Index questions on Community Vision and Pride:

• Is there a shared sense of a desired future for the community?
• Does the community have a positive self-image?
• Does the community preserve and enhance what is special and unique?

Capacity for Cooperation and Consensus Building

The public, private, and non-profit sectors, along with the broad spectrum of citizens, need to cultivate leaders who can cooperate with one another to improve their communities. The challenges to improve educational attainment, increase employment opportunities, cut crime, or any other issue faced by most communities around the world requires all sectors to work together. Communities experiencing success are erasing the boundaries between government, business, non-profit sectors, and citizens.

In addressing complex community issues, the way a community makes decisions is as important as the actual decisions made. There is no shortage of strategies or approaches to solving a community problem. The challenge is to find a means of getting the whole community to agree on an approach and move forward with it. Many communities realize they must pay greater attention to the formal and informal processes through which people talk, learn, decide, and act together.[10] These communities realize that no group will succeed unless the diverse needs of the entire community are addressed.

Most communities find there are few spaces available for interaction to take place across sectors, socio-economic lines, neighborhoods, and racial divisions. This precludes their coming together and developing agreement on direction — a requisite for shared ownership and sustained action. As disagreements arise in the community, neutral forums and processes are needed where all opinions can be heard and consensus cultivated. The ability to manage conflict is a key defining feature of community life.

Sample Civic Index questions on Capacity for Cooperation and Consensus Building:

- Are there neutral forums and processes where all opinions are heard?
- Are there informal dispute resolution processes?
- Do community leaders have regular opportunities to share ideas?
- Are all major interests and perspectives included in collaborative processes?
- Do all sectors work together to set common goals?
- Do leaders reach collective decisions and implement them?

KEY SUCCESS FACTORS

The components of the Civic Index are interrelated and synergistic. If one component is especially weak, it will diminish the strength of the others. The Civic Index is a tool to help communities address their ability to solve problems; in using it, many communities develop additional questions to help them better understand how to improve their civic capacity. The five additional components of the index not described here are Government Performance, Volunteerism and Philanthropy, Civic Education, Community Information Sharing, and Inter-Community Cooperation.

By strengthening their civic infrastructure or generating social capital, communities are investing in their long-term health. A number of communities making a serious effort to do this are part of the worldwide Healthy Communities/Healthy Cities movement.[11] Director of the Coalition for Healthier Cities and Communities, Tyler Norris,[12] has played a key role in the Healthy Communities movement. Norris has isolated "success factors" from more than 100 communities which are successfully meeting their challenges. These factors reaffirm the relevance and significance of the Civic Index components, while adding further insights for communities to consider as they strengthen their infrastructure. According to Norris, successful communities:[13]

- *Recognize that a community's health and sustainability is a product of the whole community working together, not isolated interventions in any single sector.* A community is more than the sum of its parts. In considering business strategies, public policies, buying decisions, and other issues, we need to ask, "How will a given approach simultaneously build and maximize economic, ecological, social, and human capital?" Rather than investing in narrow "fix-it" projects, successful communities orient themselves toward the allocation of resources and the equitable distribution of decision-making and power.

• *Engage everybody and build ownership across divisions.* A commitment must be made to widespread community ownership and civic engagement. Effective collaborations recognize that mobilization of all parts of the community is essential in getting away from the typical "react to the problem" and "fight the enemy" approach. They embrace processes which mobilize all citizens and institutions of civil society for continued improvement

Take both a regional and a neighborhood-by-neighborhood approach. We need to embrace multiple definitions of community and solve challenges at different levels simultaneously.

• *Know how they are performing.* Citizens demand accountability. Performance information is needed to create baseline data, to measure any progress toward or away from a community's desired future, and to track the impact of community initiatives and policy choices. Continuous quality improvement is becoming a standard objective and effective measurement is the key to its success. Strained budgets and limited public resources have exacerbated the need to maximize our return on social investment. Effective community indicators provide clear, understandable information on the status of the community as a system and assist communities to make well-informed choices. They are developed by the whole community which enables businesses, individuals, organizations, and governments to take action simultaneously toward a common agenda.

• *Start with shared values and a shared vision.* In recent decades, many community efforts have started with needs assessments chronicling a litany of problems to be solved. While these efforts can uncover and quantify problems, they often do little to mobilize action and achieve desired results. Values provide the thread for the fabric of our communities. A vision, basically a statement of values projected as a future reality, can articulate where a community wants to go and what it desires. Effective communities identify their values and generate a shared vision of the ideal future of their community. They follow this visioning with a specific action plan and implementation strategy.

• *Build on existing resources within the community.* Rather than decrying deficiencies and shortcomings, effective collaborations generate local power by clearly articulating how each person, group, organization, company, or agency can be part of the solution. They make explicit links between the work that needs to be done and those who can do it. They look at how they can do better with what they have rather than waiting for another program, grant, or other bail-out.

• *Move beyond "quick fixes" to systemic change.* They look at ways of re-allocating existing assets and resources to more productive ends. Veterans of community mobilization know that complex issues cannot be solved with categorical programs, single-sector initiatives, and dollars alone. They know the only true locus of fundamental change is people's choices grounded in their cultures, not in dollars and programs.

Communities that are successfully responding to successive challenges in the ways indicated above do so by choice, not by chance. In these communities, citizens look to one another for answers, not to external supports such as governments or the global marketplace. As these communities meet their challenges head on, they maintain and strengthen their civic infrastructure and increase their social capital. They demonstrate once again that the local level is the seedbed of civil society.

NOTES

1. Peter Drucker. "A cantankerous interview with Peter Schwarz and Kevin Kelly." *Wired.* August 1996. p. 184.

2. Peter Drucker. "The Age of Social Transformation." *The Atlantic Monthly.* November 1994. p. 74.

3. Quoted by syndicated columnist, Neal R. Peirce, "Coping with 'Flamers' and Building a Good City." The Washington Post Writers Group: 21 January 1996. Advance copy.

4. Microcredit Summit, Washington DC, February 1997. Promotional materials.

5. Lynn Marie Bell. "Microlending: Advancing Human Rights Around the Globe." *Surviving Together.* Volume 4, Issue 4, Winter 1996. p. 6.

6. Robert Putnam. "Bowling Alone: America's Declining Social Capital." *Journal of Democracy.* Volume 6, Number 1, January 1995. p. 67.

7. National Civic League. *The Civic Index: A New Approach to Improving Community Life.* Denver, CO: NCL Press, 1993. See also Chris Gates. "Making A Case for Collaborative Problem Solving." *National Civic Review.* Spring 1991. pp.105-113. For further information, contact the National Civic League at: 1445 Market Street, Suite 300, Denver CO 80202-1728, USA. Phone: (303) 571-4343, fax (303) 571-4404, e-mail: ncl@csn.net. Their websites are: http://www.ncl.org/ncl and http://www.ncl.org/anr.

8. Paul Lorentzen. "Leadership: Changing Contexts, Flexible Concepts." *The Bureaucrat.* Fall 1986. p. 3.

9. Robert Fritz. *Creating*. New York: Ballantine Books, 1991.

10. Mirja Hanson makes the point that method matters in her chapter "Facilitating Civil Society." pp. 235-247.

11. The Healthy Communities/Healthy Cities movement, which was catalyzed by a World Health Organization (WHO) conference in Toronto, Canada in 1984. According to WHO, healthy cities/communities are based on a commitment to health, require political decision-making for public health, generate intersectoral action, emphasize community participation, work through processes of innovation, and create a public health policy.

12. For further information, contact Tyler Norris, 2119 Mapleton Avenue, Boulder, Colorado 80304, USA. Phone (303) 444-3366, fax (303) 444.1001, e-mail tnorris@ncl.org.

13. Adapted from an article by Tyler Norris. Introduction to the *National Civic Review*. Volume 86, Number 1, Spring 1997. pp. 3-10.

11. Community Youth Development

Paul L. Watson, Jr.

Young people are not just the leaders of tomorrow. They are the leaders of today.

— Peter Raducha

I magine you were just hired as a youth development worker in a small community. During your first week on the job, your boss takes you on a tour of the community. As you drive into a residential area, you see a large group of teenagers standing in the middle of the road. You stop your van, park it, and walk ahead to see what's going on while trying not to be conspicuous. As you get closer, you realize there are two groups facing each other. Most of the youth have chains, pipes, or knives in their hands. You have stumbled on a gang fight.

Just then, the two groups start to walk towards each other. Suddenly, one youth pulls out a gun and points it at the leader of the other group. Quickly, the group without the gun scatter, all except the leader. Instead of running, he continues to walk towards the youth with the gun. The youth with the gun runs up to the leader, puts the gun to his head, and pulls the trigger. The gun misfires. The leader grabs the gun and the two youth start fighting. At this point, all the others come back and a large fight ensues until the police arrive.

Your boss turns to you and says: "The leader who didn't run — he's the first kid I want you to work with." What would you say? What would you do? Would you reconsider this line of work? If you decided to meet this challenge, how would you approach this young man? What method would you choose to develop this youth?

The approach used in this real-life situation was Community Youth Development (CYD). While CYD has many definitions, essentially it is an approach which embodies the best principles of youth development and community development. [See Figure 1]. Community development demands that citizens initiate and control activities to positively influence conditions affecting their lives. It calls for citizen participation, cooperation, and collaboration.

CYD takes this principle one step further. It requires that young people be actively engaged in the process by developing their own identity, self-worth, independence, sense of belonging, and connections to family, community, the Earth, and the sacred. It also develops their capacity to engage in life-long learning in order to contribute to family, community, and society, as well as to demonstrate competence in vocational choices.

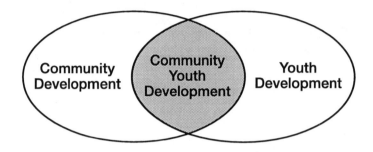

Figure 1. Community Youth Development

This approach was endorsed by the Center for Youth Development and Policy Research in Washington, DC, USA. In answer to the question, "Why should youth development and community development be connected?" director Karen Pittman replied:

> Young people should be involved in community development because they live in and belong to their community. If young people are not connected and respected, they have the power to destroy the community. Involving young people in the development of their communities encourages them to become stakeholders in their communities and to care about them.[1]

Some people think CYD can only be a prevention strategy for youth coming from a stable family with a solid economic background. For many, it is inconceivable this approach could be effective with violent, rebellious street youth. However, CYD was used in this situation and in many others like it, and it worked. In fact, the outcome produced a benefit far greater than any other commonly used intervention could have provided, as this chapter will reveal.

However, CYD is more than just an effective prevention and intervention strategy; it is an invaluable tool for building civil society.

THE SPIRIT OF UBUNTU

Why get young people involved in community processes? The fact is, they already are involved. They grow up in communities and are affected by what surrounds them. When a young person comes to a social service agency for assistance, one of the first things done is an assessment of family history, dynamics, and systems, because the way a family operates has a direct effect on its members. The same is true of communities. The conditions in a community have a major impact on every family within it, which in turn impacts each individual in that family.

In 1970, when I was working for the Black Panther Party, I used to walk through a Harlem neighborhood and talk to the people living there. One cold winter day, I left an apartment building with tears in my eyes because of what I had seen. The front door of the building was wide open because it was broken. It had snowed earlier in the week and there was more frozen snow on the stairway inside the building than outside on the sidewalk. The first apartment I entered had a family of six living in two bedrooms. There was no running water because the pipes were frozen. The family was heating the entire apartment with an electric hot plate in the kitchen. I asked myself: What kind of person would I be if I were living in these conditions? Would I be concerned about getting my homework done? Would I be compassionate towards others? Would I think anyone else cared about me, besides my family? What would I be willing to do to get heat and food for myself and my family?

My experience that day in Harlem convinced me that the conditions in our communities had to change if people were to have the opportunity to reach their full potential. It also made me think about the young gang leader I mentioned at the beginning of the chapter. That young man was not a gang leader when he moved into that small community. He was not a violent person. He had grown up in a strict, church-going family, but when he left home he moved into a community in which violence was a way of life. As a homeless street kid, he adapted to his environment in order to survive. Eventually, he began to excel in displays of violent rage, and thus became a leader.

The youth worker assigned to that gang leader realized that if the young man was not connected to the community and was not respected, he had the power to destroy the community. The youth worker saw the young man doing it every day. The youth worker realized the gang leader had the power to build that community if only he could be set on a positive course. The youth worker also knew if the youth and other young people in that community were to join in partnership with him and other adults, together they could become a powerful force that could transform their community. The youth were the key to building civil society in this place, just as they are in thousands like it around the country and throughout the world. Too often, they are overlooked, ignored, or relegated to play only minor roles in community life.

Among the native peoples of northern Natal province in South Africa, there is an approach to working and living with other people that recognizes the critical importance of being engaged with, and acknowledged by, others in the community. Referred to as "the Spirit of Ubuntu," this approach emerges from a Zulu folk saying: "A person is a person because of other people." One's identity and sense of worth and power is based on being seen and acknowledged by others.

The youth worker understood this and developed a strategy to engage the young man. He began to talk with the young man about conditions in the community and how the young man had the power to change these conditions. The worker said he would be willing to help. They soon established a partnership and went to work. They formed a youth council of gang members. They involved the entire community in obtaining adequate recreation facilities for the youth. They were successful in having Black History taught in elementary, junior high, and high schools. They organized rent strikes against slum landlords and developed a community newsletter. Within two years, there was a marked change in the conditions in their community.

I thank that youth worker every day of my life. Because of his use of CYD principles, he saved my life. You see, I was that young gang member. Through CYD I finally came to know my own identity and sense of worth and these were acknowledged by my adult partners.

That youth worker was doing more than diverting a single youth from a life of crime and violence, saving tax dollars, and even saving my life. He was developing an ally to help him change the conditions in that community. He was helping me to find and live my own calling. He was facilitating my creation of a vision or dream of a just and compassionate society because he knew it is the dream that calls us forth. He knew I would share that dream with everyone who would listen until it was realized.

Today, more than any other time in history, we need to do what that youth worker did with me. You don't have to look far to find the reasons why. The following statistics from the United States are reminders enough.[2]

- In his book *Powernomics: Economics and Strategy After the Cold War*, former United States Trade Negotiator Clyde Prestowitz stated: "On a national basis, about 25% of our students drop out of high school, consigned to a social and economic scrap heap before they even begin their adult lives. The United States is the only major nation of the world that tolerates such human waste."

- Each year through the 1980s, 5,000 youth between the ages of 15 and 25 killed themselves. Surveys show that 10 percent of adolescent boys and 18 percent of adolescent girls admit they have attempted suicide. What can one say about a generation, one million of whom have tried, or will try, to kill themselves before the age of 30, and 100,000 of whom have succeeded, or will succeed, in their final effort?

- The United States spends nearly $1 trillion annually on health care, yet nearly 75 million Americans are either underinsured or completely uninsured. Both Canada and Germany spend 30 percent to 40 percent less on health care per capita and both provide universal health care.

- Every day, the typical 14-year-old American watches three hours of television and does one hour of homework; over 2,200 students drop out of school; 3,600 teenagers are assaulted, 630 are robbed, and 80 are raped; 500 adolescents begin using illegal drugs; 1,000 begin drinking alcohol; and 1,000 unwed teenage girls become mothers.

- African-Americans are three times more likely to be killed as teenagers by gun violence than by natural causes.

- Fifteen percent of all infants born in 1994 were exposed to illegal drugs while in the womb, and over 100,000 babies were born with cocaine addiction.

- Every day, over 2,600 American children witness the divorce or separation of their parents, 90 are taken from their parents custody and committed to foster homes, 13 aged 15-24 commit suicide, and another 16 are murdered.

- In the last ten years, the number of functionally illiterate 17 year-olds in America has more than doubled. Today, seven million teenagers are functionally illiterate.

- In 1991, the United States trailed most industrialized countries in spending on social programs and led in defense spending.

- The number of guns in the United States increased from 54 million in 1950 to 201 million in 1990.

- There are three million homeless people in America, the same number as in all Europe.

KEY INGREDIENTS OF CYD

Clearly, we need to change the conditions in our communities. Traditional approaches to youth development have not done this. As Rebecca Lane, CYD Project Director for the National Network for Youth in Washington DC, points out, these approaches were based on the deductive reasoning that healthy individuals create stable families which build communities. They were focused on individuals, particularly at-risk youth, who were treated as clients of the service providers and consumers of products of the youth services system.[3]

A corollary of this system, as Lane indicates, is that service providers compete against one another for funding and clients. Efficiency is the prime value

— doing the most with the least financial and human resources. Success under this system is determined by the number of clients worked with, the number of services dispensed, and the number of service days provided. This approach focuses on changing the behavior of the client, and if this happens, it is assumed she or he is better off. While it has some value, such an approach is no longer adequate. In the words of youth and community service professionals, "It fails to provide the hope and vision for the future that people — young and old, in families, organizations, and communities — are seeking."[4]

CYD grew out of this situation and in some ways, is deceptively similar to it. [See Figure 2.] Many of the components are similar but how they fit together and the context in which they operate are radically different. CYD is a holistic approach to working with young people in which the focus is on community building. It is based on the following premises or "best practices":

- Create a culture in which youth and adults respect each other and share responsibility.
- Create a just and compassionate society in which the focus is on the individual in community, and in which peace, justice and equality are valued and supported.
- Create a space where young people feel and are safe.
- Create a culture of appreciation, in which youth can learn about relationships in a caring context, can celebrate successes, be supported in failures, and can learn about their own and other cultures.
- Transfer practical, usable skills to youth and families to use among themselves and with others.
- Be conscious stewards of relationships who value mentoring, modeling, and an openness to learning.
- Use what happens naturally in relationships as a source of learning for both the youth and the youth worker.
- Create opportunities for youth to find their own path and identity.

A key element in CYD centers around the role of the professional. Like the facilitators in Participatory Rapid Appraisal described by Marlene Kanawati in her chapter,[5] youth workers in CYD share the expert role with those with whom they're working. They work in partnership with youth and other community members to create services and systems that honor and support communities. Such partnerships necessitate changes in the behavior of our service institutions, community organizations, families, adults, and youth.

In 1996, I had the privilege of assisting a group of youth and adults working in partnership to prevent the spread of substance abuse in their communities throughout the southeast United States. This partnership group learned a process called "Condition A — Condition B." Condition A indicates the conditions in their communities as they exist today. Condition B represents the outcomes they are working towards in their communities. It was invigorating to see their plan and to see the enthusiasm with which they developed their strategies. In typical youthful style, they did not wait until the conference was over to implement their plan. They started right away by networking within the group to get the support and resources they needed.

THE CHANGING PARADIGM OF YOUTH DEVELOPMENT

Traditional Approach	**Community Youth Development**
Contract	Covenant
Economic approaches to human values	Community and participation
Debate (win/lose)	Dialogue (win/win)
Ideology	Meaning and purpose
Either/or	Both/and
Professional	Partnership
Prescriptive	Developmental
Appropriative	Evocative/calling forth

Figure 2. The Changing Paradigm of Youth Development[6]

Partnership is one cornerstone of CYD. Another is participation. As Hanson, Kanawati, Roulier, and others have shown in this book, authentic participation in community life is a defining characteristic of civil society.[7] In addition to enhancing their own self-esteem and acquiring new skills, participation gives young people an opportunity to work for social justice, to learn about their community and local government, and obtain access to valuable resources. When young people are involved, the whole community benefits from their energy, responsiveness, and accomplishments. In the long run, training youth as community-minded citizens is an investment in the community's future.

Participation and partnership don't just happen; they demand methodologies and a commitment of time and energy. In particular, they require:

- Clarity regarding the description of community conditions, resources, and processes.
- A common vision of a preferred future.
- Valuing every individual as a unique resource, which leads to valuing the whole community.
- An appreciation of our connection to one another and to the larger human, physical, and social environment.
- Equal opportunity to participate in community decision-making by all members of the community.

- A social technology which promotes inclusive participation and community learning. The *Technology of Participation*™ developed by the Institute of Cultural Affairs (ICA) is a good example.[8]

LAUNCHING A CYD MOVEMENT

CYD is not the only approach to working with young people but it has proven highly effective and it excites me deeply. I have a vision of living in a just and compassionate society that nurtures and develops people, and which supports and values human development rather than simply valuing property and monetary gain. I have a vision of a society that appreciates the richness and beauty of diversity — diversity of race, age, gender, sexual orientation, and more. The pathway I see towards realizing this vision is one of young people and adults quietly working in partnership in every neighborhood and community across the United States and throughout the world.

My vision is shared by other individuals and organizations. In the United States, the National Network for Youth is working on CYD with the ICA, the National 4-H organization, and Girls, Inc. Foundations are supporting these efforts and universities are turning their attention to CYD as well. In every region of the country, teams of people are spreading the vision and providing the skills necessary to bring about changes needed in our communities.

But CYD is not just an American phenomenon. At the international conference on the "Rise of Civil Society in the 21st Century" held in Cairo, Egypt in September 1996,[9] a global community youth development movement was launched. Conference participants from 34 countries represented a wide array of human development activities in communities and organizations. However, few of these development activities involve youth in any significant roles and fewer still involve youth as equal partners in the assessment, design, implementation, development, and evaluation of the work undertaken. To address this deficiency, a core group representing the national leadership of the CYD movement in the United States went to the Cairo conference to challenge participants to consider young people as necessary and valuable resources in the design and implementation of civil society strategies.

During a day-and-a-half CYD workshop, we introduced participants to the principles and theory of CYD. Together we developed a list of implications resulting from implementing the CYD model, created a shared vision of a global CYD movement, and outlined the strengths, weaknesses, benefits, and dangers of this vision. The group then decided what its members could collectively and collaboratively commit to, starting with the formation of the International Institute for Community Youth Development. Representatives from eight countries — Brazil, Egypt, Jordan, Kenya, Nigeria, Poland, Sudan, and the United States — were ready to begin work immediately. Another three countries are working towards making a commitment. In addition, two individuals committed to support the development of the international CYD movement. One is a consultant with experience in curriculum development, residential treatment for adolescents, and youth employment; the other is a professional with extensive experience in school-based programs dealing with multicultural issues and gang-affiliated youth, as well as police-community relations.

The CYD workshop was one of the most productive of the conference. The group affirmed a mission statement, designed organizational operations, projected long-term outcomes of the collaboration, identified key activities, and created a launch scenario. The mission of the newly-formed International Institute for Community Youth Development is "to promote and strengthen the field of CYD globally as the key to building civil society for the next millennium." The final work of the group was to develop a year-long work plan which will culminate in all interested parties meeting together in San Diego, USA, in August 1997 to further design the operations of the institute.

A GLOBAL FUTURE

The Cairo conference illuminated the common issues in youth development and community development throughout the world, and the global pathway to the future of CYD. Now is the time to clarify and identify this movement worldwide, and to link the fragmented aspects of the movement. Moreover, it is the time to identify the processes by which we can transform our neighborhoods, communities, nations, and global society. This movement transcends local and national politics, gender, generational, and racial differences, and all other natural or human boundaries. It is concerned with establishing peace, justice, dignity, and respect for all people as core values of civil society. It is also concerned with improving the quality of life for all people now and for future generations. Finally, it requires us to shift our priorities and resources so they support these ideals and principles.

At the conclusion of the conference, when the CYD workshop group presented its work to the entire gathering, they received a thunderous applause. One elderly man commented, "After many years working to improve conditions of people's lives around the world, I am convinced that youth and adults working together in partnership is the only way to truly build civil society." One leader from Nigeria, who has a long history of working on development projects in his country, decided he would quit his job to devote all his time to launching the CYD movement in his country.

Civil society is both a global and a local phenomenon. It is within the urban neighborhoods and rural villages of this world that communities grow and flourish, or die and are destroyed. Which of these two paths is followed depends on many factors; one of the most critical is the degree and quality of participation of all people in shaping the direction of their communities, particularly young people. Too often, young people have been regarded as an accessory to community development. It is time they took their rightful place as full members of civil society. As John Oyler, Executive Director of the ICA's office in Phoenix, USA, said:

> Every community is being changed by its young people. Unfortunately, most change is destructive and the few adult partners young people have do not, for the most part, guide the creativity and energy of youth towards the good of the community. No serious community development effort can possibly succeed, much less be sustained, without the creativity and energy of its young people.[10]

NOTES

1. From a personal communication with Karen Pittman. For further elaboration of this position, see Karen J. Pittman. "Community, Youth, Development: Three Goals in Search of Connection." *New Designs for Youth Development.* Volume 12, Number 1, Winter 1996. pp. 4-8.

2. Rob Nelson and Jon Cowan. *Revolution X: A Survival Guide for Our Generation.* New York: Penguin Books, 1994. pp. 210-215.

3. Rebecca Lane. "On the Journey to Community Youth Development." *New Designs for Youth Development.* Volume 12, Number 3, Summer 1996. p. 15.

4. Sara V. Jarvis, Liz Shear and Della M. Hughes. "Community Youth Development: Learning the New Story." To be published. Washington DC: Child Welfare League of America.

5. Marlene Kanawati. "Consulting Egypt's Local Experts." pp. 113-129.

6. Excerpted and adapted from the article by Rebecca Lane. p. 17. *New Designs for Youth Development,* The National Network for Youth, 1319 F Street, Suite 401, Washington DC 20004, USA. Phone (202) 783-7949, fax (202) 783-7955. Reprinted with permission.

7. (a) Mirja Hanson. "Facilitating Civil Society." pp. 235-247. (b) Marlene Kanawati. *op. cit.* (c) Monte Roulier. "Local Community: Seedbed of Civil Society." pp. 183-196.

8. See appendix for a description of the *Technology of Participation,* p. 295.

9. See page 11 for a description of the Cairo conference.

10. Cited in Paul Watson. "Transforming Communities: The Spirit of Ubuntu." *Initiatives.* Volume 12, Number 1, Winter 1996. p. 7.

12. Women Remaking Civil Society

Janice Jiggins

Women's development delineates the path not only to a less violent life but also to a maturity realized through interdependence and taking care.

— Carol Gilligan

A young farmer stood up with her daughter at a community meeting in Albany at the southern tip of Western Australia and said, "I am flattered at being consulted but I also want to be heard." During the nationwide meetings on environmental issues sponsored by the National Women's Consultative Council through 1991-92, women in Australia repeatedly stressed that merely consulting them was not enough. Like the young woman in Albany, they were angry that their time and energy were too often used to achieve other people's agendas. They wanted women's voices, values, knowledge, and skills to contribute to defining the pressing problems that face families and societies today. They wanted a part in shaping the agenda for action and in managing the search for solutions.

This same desire is repeated in the several examples described in this chapter in two quite different parts of the world, West Africa and South Asia, where women are breaking with tradition to help remake civil society. The examples underscore the importance of non-governmental organizations (NGOs) in empowering local people to access knowledge through experiential learning, to network together, to form voluntary associations, and even to impact government policies and the vested interests of the market sector. Moreover, they point to one of civil society's most important functions and defining features — ensuring the inclusive participation of all people, especially the poor, the powerless, and women, in community, national, and international life.

WOMEN'S HEALTH IN NIGERIA

During the early 1980s, my colleague Andrea Irvin and I were asked to explore and develop ways to support the priority concerns of those dealing with reproductive health issues in Nigeria.[1] During our first visit, we quickly discovered that cervical cancer was one of the main causes of death among women suffering from cancer and a leading cause of death among women in hospital. It was a major concern of both male and female doctors who made numerous requests for diagnostic laproscopes and training in their use, as well as for funding of a cervical screening program.

We considered these requests carefully but did not see how they empowered women to address the root causes of the problem. Moreover, although many doctors had been trained in cancer-related treatment in the 37 years since independence, Nigeria's public health service had no senior pathologist and only a handful of specialists trained in the early diagnosis and treatment of cervical cancer. The rest had moved to more lucrative private practice or to jobs overseas.

Most patients arriving at hospitals were too advanced even for radical surgery. A cervical screening program might catch cases early, but such programs require mass screening and follow-up to have any meaningful public health impact. In the chaotic economic and social conditions of Nigeria, it appeared impossible to mount a population-based program, or to effectively organize follow-up, referrals, and treatment. What is more, cervical cancer screening is expensive and therefore not likely to be cost-effective for a poorly funded public health service.

Phase One: Learning from the People

At the time, non-traditional women's organizations were not common in Nigeria. In our first explorations, we had met a few women who expressed a deep interest in the problems of women's reproductive health, in the context of a more general concern for the changing roles of men and women and particular difficulties facing the young. On our next visits, we talked with a wider range of men and women. The conversations often demanded courage. Matters of sexuality, the behaviors which lead to the spread of infection and infertility, and reflection on the emotional intimacies between men and women, are not normally openly discussed in African culture, nor even privately talked about between men and women or parents and children.

We met journalists, general practitioners, community nurses, market women, women lawyers, university teachers and students, feminist researchers, bar girls, commercial sex workers, young men hanging about the streets, teachers, parents, politicians, and government officials. These meetings were often adventurous. Some of our colleagues were suspicious and concerned when we sought out run-down hotels and back-street bars or disappeared into alleyways of crowded markets. Their attitudes ranged from being upset at our "improper" and "inappropriate" behavior to fascination with the topic and the effort we were making to understand it from differing viewpoints. Sadly, one of our drivers was tragically killed in the streets of Lagos one evening after dropping Andrea at her lodging, a brutal reminder of the cost of existence in a lawless environment.

While many we talked to were appalled at the distress, pain, and death caused by reproductive health risks faced by men and women in Nigeria, their fear of infertility stood out above all else. We were frequently assured that womanhood is customarily defined in terms of a woman's ability to bear healthy children and that children are the key to her access to social and economic security. Infertility is so feared that, as one woman in Lagos put it, when they fail to conceive, "Women will not just do nothing. If the modern public sector fails them, they will find money to pay private practitioners, or buy drugs over the counter, or go to a traditional healer." Childless women increase their number of sexual partners to improve their chances of becoming pregnant.

Infertility is the most common reason why women request consultation at Nigeria's teaching hospitals. In most cases, the problem turns out to be blocked fallopian tubes as a result of infection. Infections have numerous causes but most result from sexually transmitted diseases (STDs). STDs are widespread and endemic but usually go undiagnosed and untreated, or self-treated with drugs purchased over the counter, which leads to serious drug resistance. Research studies have shown STDs to be a major causal factor in infertility and cervical cancer.

Thus, a problem which had appeared susceptible to medical intervention was being defined by the way men and women in Nigeria relate to each other in the most intimate of human relationships. During the next phase of our work, our Nigerian colleagues deepened our and their understanding of these relationships and behaviors in Nigeria's many different ethnic, class, and religious settings. This was accomplished largely through women-to-women discussions in the privacy of women's homes, in the after-hours quiet at health clinics, or in the early evening lull in bars and downtown hotels.

Meanwhile, we helped Nigerian women understand the complementary but contrasting dimensions of reproductive health: medical and technical aspects of reproduction; technical options for safe management of sexual behavior and fertility; and underlying social and political factors, especially women's subordinate status which contribute to women's ill health. We negotiated our way through customs checks at airports, laden with literature which ranged from dry scientific texts to material written by women for women. We helped many women attend international and regional meetings to share ideas and experiences with health professionals and women activists dealing with similar problems in other settings. We also provided modest funding to groups of Nigerian women to develop creative local actions around the theme of women's reproductive health, such as debates on radio, in the press and in women's magazines, street marches with songs and dances written specially for the occasion, and surveys among market women and their customers, conducted jointly by market women and the few feminist university researchers.

Phase Two: Building A Civic Network

The intervention strategy which emerged from this second phase of intensive dialogue and mutual learning was quite different from our initial expectations. It was based on:

- Assisting the formation or development of women's health advocacy groups, and building a nation-wide network among them.
- Helping groups research and analyze the experience of sexuality and fertility in their own ethnic group and socio-economic context.
- Developing activities which addressed behavioral and attitudinal dimensions of the problem these studies revealed.

One of the greatest challenges of this three-fold strategy has been the high cost and unreliability of communication in Nigeria, coupled with the high cost and dangers of internal transport, and the absolute necessity of frequent face-to-face meetings of group members. Meetings provided opportunities for people to learn together the most efficient and effective ways of managing and leading their newly-established groups and to develop skills in planning, fund-raising, and financial management. For example, the necessity of making undisclosed cash payments to have a telephone line connected, and the absence of ticket stubs for many journeys by bus and bush taxi, made accounting a nightmare.

Further, although members of the various groups were united in their commitment to bring about change, they often did not initially understand or tolerate one another's cultural and socio-economic backgrounds. Meetings in different areas and discussion of local studies by some members helped the groups work through this problem. Others struggled to work cooperatively but finally decided to split into separate groups for local action and reunite with other groups for national activities. Eventually, networking became a clear mechanism with both the strength to unite and the space to accommodate Nigeria's diversity and size. Development of communicative capacity, rather than of organizations for their own sake, became the focus.

Another problem was the marked tendency to copy the habits of male-dominated meetings, which typically are held in costly hotels, with high expenditure on status symbols — dinners, printed menus, remuneration for speakers, and photo sessions with professional photographers. We had many difficult discussions about the best way to proceed. On the one hand, it is important that women demand and receive the respect of others and do not allow others to undervalue their activities. Yet all their money can be consumed swiftly in pomp and circumstance. The traditional female skills of making do with less became a strength, not a demeaning necessity.

One aspect of reproductive health which illustrates these complexities is the issue of HIV infection and AIDS. Public discussion about AIDS intensified as women considered the implications of Nigeria's first population policy enacted in 1988. The policy had two aims:

- Promotion of health and welfare, primarily through the prevention of premature death and illness among high-risk mothers and young children.
- Provision of family planning services to all couples and individuals at affordable prices. The definition of the services to be provided included help for sterile and sub-fertile couples and "individuals who want to have children to achieve self-fulfillment."

Women enthusiastically welcomed these aspects of the policy. However, they objected strongly to a number of less welcome features:

- Women were identified as the main clients of family planning services.
- The legal age of marriage was raised to 18 years
- Maternity benefits were spaced at bi-annual intervals.

In addition, it was recommended that women should plan to have children between ages 18 and 35, to a maximum of four children per woman. Although women welcomed anything that discouraged child and early teen marriages, they pointed out they prefer to marry young and get child-bearing over so they can concentrate on their economic responsibilities and opportunities.

Further, tying the "four-child norm" to women seemed to leave men free to have as many children as they want or could afford with as many women as they chose. This provision, together with the identification of women as the main clients of family planning services, seemed to absolve men of all responsibility for population outcomes while placing the burden of restraint on women. As one woman Commissioner of Health put it, "Men should also take the responsibility but they don't listen and roam free."

The women we were working with were quick to point out also the implications of the policy for the spread of sexually transmitted diseases, including HIV infection. On the one hand, they realized that when the reproductive tract was already infected, the use of certain kinds of modern contraception could lead to infertility. On the other hand, contraceptives like condoms, which offer some protection against infection, depend on their partner's cooperation and, of course, also prevent pregnancy.

The former First Lady of Nigeria, Madame Maryam Babangida, summarized neatly the complex web of socio-economic and sexual relationships that promote the spread of infection in these circumstances:

The virus has also cast a shadow over childbearing .... Infected women face a series of difficult choices, whether to become pregnant, continue pregnancy, or have an abortion. But we know that women are culturally expected to fulfill their reproductive obligations of procreation. In many African societies, a childless wife is scorned and repudiated. This may be a license for men and women to keep changing wives and husbands hoping for a child. This practice may unwittingly expose involved partners to greater risks of getting AIDS and other sexually transmitted diseases.[2]

Results of Civic Capacity-Building

The mobilization of activism around the issue of reproductive health, coupled with personal and organizational capacity-building among women, has had important pay-offs, at both macro and micro levels. Two examples follow.

Coalition of Nigerian NGOs on Health, Population, and Development

This coalition was formed at the second Preparatory Committee meeting in New York before the United Nations International Conference on Population and Development (ICPD) in Cairo, Egypt, 1994. A number of Nigerian women from non-governmental organizations (NGOs) were present to ensure women's views were adequately presented to their official representatives and to participate in intense lobbying around preparing the agenda and drafting the documentation. The women were aghast to discover there was no Nigerian government delegation present. On the spot, women from seven NGOs formed the Coalition of Nigerian NGOs on Health, Population, and Development (CONNOHPD) and developed a position paper on health, population, and development issues in Nigeria, to initiate a discussion within Nigeria on the issues to be debated at the ICPD and to help the Nigerian government prepare for the conference.[3]

The position paper articulated a cogent and influential point of view, locating women's, men's, and children's reproductive health problems in the wider context of gender discrimination, poverty, a distorted economy, and insecurity. Many of its recommendations were reflected in the official Nigerian government documents submitted to the conference. The CONNOHPD group formed a strong lobby in Cairo, giving leadership and strength to the African women's caucus which argued persuasively that "development" aspects of population problems should not be swamped in debates in the international media over reproductive technologies, contraception, and abortion. Their voice was heard again in Beijing in 1995 at the UN Conference on Women and Development, where they formed an influential part of the caucus that worked closely with official delegates to maintain and extend the gains won at previous conferences.

CONNOHPD's efforts represent a breakthrough on many fronts. They established, presented, and maintained a coherent policy position among a diverse group of organizations and became widely recognized as an authentic and legitimate voice on issues of concern to all Nigerians. They demonstrated how NGOs could work together with government at international fora to negotiate policies of benefit to all citizens. They learned with great speed the skills of lobbying, caucusing, and networking at the international level, while maintaining accountability to their own memberships. They acted with determination and courage in taking the debates to the wider public at a time of increasing political uncertainty, thereby stimulating extensive media coverage of the issues within Nigeria in a language everyone could understand.

Community Life Project

The Community Life Project (CLP) represents initiative at the micro level. It was founded by Ngozi Iwere, a teacher, journalist, and feminist activist involved in a number of women's health activities. After deep reflection on her experience, she became dissatisfied with the focus of AIDS-related activities on "high risk" groups. Risk is widely spread, especially in low-income urban areas, since both economic survival and customary lifestyles give rise to multiple sexual partnerships within and outside marriage for men and women. Drug abuse and "out of control" teenagers compound the problem, while a lack of precautionary care among street barbers and hairdressers whose salons commonly offer pedicure and manicure, leads to a risk of infection through unsterilized instruments.

CLP was conceived in 1991 and established in 1992 as a pilot community AIDS project, using participatory methods to elicit people's involvement in the development of AIDS education and control activities in the Ire-Akari and Okota neighborhoods of Lagos. The initial idea was to establish a drop-in center and outreach program using existing channels of communication and organization, focusing on hotels, schools, trade associations, barber shops, and hairdressing salons. However, the commitment to allow and support community members to initiate, plan, develop, and implement the project drove it in somewhat different directions.

The concept of "peer educators," community members trained by the project and supported to educate other community members, gave way to the concept of "peer facilitators." This transition occurred when the project staff realized the focus should be on co-learning rather than on educating, which implies a hierarchical teacher-pupil relationship and known solutions which could be transferred. The idea of an office-based drop-in center was abandoned in favor of a rented three-bedroom house to provide a welcoming, natural space for meeting with peer facilitators, confidential counseling, and an information center. As a result of the CLP's initial interactions with the community, six hairdressing salons began acting as "nodes" for information and inquiries. Twenty hairdressers took up informal AIDS education with their clients, using simple literature designed by community members and executed by professional artists. A magazine with short stories depicting "real life" dramas reflecting interpersonal relationships, and a cartoon book about a family who discover they are all HIV-positive, have proved popular.

Members of the Vulcanisers' (tire menders) Cooperative Society were shown a Nigerian film in Creole ("Nigerian English") which depicts Nigerians of different socio-economic backgrounds who had AIDS. The film sparked a discussion on condom use, which they believed would completely protect them against HIV infection. They were shocked to learn about other possible sources of infection, such as contaminated blood. They suggested stickers for their customers to paste on their car or truck windows and they became an important peer pressure group with the neighborhood's barbers. Fifteen barbers working in six salons subsequently agreed to sterilize their instruments if a client was cut and began to share information with clients on sexual infection, including HIV and drug abuse, particularly heroin and cocaine. The hairdressers and barbers collaborated in designing posters and T-shirts for use at work. The barbers were adamant that the T-shirts not mention the word AIDS and settled on the logo and motto of the CLP.

The early learning process threw up a series of further challenges. Sterilization of hairdressing implements proved unworkable, as the plastic parts melt or become distorted and street barbers have no on-the-spot facilities for boiling water. Project staff and community members investigated other ways of dealing with this problem and found the turnover of staff and apprentices at salons and barbers' shops was quite high. They felt frustrated their efforts were "getting lost."

However, they saw this as an opportunity to expand the number of those informed who could become active communicators wherever they went. As word of the CLP's work spread, broader issues began to be raised. In 1995, the CLP embarked on a series of group discussions to explore socio-cultural and economic dimensions of "safe sex" and reproductive health. These discussions are helping to mend self-esteem and to build collective energy by providing an outlet for discussion of the "unspeakable" and by offering follow-up action.

On World AIDS Day 1996, three activities further strengthened the sense of being able to make a difference in managing their own quality of life among the trade-based and neighborhood groups: a public workshop for men's groups, which led to suggestions for future work; a quiz and discussion competition for secondary schools; and a women's symposium organized by the new Community Action Committee.

PEST MANAGEMENT IN TAMIL NADU, INDIA[4]

Thousands of miles from Lagos in southern India, Mrs. Vijay Ghowri, holding a net tied to a long bamboo pole, stands in a muddy rice field with her baggy trousers rolled up to her knees. She slowly waves the net back and forth a few inches above the head of the rice plants. Women are scattered across the neighboring fields, some also with nets, others bent double with a plastic bag in hand, scooping something from the stems of the plants. Others huddled in small groups, examining with a magnifying glass something cupped in their hands. What on earth are they doing?

Mrs. Ghowri is a member of a Farmers' Field School in integrated pest management (IPM), one of 30 established around Madras in the 1994-95 season. The Field Schools, held weekly through the rice-growing season, are based on an experiential learning approach pioneered in Indonesia and the Philippines. Experiential learning is based on the principles that adults learn when they are motivated to do so by their own concerns, when the learning experience helps them discover solutions to their problems, and when the process develops them as persons.

The Field Schools are designed to help farmers learn how to make crop management decisions based on understanding the ecological processes which govern the interaction between plant growth and pest predation. The work involves taking insect samples in the crop and counting the number of each species of beneficial ("defenders") or harmful ("predators") insects present. The results are used in conjunction with individual and group analysis of the weather and stage of crop growth, to assess whether action is needed to control the pests, and if so, the type of action required. Trainees are encouraged to discover whether a hitherto unrecorded insect is a pest or predator by placing it with a known predator in an "insect zoo" and observing what happens to it. An insect zoo is made up of a rice plant growing in an earthenware pot, the whole covered by mosquito netting to keep insects in place. It is the field equivalent to the "pot cage" routinely used by entomologists in scientific experiments. Trainees also learn such things as how to determine the amount of insect-induced leaf damage that can be sustained by the rice plant before the rice yield falls to an unacceptable level.

Benefits of Experiential Learning

Advantages of this approach include reduced use of chemical insecticides, with measurable benefits to the environment, including increased populations of beneficial insects and birds and the conservation of edible frogs, snails, and fish in rice fields. Households spend less money purchasing insecticides, while rice yields tend to increase owing to better crop management. In addition, a major threat to human health and nutrition is eliminated or greatly reduced. In southern India, as in all Asia wherever intensive cropping is practiced, data on pesticide residues in market samples of rice grain, bran, and straw typically show contamination above permitted levels by chemicals hazardous to human health. Accidental death by chemical poisoning is not uncommon among farmers, while laborers frequently complain of nausea, skin rashes, and giddiness after spraying. Reliable data on the harm to women's reproductive health in particular are scarce but pesticides are implicated in a range of gynecological disorders and birth defects.

The less obvious benefits are proving to be of equal value as the program continues. The benefits are multi-dimensional, as poor men and women are empowered to take greater control of their lives, which improves household welfare and strengthens community interaction. In India, where women play a major, if unrecognized, role in agriculture but are poor, illiterate, and socially oppressed, the subtle educational effects of a program based on learning rather than instruction are of particular importance.

One Family's Experience

Mrs. Ghowri's Field School is one of four schools in Tamil Nadu especially for women. Her husband heard about the schools from friends and was keen for her to learn also when the opportunity came to attend a school in their village. Both have to work in their rice field but usually at different times of the day. Mrs. Ghowri goes to the field early after cooking breakfast and walking the children to school. The rest of the day, she works at home stitching garments. Her husband goes to the field towards the end of the day after he returns from his laboring job in a nearby brick-making business. Mrs. Ghowri feels confident enough in her new understanding to extend IPM principles to the management of her home vegetable garden. She no longer uses purchased chemical sprays. She removes the eggs or larvae of pests by hand, or uses a spray she makes herself from the *neem* tree. She has proven it is not harmful to the beneficial insects by first testing its effects in her insect zoo.

Both Mr. and Mrs. Ghowri have had only a few years of schooling and, before they started the Field School, assumed all scientific and technical knowledge had to come from educated people, such as the extension worker. Now they have an entirely different outlook. They often repeat the Field School's motto, "I can't lose. Why? Because I have knowledge, courage and enthusiasm." Mrs. Ghowri adds, "It is really exciting. Now we can see for ourselves and understand. We can also discuss observations with others in the group and together come to a decision about what to do." Mr. Ghowri says, "Before, we would rely on the extension worker to tell us, but often he did not know himself. In any case, he would only talk with a few of the better-off farmers. Now we find out for ourselves what it means and learn together." The Ghowri's enthusiasm is shared by farmers in Indonesia, the Philippines, Bangladesh, and Sri Lanka where IPM has been taken up by Ministries of Agriculture and NGOs.[5]

Strengthening Civil Society

The trainer of Mrs. Ghowri's group took a Bachelor of Science degree in agriculture and worked six years in a laboratory. She was dissatisfied with the limited opportunities open to women in scientific or technical careers so when she heard the Tamil Nadu Department of Agriculture was opening a program to support women in agriculture (TANWAP), she joined. The TANWAP officers not only conduct IPM Field Schools for women but also help them form savings and credit groups and "learn how to learn" improved vegetable and fruit cultivation methods, tree planting, chicken keeping and goat rearing. The TANWAP team's commitment to experiential learning makes a special contribution to the growing self-confidence of the largely illiterate women farmers. The program is helping women become independent knowledge-seekers capable of defending their new knowledge, to subject their findings and observations to peer review, and to put their ideas to the test.

Farmers continue to meet after they have received this kind of training because they find experiments of proven value. Increasingly, farmers who have participated in a Field School organize field schools for members of their extended families and friends, without the support of organized programs. As one farmer explained, "Before, just one or two people in the village would learn something new from the extension worker. Then we would all try to copy exactly because we thought it must be best. Now we all learn together but each person can decide for himself what to do." For example, farmers may discuss the effects on the incidence of pests of holding the water level in rice fields at a certain level, or review a field trial of the effects of using *neem* spray against a particular insect.

Another example of their new-found initiative is more dramatic. A chemical dealer introduced a new product, claiming it would avoid scouting for insects in the fields, wipe out all predators, and was completely safe. The landlord pressed his tenants to use the chemical, no doubt in return for payment from the dealer. The farmers invited the dealer and their landlord to a meeting to observe trials of the product. They sprayed an insect zoo in which they had placed both defender and predator insects and the chemical killed them all. They sprayed a day-old chick and it died on the spot. They invited the dealer to wash his hands in a bowl of the chemical and he refused. They caught a fish and put it into the bowl, and it died. More was going on here than a demonstration of a lesson learned by routine instruction. The defiance of exploitation of ignorance and the confidence of informed judgment lie close to the heart of democratic civil society.

Government extension workers are usually as enthusiastic as farmers, when they realize they too can develop their knowledge and understanding by finding things out for themselves and by learning from the analyses farmers make. They also have the satisfaction of seeing widespread changes in behavior, otherwise difficult to achieve through more conventional extension methods. The main drawback is the diminished income the extension worker might incur from the loss of kickbacks paid by chemical dealers. Indeed, illicit financial rewards for licensing the import, formulation, or distribution of agricultural chemicals are a major obstacle limiting the expansion of IPM activities. Shifts in power implicit in experiential learning can be unwelcome among power holders, especially among power holders at senior levels of government.

The disposition of agricultural bureaucracies to organize the world on the basis of their own routines and timetables is another major handicap. In Java, Indonesia, it is nearly impossible to run Field Schools in the short intermediate rice-growing season because funding for training can be authorized only during the two main rice seasons. Any use of pesticides by farmers in the short season gives rise to a higher risk of pest outbreaks in the subsequent season as the balance of defenders and predators is disrupted.

Thus, international NGOs such as CARE in Bangladesh, or indigenous voluntary organizations like Sarvodaya in Sri Lanka, have an important role to play. They may help extend the coverage of government programs to areas which governments find hard to service and they may also compensate for the limitations inherent in promoting the development of civil society through bureaucratic structures.

The social and organizational aspects of the roles NGOs play assume a particular form in Bangladesh where CARE is promoting IPM through two related projects, No-Pest and Inter-Fish (the cultivation of fish in flooded rice fields). First, women who work as CARE field trainers are still a controversial, if no longer rare, phenomenon in the non-government sector in a culture where *purdah* (seclusion) is deeply embedded. Second, as crop or water management decisions seldom can be made by a single individual, the collective aspects of learning take on special importance. CARE has developed innovative experiential learning methods through which groups of farmers construct simple physical models of the interconnected plots of the field environment in order to explore "what if" scenarios of the options for introducing seasonal fish ponds, *neem* tree cultivation for the local manufacture of *neem* spray, and water management.

Further, as one delighted NGO trainee attending an IPM training program in Sri Lanka exclaimed, "You don't have to have agricultural training to understand all these things!" The science underlying the success of the approach has been unpacked and repackaged as an opportunity for learning key principles and processes, thus making the approach accessible to a wide range of individuals and organizations who might lack specialist expertise in agricultural science. There is surely a lesson here for those concerned about the "scientific illiteracy" of civil society as the world enters the information age and the era of knowledge-based economic development.

CONCLUSION

The experiences related here focus attention on three attributes which appear characteristic of any struggle to enrich and develop civil society — acts of courage, the will and determination to persist in the face of powerful, entrenched economic and political interests, and the development of new personal and societal competencies. The key in the above cases has been to find methodologies to release the democratizing and empowering potential inherent in what some might think are solely technical issues, reproductive health and pest management.

The research-based and science-based knowledge underlying the activities presented here is essential but not sufficient. The experiential learning approach, placing knowledge in the hands of ordinary men and women, has made the real difference. Moreover, this has been done in a way that augments their capacity to shape and manage their own development as well as their capacity to create and develop further knowledge informed by their own values and meaning.

Larger claims might be made. If alternatives to authoritarian control are to be found, then we must develop mechanisms in which the diverse perspectives of individuals and of the state can be reconciled and a common definition of the "public good" can be negotiated. Without organizations in which ordinary men and women can express, and make effective, their interests, it is likely that the "public good" will be defined by the wealthy, the powerful, and the commercially self-interested.

NOTES

1. We were working for the International Women's Health Coalition, a New-York based non-profit organization which supports action research and advocacy to express women's perspectives on reproductive health issues. See (a) Janice Jiggins. *Changing the Boundaries: Women-Centered Perspectives on Population and the Environment.* Chapter 9. Washington DC: The Island Press, 1994. (b) "Report Submitted to the International Women's Health Coalition (IWHC)." Lagos: Community Life Project, 1994.

2. Madame Maryam Babangida's address to the Women's Rally, World AIDS Day, Lagos City Hall, 29 November 1989.

3. CONNOHPD. "Towards a Better Quality of Life for All Nigerians — Nigerian NGOs Speak Out." Position Paper on Health, Population and Development Issues. Coalition of Nigerian NGOs on Health, Population and Development. Lagos: National Secretariat at Women's Health Organization of Nigeria, 1994.

4. (a) Department of Agriculture. "Women Farmers Field School, Kolumanivakkam, Kunrathur Block, Sriperumbudur Raluk, Changalpattu, M. G. R. District, Tamil Nadu," 1995. (b) Joint Director of Agriculture. "Farm Women Field School, Kolumanivakkam, Changalpattu, M.G.R. District, Tamil Nadu," 9 February 1995 (mimeo). (c) K. G. Eveleens and Janice Jiggins. "Monitoring the FAO Regional Project: IPM Rice in South and Southeast Asia. Sri Lanka, India and Bangladesh (5-24 February 1995)." Wageningen: Crop Protection Centre for Developing Countries, 1995.

5. E. van de Fliert. "Integrated Pest Management: Farmer Field Schools Generate Sustainable Practices." A Case Study in Central Java Evaluating IPM Training. Research Program on Knowledge Systems for Sustainable Agriculture. Wageningen: Agriculture University, 1993.

13. Increasing Social Capital through Microenterprise

Mildred Robbins Leet

Microenterprise development is much more than providing capital to the impoverished. It is about building community, cultivating skills for collaboration, seeing human potential, and gaining control over the future. It is a reminder that a community's greatest asset is its people, regardless of educational attainment and social position.

— Monte Roulier

Dominica. April, 1979. Myld Riviere, a single mother with three children, was sitting in a field with four friends. When she spoke, her eyes were downcast. She asked, "What can we do to earn money to feed our children? After all there are no jobs around." Betty Meyer, a volunteer field worker and a Trickle Up Coordinator asked her, "What kind of business could you start?" Myld thought about it and queried, "What about all those bananas not acceptable for export that are piled on the docks? Could we use them to make banana chips and sell them in local markets?" The women became excited and started making a list of what they would need to produce and sell chips — a pot, some cooking oil, a thermometer, a slicer, and fuel. Myld became even more enthused when Betty Meyer said there was $50 available to get them started if they completed a Trickle Up Business Plan.

In 1986, seven years later, I returned to Dominica and visited Myld. She had become the leader of the business, "The Banana Bunch," and had a small office where she produced and sold the banana chips. She opened the door, stretched out her hand, looked me straight in the eye and said, "Hello, Mildred. Come in and see how our banana chip business is doing." From that time on, I knew she would never again feel helpless or hopeless. She was empowered.

Change of scene. Farmers in the Montemuro mountains in northeastern Portugal work small plots to provide for their families. Annually, they migrate to the more affluent countries of Western Europe to earn additional income as farm laborers and in service industries. In 1987, they decided to start keeping bees as a means of diversifying their agricultural base and increasing their income. They had little capital, however, for investing in hives and extraction equipment. Catherine Bayer, an Institute of Cultural Affairs staff member, encouraged them to complete the Trickle Up Business Plan. When the plan was approved, the farmers received the $50 start-up capital. In the following four years, Montemuro farmers started 88 bee and honey production businesses in nine villages.

Since then, dozens of businesses in 22 villages have started a variety of enterprises such as knitted wool clothing, tablecloths, quilts, toys, handicrafts, cheese production, postcards, and tourist hospitality businesses. In addition, people in this remote mountain area of Portugal have participated in community consensus meetings, the emergence of responsible leadership, long-range planning, and project administration.

From Europe to Asia. The Miao family of Guizhou province in China was one of many families displaced when work began to restore the wetland area in their county. Previously a nesting ground for the black-necked crane, the wetlands had been eroded by over-farming. The crane, a magnificent bird with a 12-foot wingspan and admired by many as a sign of good luck, had become an endangered species. At the same time, severe poverty and a lack of viable livelihoods had forced many people to seek assistance.

A constructive solution, to protect the environment for the cranes and to secure an alternative lifestyle for the displaced people, was provided by the collaboration of the International Crane Foundation (USA), the Caohai Nature Reserve of the Environmental Protection Agency of Guizhou Province, and Trickle Up. Challenged to think and plan, the Miao family used their skills at stove making to create an enterprise more rewarding than their previous work as farmers. They transformed discarded oil barrels that had been stored in the local village into stoves. In this way, they recycled a waste product and earned an income without further exploiting the delicate nature reserve.

In 1996 alone, 227 such enterprises were begun. The Caohai Nature Reserve-Trickle Up Partnership was formed with the realization that in order to have a sustainable outcome, the needs of entire communities had to be addressed. One way this has begun to happen is through the establishment of Community Trust Funds which have helped farmers around Lake Caohai to become increasingly involved in the long-term development of their communities. Resources for these funds were voluntarily contributed by the entrepreneurs and augmented by matching grants from the International Crane Foundation and the Environmental Protection Agency of Guizhou Province. The funds will create reserves the villagers can use to develop environmentally-sound projects that will serve the villages as a whole.

ORIGINS AND DEVELOPMENT OF TRICKLE UP

By the mid 1970s, the failure of "trickle down" economics to reach and benefit the whole society, especially the poor, was patently obvious. The international community was looking for new ways to reach the poor directly. My husband, Glen Leet, and I accepted the challenge. We created an alternative economic process called Trickle Up, designed to reduce poverty, and by extension, unemployment and underemployment. For more than a year, we talked to people in the international community about the Trickle Up process. It received much applause but no real commitment of funds. Frustrated by the lack of external financial support, we decided to invest $1,000 of our own money and selected a country in which to launch our experiment. Examining World Bank figures, we chose Dominica. It had a 45% unemployment rate, a -5% economic rate of growth and a population of 70,000. It was an ideal place to demonstrate the Trickle Up process: to award $100 conditional grants in two $50 installments and give non-formal business training to groups of people interested in starting their own businesses.

Our first meeting in April 1979 was with Sylvester Joseph, the Community Development Officer for Dominica, his field staff, and representatives of 20 voluntary agencies. He was interested in experimenting with the Trickle Up process to help put the theory into practice. Also intrigued were a British volunteer and representatives of two other agencies: the Women's Social League and the ministry responsible for community development.

Within days, ten groups of entrepreneurs identified by the agencies had completed business plans. Seven out of the ten businesses were still continuing seven years later. As one of these new entrepreneurs said, "Trickle Up gave us the push to get started" — a strong response to those who had doubted that $50 was enough to start a business.

The United Nations gave Trickle Up another push to get started. In 1980, in Denmark, at the UN International Conference on Women, we introduced the Trickle Up development process to the Non-Governmental Organization (NGO) Forum. This was the beginning of a network of women and men from voluntary national and international organizations, as well as governments and intergovernmental agencies. This network of coordinators was expanded at succeeding conferences including the UN World Conference on Women in Nairobi (1985), the World Conference on Environment and Development in Rio de Janeiro (1992), the World Summit for Social Development in Copenhagen (1995), and the UN Fourth World Conference for Women in Beijing (1995). Many of these conference participants found the process complementary to the needs of their development programs. Since 1979, over 3000 coordinators have introduced the Trickle Up process to communities in which they work.

In 1981, as a result of our presentation at the School of International Training in Brattleboro, USA, Robert Lawson learned about Trickle Up. As a student intern, he was assigned to work in Geneva for the United Nations Development Programme (UNDP) publication, *Development Forum*. He wrote an article about Trickle Up which received wide circulation in English, French, and Spanish and attracted many new coordinators.

Initially, the UNDP provided Trickle Up with small but encouraging grants. A more substantial grant was received in 1987 from the government of the Netherlands through the UNDP. In the Ruai squatter settlement in Kenya, a member of the Netherlands Embassy had seen the transformation of a community from economic survival to economic growth. In one year, people had started over 40 businesses. As the coordinator Humphrey Sikuku said, "The Trickle Up plan is laid down in plain facts. By following them, they work. The money goes right to the people themselves. It comes as a shock when people see others united and pushing off poverty. This is what makes the difference." Word of their achievements reached The Hague and Trickle Up received a grant of $1,600,000 over nine years to reach the poorest of the poor.

In 1989, at the suggestion of Suzan Habachy, then with the United Nations Department of Technical Cooperation for Development, the UN published a document, "Liberating the Potential for the Poor: An Approach — The Trickle Up Program." It was translated into the six official UN languages and circulated throughout the world. In 1994, Suzan Habachy became the Executive Director of Trickle Up.

In 1991, in cooperation with the Dutch government, the UNDP produced a 25-minute film on Trickle Up entitled, "If Given the Opportunity." This dramatic and moving documentary has proven an excellent educational tool, widely distributed to UN Resident Representatives and the general public. One result of showing the film was the initiation of programs in Laos, with a Japanese UNDP staff member as coordinator.

As a result of an expanded Trickle Up program in Liberia, a cost-sharing project between Trickle Up, the United Nations Volunteers (UNV), and UNDP Liberia, 865 businesses were started in 1995. This cost-sharing agreement involved promotion and support for income-generating enterprises among vulnerable groups in the country. It created another 1300 businesses in 1996 and has involved nearly 30 local NGOs as coordinating agencies. It was an example of many sectors of society working together to meet a crisis of persons displaced by civil strife. Unfortunately, Liberia's move toward peace came to an abrupt halt in April 1996 due to further civil disturbances.

Since 1979, over a quarter of a million women and men have started or expanded more than 55,000 businesses. The total number of entrepreneurs and family members assisted by Trickle Up exceeds 530,000. More than two-thirds of the entrepreneurs are women. This information is documented in Trickle Up's computer database, which allows input and analysis of data from 113 countries. This illustrates the core of the Trickle Up paradox — it is both a simple idea based on human needs and simple skills and yet it is sophisticated in its interpretation, potential, and execution.

THE TRICKLE UP PROCESS

Entrepreneurs working with Trickle Up learn by doing. A non-formal education process combines a basic business plan and a conditional start-up grant of $100 issued in two installments. The first $50 check is issued upon completion of the Business Plan. The second $50 is issued upon completion of the Business Report after the report is approved and entered into the Trickle Up data base.

There are two benefits from the way this cost-effective program is set up. One is short-term — the ready availability of seed capital, which is the incentive to start a business and produces immediate income. The other is long-term — the requirement that entrepreneurs save and reinvest at least 20% of their profits. This encourages new entrepreneurs to create their own capital and to keep their businesses growing.

The Trickle Up Business Plan asks simple questions about the contemplated business. Step by step, with each response, new entrepreneurs are able to complete the Trickle Up Plan on their own, or with minimal guidance from the coordinator. The ability to complete this business plan begins with the crucial process of giving entrepreneurs confidence in their own idea and their ability to implement it. Another important factor is the requirement that a group work together. People think together to create a plan that results in productive action.

The Trickle Up Business Plan puts the new entrepreneur face-to-face with these questions in a step-by-step learning process:

1. Choosing a Business
   - What will our product or service be?
   - Who will our customers be?
   - Where will we sell our product?
   - What will be the name of our business?
2. Planning Initial Investment and Costs
   - Initial investment (What will be put into the business in addition to hours of work? e.g. money, land, equipment, tools.)
   - Start-up costs and operating costs
3. Planning Sales and Profits — How much profit will we make, given costs and time?

4. Planning Reinvestment and Savings — at least 20% of profits.
5. Business Information (Who, where, when, why, and how?)

Cashing a check can pose many problems, particularly for people who are not familiar with banks. One problem concerns check cashing charges. In some cases, banks have waived these charges as a philanthropic contribution and in other cases, coordinating agencies have covered the cost. Regardless of these difficulties, cleared bank checks which Trickle Up receives prove that most people succeed in cashing their checks. Introducing the bank to the entrepreneur as well as the entrepreneur to the bank is another important learning experience. The coordinator works with the bank, the entrepreneurs, intergovernmental agencies, and Trickle Up to make banking a positive experience. Another problem is the long clearance time imposed by banks which require checks to be deposited for 30 to 45 days. Trickle Up's practice of disbursing checks to coordinators in advance reduces this time lapse.

One of the unforeseen benefits of depositing their savings into bank accounts is that entrepreneurs learn numeracy, a first step to literacy. Over 40% of Trickle Up entrepreneurs have opened bank accounts. This represents private sector savings, which add to the GNP of the country and provide capital for national economic development. Even though it may be somewhat intimidating at first, opening a bank account is a highly significant step in moving out of poverty and into the economic mainstream. This is especially true for women, for whom a bank account has far-reaching and profound economic, social, and legal implications. In countries where women are not permitted to own or inherit property, it is an opportunity for peaceful social change.

UNIQUENESS OF TRICKLE UP

In a world where so many businesses fail, people often ask how 83% of Trickle Up businesses continue after a year. What is unique about the Trickle Up process resulting in successful and sustained economic and social development?

Trickle Up has many unique features, but two principal ones predispose a business to succeed — people create their own jobs and they are self-employed. However, there are other built-in advantages. When a group of three or more people start a business they have planned themselves and for which they commit to invest 1,000 hours of time, initially there is no payroll to meet. There may be no rent and little travel time or expenses. Since the people creating the plan will do the work themselves, a group can find time to invest in the business without having to abandon other work that has been producing income, so any income the new businesses earn is additional income. Seventy-eight percent of Trickle Up entrepreneurs report their businesses are their main source of income. Since the people who do the work are the owners of the business, there is little discrimination or conflict of interest between owners and workers. This contributes to more productive and happier working relationships.

Entrepreneurs learn how to solve problems themselves, how to continue in their business by using their own judgment, and to learn from their mistakes. The goal is for them to become independent and self-reliant. Trickle Up provides one-time conditional grants, not loans. The condition is that they will fulfill the Trickle Up Proposition as prepared. Hence, there is no continuing dependency on external direction or funding.

The process also adapts itself to diverse political, economic, social, cultural, and environmental conditions, and is shaped by the people themselves. A good example of how the Trickle Up process is influenced by these factors is in the East African country of Malawi. Malawi ranks as one of the world's least developed countries with more than half its people living below defined poverty levels. Food shortages are endemic among traditional subsistence farmers.

Starting in 1990, a Trickle Up coordinator, a Peace Corps volunteer, and a Trickle Up program officer, working with local organizations, introduced "enterprise zones" as a development tool. A Trickle Up enterprise zone is a cluster of 25-100 small businesses in a village or community. Today, there are over 100 such enterprise zones globally. Their main purpose is to improve the social and economic conditions of the community and to gather information on these improvements. The progress of each business in an enterprise zone is monitored for at least three years in order to evaluate the long-term sustainability of the business and to track the impact of the Trickle Up process on both the participants and the wider community.

Now in their sixth year, the 13 enterprise zones in Malawi have already dramatically increased food production and spurred further community development efforts. Income from the enterprise zones, coupled with the 20% savings requirement of Trickle Up, has attracted a mobile rural savings bank to the villages. The Malawi Union of Savings and Credit Cooperatives has set up an account for each business group and provided members with various services including crop and livestock insurance, interest and dividends from passbook savings accounts, and bank and life insurance. As a result, 225 villagers who had been unable to secure access to credit received loans during the bank's first year of operation.

Forming an agricultural cooperative enabled grant recipients in Malawi to collectively purchase supplies at lower prices and to sell their harvested maize at higher prices. Through the collaborative efforts of both community members and Trickle Up businesses, the central village was able to build a marketplace, a new drinking well, and a new elementary school block.

For many farmers in the enterprise zones, maize storage bins have been full nearly year round, providing food security for the first time in recent memory. Health conditions, too, have significantly improved due to the availability of clean drinking water from the community-built well. Child malnutrition has been reduced and the number of families able to send their children to school has increased. As a result of so many village-wide activities, income levels have substantially increased.

Given that typical village families earn only $39 a year, the average family income in the enterprise zones more than doubled during the program's first year. Through cooperative efforts, villagers who rarely had enough collateral to even be considered credit-worthy now have substantial access to credit within their own community's credit programs. This program is run by the participants themselves, who select officers for the Savings and Credit Cooperative.

Another unique feature of Trickle Up is that it is not restricted to "less developed" countries. In recent years, it has been successfully applied in the United States, where it reaches entrepreneurs who not ready or are ineligible for credit. It allows them to gain valuable business expertise and accrue assets. One of these entrepreneurs was Mary Fung who came to the United States from Hong Kong in 1989. She soon discovered the need many Asian-American families have for child care while parents are at work. After completing a childhood education and training program, Fung succeeded in obtaining a permit to open her own child care center. However, when she applied for finance and business advice to the Manhattan Neighborhood Renaissance, a Trickle Up coordinating agency, she did not qualify for a loan. Instead, they referred her to Trickle Up. With Trickle Up seed capital, she was able to purchase the supplies she needed and has now been operating successfully for over two years.

PIVOTAL ROLE OF COORDINATORS

In the 17 years since Trickle Up was launched, over 3000 agencies have been accepted as volunteer coordinators. They are a part of civil society growing in number and voice worldwide who know who and where the poor are. They are in a position to offer them an opportunity for a better life. Trickle Up seeks to enhance the ongoing work of local development agencies by providing a basic business development program they can incorporate into their services to poor communities. These local agencies serve as the link between Trickle Up and low-income people. At the same time, the process helps them carry out their own development mission.

These coordinating organizations are primarily local NGOs but they also include government agencies and international organizations. The coordinating agency designates one or more staff members or volunteers as the coordinator to implement the Trickle Up program on behalf of the agency.

Some international agencies working closely with Trickle Up include the United Nations Volunteers, Peace Corps Volunteers, UNICEF, the International Labor Office, and the World Food Program. However, for the most part, local agencies have been primarily responsible for the expansion of the Trickle Up program. Coordinators are provided with Trickle Up guidelines to facilitate the practical application of the process. In India, for instance, Trickle Up has collaborated with more than 270 NGOs serving as coordinating agencies to assist disadvantaged groups in organizing microenterprise development businesses.

Dr. Ajaga Nji of Dschang University in Cameroon is a good example of a volunteer coordinator. He has helped groups start over 300 businesses in that country. He recently reported on 14 businesses still operating after ten years. "In Cameroon," Dr. Nji reported, "the small-scale project approach to rural development offers more potential for self-reliant and sustained development than large-scale enterprises." His study comparing 25 small-scale projects funded by Trickle Up with 20 Cameroonian large-scale agro-industries revealed that small-scale, labor-intensive projects in agriculture, manufacturing, or commerce are not only possible, but also highly efficient in relation to large-scale, capital-intensive enterprises. Such projects created employment, generated income, and built institutions.

BENEFICIARIES OF TRICKLE UP

Over the years, particular groups of people have emerged as major beneficiaries of the Trickle Up process. These include women, youth, refugees, and displaced persons.

Women

Although access to Trickle Up is available equally to women and men, women respond more readily. Traditionally, women are the last to be given an opportunity for education, land, finance, or training but are the first to accept responsibility to care for and feed their families. Women produce most of the goods and services poor people consume. They comprise a majority of the poorest of the poor.

Trickle Up provides women with an opportunity to increase their incomes and to improve living conditions for their families. When members of a group complete their plan and select their group leader, they can decide to work at times and places that fit their family and household obligations. This gives an advantage to women, since they are able to have flexible work schedules. This would not be possible if work were controlled by a separate owner who could require people to work during fixed hours or at locations determined by the owner or a creditor.

For example, the Associacion de Artesanas (women artisans) in Tecpan, Guatemala — a town where 84% of the population live in extreme poverty — created an enterprise zone of 42 businesses. These low-income women, many of them widowed as a result of political violence, have organized themselves into groups to increase production and marketing of handicrafts.

Sixty-two percent of Trickle Up entrepreneurs in the Americas are women. In addition, a number of Trickle Up coordinating agencies are organizations dedicated exclusively to serving women's needs, such as OEF of El Salvador and the Programa Nacional de Promocion de la Mujer in Peru. In Honduras, rural women's organizations have coordinated the Trickle Up Program through the UNDP since 1985, resulting in the creation of 321 businesses.

In addition to the tangible benefits of having a profitable enterprise, OEF's evaluation of the enterprise zones in El Salvador noted women entrepreneurs increased in confidence and improved their decision-making skills, which motivated other women to start enterprises of their own. Entrepreneurs also have higher status and are more integrated into the community. One Salvadoran single mother told us, "With Trickle Up, I established a tortilla business two years ago. Since then I have been able to support my children, start repaying my debts, and open a savings account at the bank."

Youth

While unemployment is a widespread problem, the shortage of jobs for young people is particularly acute. For example, in Sri Lanka, a group of seven unemployed teenagers, both male and female, were looking for jobs but none were available. They accepted an offer to use of a plot of cultivable land from a neighbor. They decided to plant peppers and other fast-growing crops in order to make a quick return on the sale of their produce.

Holly Wilson, a coordinator from the School for International Training, presented them with the $50 start-up capital after they had completed the Trickle Up Business Plan. With the grant money they bought seed, fertilizer, and tools.

Later, when they noticed that animals were eating their young plants, they built a fence to keep them out. When the crop ripened, they discovered a new problem — how to keep people from stealing the crops. They then built a lean-to so two members of their group could stand watch at night. Through a national competition, government officials learned of the group's persistent efforts to succeed, offered them a two-week training session on growing seedlings, and presented them with a grant of land. The government benefited by having young people self-employed and producing a needed product. The group learned how to start and continue a business. They didn't wait for someone to give them a job. They discovered they could make their own.

Refugees and Displaced Persons

Each year, thousands of people are killed in civil wars in many parts of the world. Thousands more become homeless. For example, in Cambodia, civil war has posed severe challenges to the people and the economy for the past 30 years. With a population of about eight million, half of whom are 19 or younger, Cambodia's per capita GNP ranks among the lowest in the world. It is estimated to have the highest per capita incidence of land mine victims of any country.

In response to these circumstances, Trickle Up, in association with the American Women's Economic Development Corporation (AWED), launched 152 new micro-enterprises. At a training center in the rural province of Kampot, AWED is working with Cambodians wounded during the war years, widows, and physically disabled survivors. The Kampot Training Center helps the disabled obtain artificial limbs, trains them in new skills, gives courses and counseling on human rights and family responsibility, and turns them into business people.

Having heard about Trickle Up, Ronnie Yimsut, the only one of eight siblings to survive the Khmer Rouge massacres in Cambodia, returned to home after graduating from an American university, to fulfill his ambition to help his country. He has since become a coordinator and helped launch five businesses in Phnom Penh with Trickle Up grants. One of them is run by Mrs. Sin Sinoum, whose husband, a metal worker, lost everything during the war. With the Trickle Up grant, his wife became an income earner by selling cooked foods on the sidewalks of Phnom Penh. The income from her business enabled Mr. Sinoum to resume his trade, and with two incomes, this family found a way out of poverty.

Trickle Up grants to displaced persons and refugees can have several different but equally important outcomes. They can provide early income for the displaced person or refugee in his or her new community or camp and they can provide long-term reconstruction assistance to their communities if and when those persons return home.

In northeast Uganda, Trickle Up helped start 100 small businesses in a camp comprised of people displaced by local conflict along the Karamoja/ Teso border. The participants had been living in the camp for six years in difficult conditions. Land for farming is accessible, however, so the majority of the businesses involve small-scale farms. The infusion of capital and business activity in the camp has sparked economic recovery in the area, with the majority of the participants using their profits to engage in animal husbandry. In addition, small retail stores selling essential items such as soap, cooking oil, and medicines have also been started.

CONCLUSION

Microenterprise development has been receiving a great deal of attention of late. It is now being recognized as a key building block of international development and civil society. The Microcredit Summit in Washington DC, USA, in February 1997[1] was a sign of this. It attracted presidents and prime ministers, representatives from business and funding agencies, along with numerous development practitioners. Participants pledged to reach 100 million of the world's poorest families by 2005 through credit for self-employment and financial and business services. Trickle Up was among the 2,500 attendees at the event.

However, Trickle Up differs in philosophy and practice from many of the groups present. It is not in the business of issuing loans to the poor. It is concerned with helping the poorest of the poor to take first step out of poverty to self-employment by providing start-up capital in the form of conditional grants and the basic skills to launch successful enterprises. Once people have taken this step, they may then be able to secure other resources, join a savings group, or qualify for a loan.

In some areas, Trickle Up partners are microenterprise organizations which run credit programs but they use Trickle Up with people who are not able to qualify for loans. The 1993 United Nations Human Development report notes that most NGOs do not reach the lowest 5-10 percent of the 1.5 billion poorest people in the world. Trickle Up gives these people a means to go into business.

It also does a lot more than this. It has a significant impact on the lives of individuals and communities, way beyond its economic value. As Monte Roulier points out:

> Microenterprise development ... is about building community, cultivating skills for collaboration, seeing human potential, and gaining control over the future. Where economies are developed and controlled locally, and where the impoverished have access to capital, is where you find communities looking inward for solutions rather than outside themselves .... [It] is a reminder that a community's greatest asset is its people, regardless of educational attainment and social position.[2]

Trickle Up started with a belief in and respect for people and their ability to work together. It recognized the untapped human resources and the existence of local support agencies and knew that such partnerships can be productive and mutually beneficial. It continues to strengthen these partnerships and to create new ones as the number of organizations expand locally and nationally. In so doing, it is laying the foundation to build civil society in thousands of communities around the world.

NOTES

1. The Microcredit Summit was held in Washington DC, USA, February 2-4, 1997. It was organized by the RESULTS Educational Fund and backed by several American multinational corporations.

2. Monte Roulier. "Local Community: Seedbed of Civil Society." pp. 183-196.

14. Facilitating Civil Society

Mirja Hanson

*Facilitation is not a collection of group techniques. At a
deeper level, facilitation gives birth to new public vitality. It
is about the rapid change of society.*

— Duncan Holmes

C ivil society is being created one meeting at a time. Every human encounter, every discussion and every gathering is an opportunity to advance or retard the shaping of cooperative community. This chapter
focuses attention on the importance of managing that building block of civil
society. The ideas and insights come from over 20 years of "mental field notes"
and lessons learned in the course of working as a facilitator in hundreds of
meetings, projects, think-tanks, retreats, work days, transitions and roundtables
where participants worked to blaze new trails in teamwork. The central realization is that collective genius doesn't just happen. Method matters.

DEFINING CIVIL SOCIETY

"What is civil society?" is a question that fills seminars and attracts academics, social commentators, and journalists. The question was big enough for me
to travel from Minneapolis, USA, to Cairo, Egypt, for the conference on the
"The Rise of Civil Society in the 21st Century," sponsored by the Institute of
Cultural Affairs International in September 1996. Over 300 participants from
around the world attended. As the presenters spoke, my notebook filled with
an avalanche of definitions but my question still persisted when it came time
for my workshop session on the subject of facilitation and civil society. I decided to demonstrate facilitation by conducting a discussion about the definition.

I was delighted when over 30 participants crowded the room and enthusiastically supported the proposed agenda. We were a microcosm of the global
village, representing all continents, sectors of government, science, academia,
the private sector, non-governmental organizations (NGOs), and local communities. We were a mix of field practitioners, policy makers, private citizens

and everything in between. The one thing we had in common was our lack of a consistent working definition of civil society.

The small groups spun into a whirlwind of discussion and then came together in a large group, each bringing seven to eight ideas they agreed were key elements of civil society. Five common characteristics of civil society emerged:

- Active and inclusive participation
- Respect for differences
- Access and opportunity to meet basic needs
- Empowered community with broad-based responsibility
- Ongoing creative process

We defined civil society as a set of five cultural values and practices rather than economic or political structures as other presenters had done. Cumulatively, these practices and values define civil society as a relationship — a way of relating in community which fosters inclusive, respectful, and responsible participation. It offers fair citizen access to resources, to power, and to personal freedom. It is a reality that constantly evolves and needs to be redefined and developed forever. Civil society shapes its thinking, organization, and action by institutionalized, non-violent, and inclusive values and practices of give-and-take between citizens at all levels and at all times.

EMERGENCE OF THE PROFESSIONAL FACILITATOR

If civil society is based on the practical give and take between citizens — the ability for people to engage in dialogue, inquiry, analysis, and decision making — the process for interaction is of utmost importance. Yet, even in the most democratic nations, there is a dearth of "public spaces" where ideas can be shared and mobilized into collective action, where there are "opportunities for the articulation of multiple perspectives in multiple idioms, out of which something common can be brought into being."[1]

Even when public forums are conducted, old methods of decision-making are not able to honor the diversity of viewpoints and complexity of situations. Group facilitators and facilitative leaders have emerged to fill the urgent need for more effective methods of interaction. The growth of the profession of facilitation may be one of the strongest indicators that society wants to take civic participation seriously. Statistics about this rapidly developing and unregulated industry are not available, but having been part of the evolution, I can attest to the fact that the new profession of facilitation is rapidly taking its unique place alongside those of the consultant, coach, and trainer in organizational and community development.

When we gather at professional events, we realize most of us did not become professional facilitators based on some theoretical understanding of civil society or anything else. In fact, the fascinating thing about facilitators is that, like pilgrims and nomads, we have traveled on separate, solitary pathways in multiple fields, settings and disciplines. Facilitation has evolved from the necessity to make sense of life in many different contexts.

My own story may be fairly representative of the evolutionary nature of the profession. In the early 1970s, I worked for the Institute of Cultural Affairs (ICA) in Osaka, Japan, as well as in Minneapolis and Kansas City, USA. The ICA is a non-governmental research and training organization seeking to empower communities to take responsibility for their destiny.[2] In the process of working with people to shape their future, my colleagues and I learned how to successfully get people talking, thinking, and working together. We were all volunteers. Often we had to beg communities to come together and try out a new way of planning the future together. Not only did we pay to work, we sometimes had to bring the meeting snacks as well. Now, two decades later, I can make a living conducting meetings.

There are thousands of stories like mine in every field where facilitators are active. The following is a representative list of areas within which professional facilitators are appearing:

International relations. "Dual track" diplomacy which uses methods for negotiating peace, treaties, and agreements outside the traditional diplomatic channels and protocols.

Law. Cases are settled outside the court through alternative dispute resolution.

Community mediation. Conflict resolution and mediation have become broad-based activities, with increasing numbers of community dispute resolution centers staffed by volunteers who are trained to mediate arguments in their neighborhoods.

Community governance. Facilitators are active in local community development, neighborhood decision making, and other community-based efforts to deliver economic and human services as an alternative to centralized bureaucracies.

Government. In progressive governments, agencies are moving away from being resource providers or regulators to becoming coordinators and facilitators of constituent dialogue and public service.[3]

Business. As the pressures of competition have forced companies to become more flexible, market/customer driven entities, the ability to invent products and services to meet ever-changing needs has heightened the need for teamwork and shared leadership, in place of traditional hierarchical systems of authority and decision-making. Companies that invest in employee involvement are staying profitable.

Partnerships. In the private, public, and non-profit sectors, there is a huge market for facilitating consortiums, alliances, partnerships, councils, associations, and other mergers as a way to "work smarter not harder" in an environment of diminishing resources and increased user demands or expectations.

School peer mediation. Students are learning skills for cooperation in schools, clubs, and sports. My fourth grader is being trained as a peer mediator on the playground.

The experiences, techniques, theories, and models for facilitation vary in each field of application but similar lessons have been learned about the make-or-break variables of civilized public interaction. I will present these lessons as *core assumptions* about participation in civil society, *core activities* which make up public discourse, and some *rules of thumb* about conducting those activities effectively.

CORE ASSUMPTIONS

Interrelatedness. Today, communities are coming to terms with the reality that all life is intensely interrelated. In previous eras, we were able to live in an illusion of independence because we could escape to new frontiers. Now most corners of the world have been staked out, owned, and lived in. The Earth can no longer be viewed as a limitless terrain to explore, expand, and exploit. It needs to be viewed as the crowded planet it is. Scientists agree that our global village with six billion inhabitants will double in population in 50 to 100 years or even sooner.

The challenge of facilitating participation will grow in tandem with the crowding of our planet. Living at the intersection of diverse interests, needs, endeavors, opinions, and trends is the ultimate challenge of our time. The quest for civil society is synonymous with the need to declare our interrelatedness at all levels — global policy, local action, and individual relationships. In many places, we *implicitly* admit to the cost of conflict and the urgency for participation. Facilitation is part of the trend to *explicitly* acknowledge our interrelatedness. It is the art and science of forging new values, protocols, etiquette, and formal methods for a small planet.

Respect. The search for meaningful ways to work together in a complex and changing society is a universal cultural challenge. Naive notions of cross-cultural interaction, such as admiring one another's national customs, cuisines, and clothing are being replaced by the understanding that "multicultural" means every human being is totally different from every other. There is as much diversity between marketing and engineering, between parent and child as there is between Filipinos and Finns. A truly global citizen is one who respects all other human beings — not just tolerates, not just understands, not just accepts, but respects them. We live in a time when the corollary to "the only constant is change" is "the only normal is diversity." Respect is believing that. Dr. Harlan Cleveland, former dean of the Hubert Humphrey Institute of Public Affairs in Minnesota, USA, pointed this out in his story about his little nephew who made an insightful mistake with a traditional prayer. Instead of saying "Oh Lord, let us be mindful of the needs of others," he said "Let us be needful of the minds of others."

Participation. Facilitation is everybody's business, not just a domain of new professionals. If facilitation is the practice of enabling effective public discourse and civic engagement, everyone has a role. According to Roger Talpaert, a European management expert: "It is unthinkable today for people to contribute to any form of collective action without being able to influence choices."[4] The graffiti I found in a school rest room expresses the same sentiment. "Tell me, and I will forget. Show me, and I may remember. Involve me, and I will understand." Participation has become "that-without-which" for our time. Sociologist Daniel Bell underscores this when he speaks of axial principles which have fueled various historical periods: in the 18th century it was equality and rationality; in the 19th century it was industry and mechanization; and in the 20th century it is participation.[5]

CORE ACTIVITIES

The overall duty of the facilitator is to help a group discover common ground and move beyond conflict and compromise to collaboration. Compromise is the costliest way to get to a solution neither side wants. Collaboration, on the other hand, implies a situation in which everyone wins, rather than bargaining over whose hopes will be lost. Three main activities are involved in the quest for common ground: building shared awareness, creating consensus agreements, and mobilizing productive action. Every successful episode of public discourse needs to emphasize one or two activities but should include some of all three.

Catalyzing shared awareness

A shared picture of current reality. Discourse and decision-making on a crowded, complex planet assumes that the safest definition of the situation at hand is one constructed from the multiple views of participants who have a stake in the situation and its outcome. In the facilitator's dictionary, the "right" reality to work from is the one described, named, assessed, and labeled jointly by the participants. The facilitator's duty is to provide a comprehensive, blank framework and open questions which help people unlock what they know. Whether you are conducting a meeting with public housing residents, assessing the results of a fund-raiser, analyzing the status of old growth forests, scanning the marketplace for product development, or identifying regional resources for starting a village pig farm, don't assume everyone has the same view of reality. The goal is to build the big picture by assembling the experiences and observations about the topic and its context.

Sometimes, this picture is created from scratch. Sometimes, facilitators and meeting sponsors spend part of their preparation time deciding what materials, presentations and background information need to be made available in order to avoid a hierarchy based on information where those most versed in the subject have the edge and the power in the conversation. When people are given the time and information to see the whole scope, the contentiousness and conflict we have grown to expect and dread at meetings is reduced significantly. As participants understand where people are coming from and identify together what they are up against, relationships are realigned. The usual contest for the winning position converts to a search for the best ways to address the common challenges at hand.

Deciding what is meaningful. Once there is a shared understanding of the situation, the next task is to engage in collective analysis, heeding the advice of American industrialist Charles Kettering that "a problem well-stated is a problem half solved." The facilitator works to foster a forum for critical thinking which allows a dialectical exchange between the topic and its broader social context; which questions, probes, explores, tests, and explodes options; and which catalyzes creativity.

It is extremely challenging to customize processes that enable this kind of thinking, not because people are dull or incapable but because we show up at a meeting immersed in our everyday lives and familiar paradigms. It takes effort to focus beyond the edge of our rut and see the horizon. A facilitator's duty is to find ways to trigger whole brain-thinking. I once observed a facilitator begin a teachers' session on site-based management by asking the question, "Now let us engage in some 'out of box' thinking. What are your ideas about managing the site?" Dead silence ensued because the facilitator minimized his homework. It helps to bring in thought-provoking stories, experiences, literature, and theories in addition to well-orchestrated questions and discussion processes.

Andrew Robbins, a contemporary inspirational speaker, suggested that people move into the future as a result of two things, inspiration or desperation. Effective public dialogue needs to surface the driving desperation or inspiration in a given situation. Good process is a drama which engages people. It builds momentum in the world of facts, observations, feelings, and reactions. It climaxes in debating and constructing interpretations, meanings, and implications. The flow of the discourse should mirror the multilevel process of consciousness within every human being. As one facilitator observed, "Stuff starts to happen if you bring out all dimensions of the topic — the what, the gut, the so what and the now what."

Building Consensus Agreements

Traditional methods for decision-making are based on proposing motions, discussing them, voting on them, and implementing some form of majority opinion. Another format has members providing input and leaders determining the final choice. These approaches are irrelevant today. Perhaps Robert's Rules of Order and executive decision-making are appropriate ways to symbolize or formalize the collective will. The issue with respect to empowering civil society is that these methods tend to produce decisions which are unaccompanied by the constituents' will to implement them. When situations are complex and stakeholders diverse, making choices based on one brain or a fragment of the group reduces the "buy-in factor" required to actualize decisions. One state manager put it this way: "In the good old days, a leader could simply decide, announce, and defend decisions. Now things are too complex. You can't get others to do your decisions. To be successful these days, you have to negotiate, agree, and implement with all the stakeholders … if you're going to get anything done."

Often clients will say to me, "We've got a plan but what we really need is the buy-in. You need to help us with that." There is no magic method for that. The only way to achieve buy-in is to have a product people want to buy. That means making choices that represent the public good and/or meet the private needs of all those concerned. It means building decisions that generate commitment.

Such decisions must be arrived at by *consensus*. Like the term "civil society," definitions of consensus abound. As the quest for civil society continues, there will no doubt be more efforts to institutionalize protocols for building consensus. Such efforts are underway as I write, including one referred to as "Roberta's Rules," a set of guidelines for developing binding public decisions using consensus. However, until the formal and legal definitions are in place, each group needs to define consensus appropriate to its particular situation. Some commonly-used definitions include "the agreement to agree for a period of time," "unanimous consent," and "the collective opinion."

My most memorable experience with consensus was facilitating a year-long timber-harvesting mediation between 26 interest groups where the working definition of consensus was "something we can all live with." A plan was formalized at the end by having all players sign the consensus document. While definition was important, what really made the consensus binding was the willingness of all representatives to continue to return to the table and put in the time — close to 200 hours each — to understand, to hold interest group caucuses, and to craft a recommended public agenda for managing Minnesota forests. The plan was put in statutory language and sailed through the legislative process because all 26 lobbies supported the collective product.

The art of group decision-making involves framing the options into manageable scenarios without oversimplifying the systemic nature of the actions. One of the key constraints of voting or Robert's Rules of Order is that situations are impossible to frame into one motion or a few voting choices. A good facilitator puts a great deal of design time into finding techniques that allow people to analyze their complex situation and develop a system of solutions to address underlying barriers, pressure points, or places where they are stuck. This fundamental shift in planning and decision-making is described aptly by Russell Ackhoff, formerly of the Wharton School of Management of the University of Pennsylvania, in the following ways:

> In a real sense, problems do not exist. They are abstractions from real situations. The real situations from which they are abstracted are messes. A mess is a system of interacting problems.

> The solution to a mess is not equal to the sum of the solutions to its parts. The solution to its parts should be derived from the solution to the whole, not vice versa.

> The question of priorities is misleading. All messes should be dealt with simultaneously and interactively.

> We waste too much time trying to forecast the future. The future depends more on what we do between now and then, than it does on what has happened up to now. The thing to do with the future is not to forecast it but to create it. The objective of planning should be to design a desirable future and invent ways of bringing it about.[6]

Mobilizing Productive Action

The third major component to good public discourse is mobilizing action. It is the final step that allows for a true democracy. This is easier said than done. Just because decisions are agreed to, understood, and overwhelmingly supported, they are not doomed to success. As a Chinese proverb suggests, "Action removes the doubt that theory cannot solve." Implementation, like any other part of public discourse, happens best by design rather than default. The facilitator's duty in empowering civil society is to work with the discourse sponsors to assure collective decision-making about the next steps, schedule, and staffing for implementation.

In addition to managing public discussion and decision-making, facilitators and facilitative leaders are being called upon to advise and guide long-term civic engagement, more commonly referred to as whole system transformation, reorganization, cultural change, public initiatives, and campaigns. Facilitators serve as change agents for enabling a system to get on a self-conscious, self-correcting, and self-organizing path, but everyone in civil society needs to play a role. American sociologist James Brian Quinn's research summarized the necessary process and leadership needs of long-term innovation in a simple but solid way:

> Every innovation [development effort] is like a baby. In order to grow it needs three leadership roles: a father who blesses the innovation with authorization and resources, a mother who loves the innovation unconditionally, and a pediatrician who understands the general process of growing babies [innovations].[7]

The task of empowering civil society is a long-term undertaking, sometimes called human development or initiating a "learning community" — a group of people who are engaged together, reflect, and learn from their engagement, and who continuously change, adapt, and improve their existence. In similar vein, the Total Quality Management movement speaks about building a discipline of Kaizen — a Japanese term for constant, ongoing, relentless, and incremental improvement.

RULES OF THUMB

Facilitating collective effort is simple but not easy. In fact, some participants have been known to ask, "Why do we have to pay so much for a facilitator? Anyone can stand up there and scribe the conversation on a flipchart!" However, upon taking their turn at the head of the table, those same persons usually discover there is more to the job than meets the eye. If we had the luxury of consistently small groups and unlimited time, anyone could bring dialogue and group decisions to a successful closure. But when the challenge is to manage hundreds, or sometimes thousands of pieces of data, with 25 perspectives on each piece, changing space conditions, shifting moods, interaction effects, and finite time frames, facilitation skill, method, and experience can make or break the effectiveness of public discourse. If method is important, what are the make or break practices that assure effective facilitation? Answering that question fully is beyond the scope of this chapter. However, here are a few key rules of thumb for facilitating in a way that truly empowers civil society.

Process is not a substitute for thinking. While structure is essential to public discourse, it is not the magic. The magic is catalyzing the amazing human energy of the participants around the table. A colleague of mine made it a point to remind planning groups about this fact with the introduction, "There is nothing that can ever substitute for critical thinking and hard work. I am here to provide a process for organizing and surfacing the collective thinking and creativity." The role of the facilitator is a decision support function. Just getting together doesn't assure "spontaneous combustion." A meeting with and without effective process is like the difference between car parts in a pile and a finished car.

I experienced this long ago at the White House Conference on Children and Families in Madison, Wisconsin. Other conferences in neighboring states had failed due to the domination of the pro-life and pro-choice activists. The one in Madison succeeded because the process was robust enough to include the activists but enable everyone to participate and therefore create a balance to the discourse. Maybe some day, facilitation and process design will become an institutionalized decision support function where organizations will consider it automatic to have their certified public accountant, their attorney, and their certified public facilitator.

Build processes that embrace complexity. Processes need to be simple but not simplistic. They need to fit the complexity, change, and interrelatedness of the situation. Issues resist being framed into no/yes formats. The facilitator needs to decide what is the scope of the discourse and find the best ways to address all the issues and people within it. The prerequisite stance of a facilitator is to embrace complexity and believe in the notion that "freedom means picking your way painfully through a veritable jungle of alternatives, few of which are satisfactory, none of which is perfect."

Prepare thoroughly. The work of the facilitator begins long before he or she arrives at the meeting site to rearrange tables and stand in front of the flipchart. A standard guideline that has stood the test of experience advises that every hour of facilitation requires two to four hours of preparation and documentation surrounding a meeting. This includes desk work, pre-meetings and phone conversations to carefully understand the situation, audience, players, and subject matter and to produce the right procedures, questions, examples, stories, and materials that assures a rich and rewarding meeting of minds. My son was once asked what his mother does, and he quickly replied, "She talks on the phone and says u-huh." A recent book on negotiation, *Getting Ready to Negotiate*,[8] emphasizes the fact that determining the who's, how's, and why's of the public discourse before a meeting is a major task in moving the agenda forward *at* the table.

Respect processing time. The facilitator's task is to minimize time while maximizing group effectiveness. However, there is no way to get around the fact that participation takes time. It is not efficient, like a dictatorship. Listening to and hearing the whole situation takes time. As one proverb says, "You can't make beans grow by pulling on them." Carving out the time and patience to build civil society is a challenge. Often a client will say: "I'm not a process person, I just want to get right to the point." I suggest they go right ahead. The choice is whether you want the rest of the group to help get the point *imple-*

mented once you get to it. Another way to answer such a request is to compare it to a more familiar kind of public discourse — a court trial. "Getting right to the point" would be like someone saying, "Let's just do the opening and closing arguments and skip all that stuff in between." Nobody would think of determining the fate of a defendant without putting time into a thorough process.

Admittedly, process has acquired a bad reputation when facilitators stifle group dialogue with canned and pre-set methods or overplaying games. Once a manager declared he would refuse to participate in a retreat if this was "one of those touchy-feely sessions where we put our shoes in the middle and sit around in a circle." The keys here are: Don't waste participant time but don't circumvent critical thinking and creativity in the interest of expediency.

Pay attention to the needs of insiders. The dialogue in civil society belongs to community members. As an instrument of empowerment, the facilitator's duty is to understand that the work of carrying on the empowerment goes on after the facilitator leaves. It is important to make sure every step of the process makes sense to those whose life it affects. Managing dialogue in civil society is a partnership between the inside leaders and the outside catalysts.

Optimize everyone's contributions. The facilitator assures that all voices are heard. Often these are voices that have not spoken or been allowed to speak for a long time. A major part of the magic results from the answers and insights which have been part of the system all along but never been aired. The facilitator understands that solutions to issues are usually around the table or somewhere within the system. This dimension of modern public discourse may be the key to avoiding many of the pitfalls of the past — the tendency to subjugate the knowledge of many groups and individuals to the powerful few.

Continue to stand at the center of the chaos. Facilitators must be willing to stand in the mess of human discourse and "direct traffic" until the creative process yields a desired outcome and until resolve is built. They trust the self-organizing capacity of the group and the ability for every system to heal itself. Marvin Weisbord, an American organization development consultant, speaks of the role of facilitator as a stage manager:

> On my bookshelf I find more models for fixing things than there are stars in the galaxy. Yet I am strangely undernourished by this intellectual cornucopia. My objective, I keep reminding myself, is not to diagnose and heal sickness but to help people manage their work lives better and enact productive community .... The consultant negotiates a role ... always limited by the willingness of others to play along ... the consultant's role is to help people discover a more whole view of what they are doing than any one discipline or perspective can provide .... The task is to see confusion and anxiety through to energy for constructive action and learn along with everyone else.[9]

Study maps and methods to improve discourse. Staying abreast of new techniques and technologies is part of a facilitator's job. The more experiences and methods are stored in the brain and files of a facilitator, the more able she or he is to find the right tool to fit a given situation. Facilitation, like management, is a knowledge-intensive profession. However, unlike law or accounting, there are very few constants, laws, absolutes, or precedents. Wisdom comes from applying theory and methods to numerous situations and learning from those experiences. It is said that professionals who have practiced 10-20 years have about 59,000 bits of useful information in their brains which they can access quickly as needed to fit an oncoming situation.

CONCLUSION

The participants in my workshop at the Cairo conference defined civil society as an evolving relationship based on inclusiveness, respect of differences, equal access to basic needs and shared responsibility. The work of the facilitator is the work of every member of civil society — to use every small and large interaction as an opportunity to pioneer, experiment, learn, and invent ways to bring about such a relationship. The magic word is "work." In a recent movie and book, *Dead Man Walking*, a true story about a nun who counseled a death row inmate, there is a scene at the funeral of the inmate where she notices the father of the dead victim waiting beside his car. She walks to him and says, "I'm glad you came. Perhaps we can work together to get rid of the hate." He replies, "I don't think so. You have a lot more faith than I have." She looks him straight in the eye and says, "It's not faith. It's work."[10]

This notion of collective work is critical to building civil society and implies a change in the concept of leadership. In the past, a leader has been seen as someone in a leadership position or a charismatic person with unique traits and abilities. Civil society requires that leadership be shared — the process and product of collective thinking, organization, and action. This is the thesis of a recent book, *Making Common Sense: Leadership as Meaning-Making in a Community of Practice*:

> With the shift to seeing meaning-making as the basis of leadership, influence is no longer considered the essence of leadership; it becomes, rather, an outcome of leadership …. The purpose of the process of leadership in this view is, therefore, not to create motivation; rather it is to offer legitimate channels for members to act in ways that will increase their feelings of significance and their actual importance to the community…. We refer to leadership as a social process in which everyone in the community participates …. This in turn implies that leadership is intimately connected to processes of group, community, nation-state, and even species-wide integration and togetherness and ultimately to

communal survival, growth and enhancement. Leadership is uniquely human; it is a key component, perhaps the key component, in our survival strategy.[11]

When every human being sees her or himself as a member of the leadership team, we will have a chance to solve the most complex problems and the most troubling trends of our planet. The facilitator's role in enabling the process of collective leadership is to initiate or speed up the self-organizing capacity of civil society.

NOTES

1. Maxine Greene. *The Dialectic of Freedom*. New York: Teachers College Press 1988. p. xi.

2. For a description of the Institute of Cultural Affairs, see pp. 299-300.

3. James Troxel. "The Recovery of Civic Engagement in America." pp. 97-111.

4. Roger Talpaert. "Looking Into the Future: Management in the Twenty-first Century." *Management Review*. March 1981. pp. 21-25.

5. *Ibid.* p. 25.

6. From a variety of sources and acknowledged by Russell Ackhoff as his statements.

7. James Brian Quinn. "Logical Incrementalism." Tuck School of Management, Dartmouth Strategic Management Research Center Colloquium, 17 March 1987.

8. Roger Fisher and Danny Ertel. *Getting Ready to Negotiate*. New York: Penguin Books, 1995.

9. Marvin Weisbord. "Toward Third Wave Managing and Consulting." *Organizational Dynamics Journal*. (1987) pp. 5-24.

10. Tim Robbins. Director of the film based on the book by Sister Helen Prejean. *Dead Man Walking*. Polygram Filmed Entertainment. 1995.

11. Wilfred H. Drath and Charles J. Paulus. *Making Common Sense. Leadership as Meaning-Making in a Community of Practice*. Greensboro: Center for Creative Leadership, 1994. pp. 13, 14, and 18.

15. Indicators of a Healthy Civil Society

Robert O. Bothwell

The indicators a society chooses to report to itself about itself are surprisingly powerful. They reflect collective values and inform collective decisions.

— Donella H. Meadows

C IVICUS is a new international organization dedicated to advocate, promote, and protect civil society organizations and the autonomous citizen action they advance. In mid-1996, it initiated an exploratory project to investigate the feasibility of a Civil Society Watch. This project was to be modeled after the Human Rights Watch and the World Watch Institute's *State of the World*[1] reports which have had powerful effects on world leaders' thinking and action.

Shortly into the project, it became clear that measuring the status of civil society in various countries required an operational definition of what constitutes *healthy* civil society. This paper is a beginning attempt to provide that definition. It is a "work in progress" that needs input from academicians and practitioners around the world.

APPROACHES TO DEFINING CIVIL SOCIETY

In surveying the literature on civil society, four different emphases in defining civil society can be discerned. First, scholars such as Robert Putnam, Larry Diamond, and Francis Fukuyama[2] focus on what they see as the *results* of a strong civil society — the behaviors they believe healthy civil society produces including trust, reciprocity, tolerance, and inclusion. Other writers highlight peaceful dialogue, transparency, flexibility, and listening. These traits and the networks of civic engagement they develop add to a society's *social capital*. The more social capital a society has, the more efficient its transactions and the more productive it is. The government runs better. The economy functions better. Thus, measurement of the levels of trust, tolerance, and these other individual behavioral traits might tell us a lot about how healthy civil society is in different countries.

Government operations and economic interactions, historically and currently, also contribute to social capital. For example, if government historically has respected and adhered to a country's constitution and laws, then trust and reciprocity could be at high levels, even if civil society has been functioning only nominally. Or, historically, if an economy has functioned with substantial efficient transactions among individuals and groups who are not related to one another through family, tribe, or clan, then again trust and reciprocity could be at high levels, even if civil society is not significant. Thus, examination of a society's behavioral traits may not tell us definitively whether a country has a healthy civil society or not.

Second, other students of civil society, such as Rajesh Tandon, David Brown, and John Clark,[3] focus on the *preconditions* that must be met before a healthy civil society can come about. These might also be called the *foundations* for a healthy civil society. Note that these are preconditions or foundations for a *healthy* civil society, not for any kind of civil society. Civil society can develop in the absence of these preconditions, or at least in the absence of some of them, but it cannot become healthy unless certain preconditions are met.

Several preconditions are often cited: freedom of speech, freedom of association, general rule of law, absence of political violence or war, and effective, capable government. Others have been suggested: freedom of religion, absence of tribal/ethnic/racial violence or war, multi-party politics, substantial literacy, lack of famine, a sizable middle class, and a healthy, participatory political culture. Citizen action to seek these conditions may be crucial; citizen buy-in certainly is. However, these preconditions are primarily secured by the state and the economy.

Such preconditions constitute an enabling environment for the development of civil society. Once met, they must also be maintained as foundations for a healthy civil society. Having achieved a healthy civil society, a country cannot expect to continue in this state, if, for example, freedom of speech or freedom of association ceases, or if political violence or war dominates the country.

Third, many who have considered what is a healthy civil society have sought to define it as a desirable state of *all* society. They suggest that only a small percentage of people can be poor, that free public education must be available to all, that income and wealth not be disproportionately distributed among the population, and that free or nominal cost health care be available to all. The United Nations Development Programme *Human Development Index* offers a more limited definition which measures a modified version of Gross Domestic Product, life expectancy at birth, adult literacy, and education enrollments as a way to compare development efforts in broader terms than those offered by the traditional economic income model.[4] The San Francisco-based organization Redefining Progress and others go much further by including measures of sustainability.[5] Nevertheless, while these schemes have great value in telling us how we are doing in socio-economic terms, they report on integrated, whole societies, not just on civil society as part of the whole.

Fourth, most who write about civil society define it in terms of its *composition*. While they agree that civil society is the realm between the individual and the state (government), there is wide disagreement about who is part of civil society and who isn't.

Most commentators exclude the family, tribe, and clan from civil society, as the connections between people within these groupings are hereditary and not transactions between strangers. Many exclude commercial, for-profit activities and business interest associations from civil society because for-profit motivations supersede "public good" impulses. Many also exclude political parties from civil society, especially political parties of the ruling government, because they are a critical part of the governing of the state. However, prominent academics disagree with each of these propositions. There is also considerable debate whether to include or exclude groups which exhibit "uncivil" behavior, such as extremist political and religious groups.[6] Most agree the following are part of civil society:

- Religious organizations, churches, mosques, temples
- Social clubs
- Social movements
- Community based organizations (CBOs)
- Private schools and colleges
- Free press and independent media
- Consumer associations
- Labor unions
- Professional associations
- Non-governmental organizations (NGOs) not otherwise identified above

However, agreeing who is and who isn't a part of civil society tells us little about the status or health of civil society.

DEFINITION OF A HEALTHY CIVIL SOCIETY

While many define civil society in terms of its composition, few define what is a healthy civil society.[7] This chapter seeks to remedy this situation by proposing a definition, and suggesting possible indicators, drawing heavily from observations and postulations in the existing academic and practitioner literature. The focus is on organizational activity for the public good. Individual activity, no matter how compelling, is routinely magnified and multiplied through the organizational activity that is the essence of civil society.

The first step is to define the significant indicators of civil society in *qualitative* terms, then, when appropriate, to suggest possible *quantitative* indicators.

Qualitative indicators were identified from searching the literature and reviewing the results with diverse focus groups, including the senior staff at World Learning and Partners for the Americas, and a group at the 1996 Cairo conference of the Institute of Cultural Affairs International.[8]

Quantitative indicators were extracted from world and regional indices such as the United Nations Development Programme's *Human Development Report,*[9] world surveys such as the *World Values Survey,*[10] and the literature on civil society. All possible quantitative indicators which fit the qualitative definitions are included. Some indicators are readily available for many countries; others will require future research.

None of these indicators, by itself, should be considered an adequate measure of a healthy civil society. Empirical research will be needed to identify the best indicators for each aspect of a healthy civil society.

To arrive at a definition of a healthy civil society, six basic aspects were identified. Each of these will be discussed below in detail.

- Organizational activity and resources
- Civil Society Organizations' (CSOs) relationships with government
- CSOs' relationships with the for-profit economy
- CSOs' relationships with tribal/ethnic/racial/religious divisions of a society
- Relationships among CSOs
- Communications among and about CSOs

Organizational Activity and Resources

High numbers, activity, and resources of each type of CSO might suggest a vibrant civil society, or even a healthy civil society, though some would disagree. Certainly, the obverse is true, that low numbers of CSOs or low activity or resource level among CSOs would indicate lack of a vibrant or healthy civil society. Activity and resources of CSOs can be measured in many ways:

- Number of CSOs per capita
- Number of members per capita
- Number of contributors (of money) per capita
- Number of beneficiaries per capita
- Number of people involved per capita (as volunteers, staff, board members, conference participants, program planners, beneficiaries, etc.)
- Annual expenditures per capita
- Annual expenditures as a percent of Gross Domestic Product (GDP)
- Annual expenditures as a percent of government expenditures
- Annual revenues from indigenous sources per capita

- Annual revenues from indigenous sources as a percent of GDP
- Annual revenues from indigenous sources as a percent of government revenues
- Employment as a percent of a country's total employment
- Employment as a percent of government employment
- Geographical dispersion of CSOs
- Sectoral variety (health, education, environment, etc.)

None of these measures tells with certainty whether civil society is healthy or not. Even if there is a norm for a given region, a single indicator may tell us little. Over time, however, empirical research might separate out which of the above indicators are the best predictors of a healthy civil society.

Also, all the above indicators are not applicable to each type of CSO. For example, the number of members per capita (i.e., dues-paying, active members) might well apply to religious organizations, social clubs, community-based organizations, consumer organizations, trade unions, and professional associations, but it is not necessarily applicable to social movements, NGOs, private schools/colleges, or media.

Data are available from many sources. Johns Hopkins University Comparative Non-profit Sector Project, headed by Lester Salamon and Helmut Anheier, is collecting data on annual operating expenditures, revenue sources and employment of CSOs in 25-30 countries, including the developing world and Eastern Europe. The project's definition of CSO is more limited than that proposed above, but broad enough to be useful.[11] The *State of the World Atlas* by Michael Kidron and Ronald Segal provides data on trade union membership and the status of trade unionism around the world.[12] Association membership in 45 countries can been obtained from the *World Values Survey.*[13]

CSOs' Relationships with Government

Fundamental to most scholars' observations on civil society is a description of CSOs' relationships with government. Seven basic relationships are:

Legal Protections Offered by Government

Indicators of legal protections offered by government include:[14]

- Extent to which separate legal entities can easily be formed as an exercise of the freedoms of speech and association.

In many countries, a CSO has to gain approval for its legal existence by securing the consent of a government agency or department, or sometimes of a legislative body. Thus, conformance with the general political direction of the government is often the price of official approval. On the other hand, when legal requirements for establishment of a CSO are published, generally adhered to, and administered by a government body neutral to a CSO's program, CSOs can be easily organized.

- Extent to which government registration and reporting requirements are limited to those minimally necessary to instill public confidence in the openness and accountability of CSOs.

Overly demanding requirements set the stage for the government to manipulate the process for granting continued approval of CSOs. Also, extensive reporting requirements might call for sensitive or proprietary information to be made available, thus opening up the possibility that a government could misuse this information by providing it to the media or to rival CSOs.

- Extent to which CSOs' acts and decisions are subject to the same rights of administrative and judicial review that are applicable to other legal entities.

Ideally, CSOs are not treated as second class citizens but receive the same treatment as other businesses and legal entities.

- Extent to which CSOs have the same rights to participate in public hearings and comment on published governmental regulations as other legal bodies.

Opposition to Government

It is generally agreed that elements of civil society must be able to oppose the government if civil society is to be considered healthy. If civil society is the aggregation of diverse citizen interests between the individual and the state, some of these diverse interests surely would contradict state policies. If these interests cannot be expressed publicly, how would governments' power ever be checked?

This opposition can be discerned in many ways. Three are:
- Extent of CSOs' public opposition to government policies or practices.
- CSOs' success in publicly opposing government policies or practices.
- Government opposition to CSOs' policies or practices.

Indicators could be measured by content analysis of key media, counting the number of distinct cases for each item above, the sectoral variety of cases (for example, in education and health), and the number of column inches in newspapers or prime-time news minutes on radio and television devoted to each case. Legislation passed, averted, or defeated could also be a measure of opposition.

Cooperation with Government

Cooperation with government can be indicated by government inviting CSOs to participate in governmental activities, or by CSOs obtaining governmental participation in CSO activities. Policy and program planning, evaluation, and implementation are all possible activities.

Most agree that CSOs' cooperation with government is as essential to a healthy civil society as their opposition is. Having both indicates government and CSOs take each other seriously and accept that differences must be aired to be properly dealt with.

Again, a variety of indicators are possible. Several are:

- CSOs' participation in legislative or administrative hearings.
- CSOs' participation on government study or oversight commissions.
- Government participation on CSO-initiated study or oversight commissions.
- Government participation in CSO programs.
- CSOs' responsiveness to government registration and reporting requirements.

Indicators could be measured by content analysis of key media, as with "opposition to government" above. Also, the number of CSOs and government representatives participating in the first three items above can be tallied.

Autonomy from Government

Cooperation with the government often raises questions about CSOs' autonomy from the government. All the "cooperation" indicators above may be seen as government co-optation of CSOs rather than as autonomous parties working together. Therefore, there must be some evidence of substantial CSO autonomy, other than opposition to government, if there is to be healthy civil society. Such autonomy could be indicated by CSOs receiving a preponderance of their funding from non-governmental sources or by having CSO staff and board members known for their opposition to relevant government policy.

Alternatives to Government

When CSOs organize health clinics in low-income neighborhoods, when mothers organize food kitchens in *favellas*, or when neighborhoods organize community policing and court systems, they are initiating alternatives to what many think governments should do. Some indicators of this might be:

- Variety of alternative services such as health, education, public safety, and social services provided by CSOs.
- Magnitude of alternative services as measured by money spent and the number of participants involved.

Formal Encouragement by Government

Legal protections offered by the government are a form of encouragement. So, too, are some of the modes of cooperation noted above. Other more direct forms of encouragement include:

- Tax exemptions for CSOs, in recognition that they seek the "public good" rather than individual private gain.
- Tax deductions or credits available for private contributions to CSOs.
- Government funding of CSOs.

Holding Government Accountable

Both opposition to and cooperation with the government can involve holding government accountable. Many commentators have identified this activity to be a primary one for CSOs in a healthy civil society. Holding government accountable means tracking a government's major policy pronouncements, speaking out when government practices do not live up to policy, and initiating action to correct discrepancies between policy and action.

CSOs' Relationships with the For-Profit Economy

Since most scholars exclude the for-profit economy from civil society, then CSOs' relationships with it are crucial. Four basic relationships are:

Opposition to Major For-Profit Interests

Opposition to major for-profit interests should be seen in the same vein as opposition to government — it is legitimate, inevitable, and desirable.

There are many examples of civil society opposition to major economic interests. One is an organization advocating that large growers use natural pest control agents rather than pesticides. Another is United States consumer advocate Ralph Nader and his multiple public interest organizations challenging the automobile industry because of its disregard for the safety of drivers. Still another is Chico Mendez and hundreds of environmental organizations challenging clear-cutting by logging companies in the Amazon rain forest. Indicators include:

- CSOs' public opposition to major for-profit interests.
- CSOs success in their public opposition to major for-profit interests.
- Major for-profit entities' opposition to CSOs.

Indicators could be measured by content analysis of key media, as with "opposition to government" above.

Cooperation with the For-Profit Economy

Cooperation can take place in a multitude of ways. A women's organization can work with businesses to provide training, motivation, and support to women executives who want to crack the "glass ceiling." An environmental organization can work with a fast food business to substitute recyclable paper cups and plates for Styrofoam™ ones. Not-for-profit hospitals can work with for-profit hospitals to more efficiently offer medical services that require high cost equipment. Many indicators are available, six of which are:

- Public support by business for CSOs' public policy campaigns.
- Business funding of CSO activities.
- Cause-related marketing by business, such as a business paying a CSO to help sell products or services in return for payment.
- Business participation in CSO-initiated study commissions.
- Corporate representatives serving on CSO boards of directors.
- CSOs providing contract services to business.

Indicators could be measured by content analysis of key media. Annual reports of corporations and CSOs could be examined on a sample basis.

Autonomy from the For-Profit Economy

Cooperation with for-profit business often raises questions about CSOs' autonomy from business. All the indicators in the above category may be seen as business co-optation of CSOs rather than as autonomous parties working together. Therefore, there must be some evidence of substantial CSO autonomy, other than opposition to business, if there is to be healthy civil society. Such autonomy could be indicated by preponderant funding coming from non-corporate sources or by issuing research reports critical of corporate practices.

Alternatives to the Traditional For-Profit Economy

Many CSOs offer alternatives to people not served by the for-profit economy. CSOs make food and shelter available to the hungry and homeless because of a failure of economic systems to provide them. Many CSOs are focusing on microenterprise development because of the unwillingness of conventional banks to loan money to the poor, especially women. Non-profit recycling centers have been set up because the initial cost of collection and recycling is uneconomic in conventional terms. In some northern hemisphere locations with severe winters, non-profit consumer buyer clubs sell fuel more cheaply than commercial sources. Possible indicators include:

- The variety of industries with CSO-generated alternative products and services.
- The magnitude of alternative products and services, as measured by money spent and the number of consumers involved.

CSOs' Relationships with Tribal, Ethnic, Racial, and Religious Groups

Most wars being fought today are internal battles within nation states and among tribal, ethnic, racial, or religious groups. A healthy civil society ameliorates or prevents conflict, violence, and war among tribal, ethnic, racial, and religious divisions of society. Two possible indicators are:

- Number of formal efforts to bridge differences among tribal, ethnic, racial, and religious groups.

  Existence of effective organizations whose mission is to bring together key representatives of different tribes, ethnic, racial and religious groups can do much to develop critical communications among them, thereby expanding trust, tolerance, reciprocity, inclusion, peaceful dialogue, transparency, flexibility, listening, and other behaviors that build social capital.

- Number of informal efforts to bridge differences among tribal, ethnic, racial, and religious groups.

  Most organizations do not have a formal mission to bring together the strangers from different tribes, ethnic, racial, and religious groups. Nevertheless, many CSOs do bring together diverse people —as employees, volunteers, board members, or program participants — thereby bridging cultures on a one-to-one basis.

Relationships Among CSOs

Connections among CSOs across sectoral lines and through civil society infrastructure organizations is critical to healthy civil society. Individuals as staff, volunteers, and boards of directors also provide critical bridging across CSOs. Indicators include:

- Organizations bridging with different types of CSOs.

  CSOs connecting with other similar CSOs, for example, a metal workers trade union with a seafarers union, builds relationships among strangers and increases the stock of social capital. It is relatively easy for a union to connect with another union, regardless of the type, but for a union to relate to a college, church, or international relief agency is a professional and social leap. Successful relationships among different types of CSOs are more difficult to achieve and therefore, can potentially generate more social capital.

- Organizations bridging sectors.
  Similarly, bridging communications gaps between sectors — such as health, education, social services, and environment — also has its challenges but expands the possibilities for strangers to trust one another, which is a key to building social capital.

- Development of infrastructure organizations dedicated to protecting and expanding civil society.
  Such organizations are the Independent Sector in the United States and the Asian Pacific Civil Society Forum in Asia.

• Individuals' propensity to cross CSO boundaries.

Individuals play a huge part in connecting CSOs. A staff person of one CSO may serve as a volunteer on a totally different type of CSO, as well as on the board of directors of a CSO in another sector. For example, in Brazil members of Christian-based communities are often simultaneously leaders of unions, women's groups, and social movements. This cross-fertilization may be even more powerful than CSOs bridging the gaps among CSOs because the multitude of individuals involved may be much greater than the number of bridging organizations.

Communications Among and About CSOs

Communications play a powerful role in everyone's lives. Governments, businesses, CSOs, and individuals have been made and broken by communications. When there was no Internet, e-mail, fax, television, radio, telegraph, or telephone, communication consisted of the printed word and face-to-face conversation. The communications revolution has changed all that. Availability of fax and e-mail is reported to have played a significant part in the breakdown of the Iron Curtain in Eastern Europe and Russia. Reports from Latin America and Africa confirm the power of these new media to connect the dispossessed to the rest of the world, despite the desires of ruling despots.

There can be no healthy civil society without good communications. Four types of indicators stand out:

Independence of Media

The media must be free to report what's happening. Control of the media by government does not permit the communication necessary for a healthy civil society to develop. Similarly, when the media considers only profit and does not report news that may offend advertisers or other powerful interests, communication is stifled and civil society suffers.

Freedom House, a New York non-profit organization, publishes *Freedom in the World: The Annual Survey of Political Rights and Civil Liberties,*[15] which measures the freedom of a country's media to criticize local and national governments in 187 countries. Also, data on censorship are available in the *State of the World Atlas.*[16]

Media Attention

The media can be free and independent and still not report what is happening within civil society. In the United States alone, almost all CSO activities go unreported by the media. Nevertheless, some news gets through, and when it does, the effects are powerful for the CSOs involved.

Even if the news of CSO concerns and activities does not reach mass audiences, the leverage of media attention usually can be felt by key opinion maker audiences. No other means of communication can reach so many so efficiently. Thus, when CSOs receive no media attention or are invisible to the media, it is harder for civil society to function. A healthy civil society needs media attention.

Newspaper Usage

Robert Putnam's research on Italy reveals that newspaper readership is a prime correlate to healthy civil society.[17] On the other hand, he suggests television is a negative influence on social capital. Newspaper circulation per capita data are available from *The State of the World Atlas*.

Use of New Technology

Fax, e-mail, and the Internet are the liberating modes today that the telephone and telegraph were in the late 19th century or that radio and television were earlier this century. Governments can control the telephone system, through which faxes, e-mail, and the Internet are connected. However, government control can inhibit the market sector as well as civil society, so governments are unlikely to restrict telephone systems if they want to promote strong economic development. As telephone lines and satellite connections become more available worldwide, national boundaries are less able to prevent communications across them. CSOs' use of new technologies is critical to the growth of a healthy civil society. Possible measures could be:

- Ratio of CSO fax users to CSOs per capita.
- Ratio of CSO Internet users to CSOs per capita.
- Ratio of CSO cellular phones to CSOs per capita.

Fax machines and mobile cellular phones per capita data are available in the United Nations Development Programme's *Human Development Report 1996*,[18] for 83 and 54 countries respectively. Information on computers and computing power per capita is available in Lester Brown's *State of the World* report.[19]

CONCLUSION

The indicators of healthy civil society suggested above are somewhat ideal and data are not readily available for most of them. When data are available, they may only be for a limited number of countries. Nevertheless, most of these indicators listed have been suggested by academics and practitioners and deserve serious attention.

I welcome feedback from readers to enable me to take these indicators another step closer to application.[20] Perhaps over time, as this set of indicators is revised and refined, researchers will be encouraged to collect more appropriate data. Eventually, publication of an annual *State of Civil Society in the World* report would encourage the development and protection of civil society and the concomitant advancement of vitally important citizen participation.

NOTES

1. Lester R. Brown et. al. *State of the World 1994: A World Watch Institute Report on Progress Toward a Sustainable Society.* New York: W. W. Norton & Company, 1994.

2. See for example (a) Robert D. Putnam. *Making Democracy Work: Civic Traditions in Modern Italy.* Princeton: Princeton University Press, 1993 and "The Prosperous Community: Social Capital and Public Life." *The American Prospect.* Number 13, Spring 1993. (b) Larry Diamond. "Toward Democratic Consolidation." *Journal of Democracy.* Volume 5, No. 3, 1994. pp. 4-17. (c) Francis Fukuyama. *Trust: The Social Virtues and the Creation of Prosperity.* New York: The Free Press, 1995.

3. See for example (a) L. David Brown and Rajesh Tandon. "Institutional Development for Strengthening Civil Society." Volume 11, Number 9. IDR Report. Boston: Institute for Development Research, 1994. (b) L. David Brown. "Creating Social Capital: Non-governmental Organizations and Intersectoral Problem-Solving." In W. W. Powell and E. Clemens (ed.) *Private Action and the Public Good.* New Haven: Yale University Press, 1995. (c) John Clark. *The State and the Voluntary Sector.* Washington DC: The World Bank, Human Resources Development and Operations Policy, October 1993.

4. United Nations Development Programme. *Human Development Report 1996.* New York: Oxford University Press, 1996. pp. 135-137.

5. Clifford Cobb, Ted Halstead and Jonathan Rowe. *The Genuine Progress Indicator.* San Francisco: Redefining Progress, 1995.

6. See Saad Eddin Ibrahim. "Populism, Islam, and Civil Society in the Arab World," regarding the role of Islamic militants in the Middle East, particularly Egypt. p. 53-66.

7. However, some who have written about the so-called "third wave" of democracy, such as Larry Diamond and Samuel Huntington, have examined the role and function of civil society in democracy in detail.

8. For more detail about the conference see Introduction p. 11.

9. United Nations Development Programme. *op. cit.*

10. World Values Study Group. *World Values Survey, 1981-1984 and 1990-1993.* Ann Arbor: Inter-University Consortium for Political and Social Research, 1994.

11. Lester M. Salamon and Helmut K. Anheier. "Social Origins of Civil Society: Explaining the Non-Profit Sector Cross-Nationally." Working Papers of the Johns Hopkins Comparative Non-Profit Sector Project. Number 22. Baltimore: The Johns Hopkins Institute for Policy Studies, 1996.

12. Michael Kidron and Ronald Segal. *The State of the World Atlas.* London: The Penguin Group, 1995.

13. World Values Study Group. *op. cit.*

14. This section is derived from Karla Simon. "Legal Principles for Citizen Participation." Washington DC: International Center for Not-for-Profit Law, 1996. (Draft, October 10).

15. James Finn. (ed.) *Freedom in the World: The Annual Survey of Political Rights and Civil Liberties, 1993-1994.* New York: Freedom House, 1994.

16. Kidron and Segal. *op. cit.*

17. Putnam, Spring 1993. *op. cit.*

18. United Nations Development Programme, *op. cit.*

19. Brown et. al. *op. cit.*

20. Contact me at the National Committee for Responsive Philanthropy, 2001 S Street NW, Suite 620, Washington DC, 20009, USA. Phone 202-387-9177, fax 202-332-5084, and e-mail NCRP@aol.com.

16. Organized Religion: The Forgotten Dimension

Koenraad Verhagen

*The creation and development of the third sector is rooted in
religious principles and moral thought.*

— Amani Kandil

I n most parts of the world, the culture of ordinary people is profoundly
rooted in religion. Their vision of reality and aspirations for social transformation are related to religion and may differ from the mindset of progressive social actors — non-governmental organizations (NGOs) and people's
organizations — who have put their faith in civil society as the new development paradigm.

Without integration of the religious factor and strategic alliances with organized religion, civil society is not likely to gain sufficient strength to
effectively counteract secular and religious fundamentalism. Conceptually,
organized religion and its structures might be conceived as a sector in its own
right, different from the first sector (the state), the second sector (the market)
and the third sector represented by civil society.

There have been many attempts at social transformation which, implicitly
or explicitly, have tried to relegate religion and its symbols to the exclusive
domain of private life. Such a policy is short-sighted and counterproductive in
the long run. It plays into the hands of fundamentalists by creating a dichotomy
between religion-free promotion of development and reactionary, religion-
based conservatism.

HOW SECULAR IS THE WORLD?

Secularization as an organizing principle for the division of powers in society
has, in many countries, effectively counteracted the accumulation of worldly
powers by leaders of religious communities. At the same time, at the level of

the individual and society, it has led to a separation between believing and acting. Religion and religiously inspired practice have had to give way to rationalism and economism which have become the two dominant forces for shaping present-day, modern society. Yet, in spite of their hegemony, there are other contemporary realities and movements which can help restore balance and counter the devastating effects of unbridled capitalism. Religion can provide the necessary counterweight, considering that:

- Most of the world's people consider themselves religious and belonging to a religious community, with concurrent religious practice and rituals basic to their existence, their being, and their sense of well-being.

- Faith-based communities are potentially powerful agents of change. They can humanize society, contribute to tolerance, and call for justice. However, religious diversity and differences can also be misused in pursuit of conflict and war.

- All religions promote a systematic reflection on human behavior from the viewpoint of good and bad, values and norms, responsibility, and life choices. They provide the ethical basis of society, even if, as history has shown, they provide no guarantee that people will live up to those values and ethics which, in principle, they endorse.

- In Western countries, there is a renewed interest in spirituality. It is a reaction to a modern way of life which, for many, has lost its purpose and meaning. The spiritual view is a different, almost forgotten way to look at things. While recognizing the value of human rationality and its achievements in technology and science, the spiritual mind also sees certain forms of rationality as an obstacle to full humanity. It is critical of the blatant rational approach for its one-sidedness and its claim of autonomy. The intense longing and search for the spiritual dimension of life is a global phenomenon which re-emerges where it had almost disappeared from customary thinking.[1]

A FOURTH SECTOR

In *Citizens, Strengthening Global Civil Society*,[2] de Oliveira, Tandon, Isagani and others make a commendable effort to describe "the third sector" and civil society. According to them, the third sector brings together non-profit service organizations and membership-based civil associations. Perhaps to the surprise of some, but not without justification, social initiatives which have emerged from the business community, such as foundations and corporate grant-making organizations, are included in their global citizen alliance known as CIVICUS.[3]

They distinguish the third sector from the first and second sectors by its non-state and non-profit nature. What is innovative in the CIVICUS approach is that it sees itself not in opposition to, but as complementary to, the first and second sector with which it seeks to foster alliances at a personal and institutional level. No longer has it the pretentious claim, not to say the arrogance, of being the sole protector of human well-being and the only valid expression of social concern.

As a person belonging to one of the largest Christian denominations, my question is: Where in this triangular framework of the first, second, and third sectors do we, or should we, locate the organizational structures of the faith communities of the world religions? These structures exist with different degrees of centralization and organization in all religions and some of their representatives are influential actors in the social and political field. The question is not purely theoretical, but also practical. Is it possible to bring to life proclaimed third sector values such as solidarity, compassion, responsible behavior, refusal of violence, and oppression without seeking strategic alliances with the major world religions — Buddhism, Christianity, Confucianism, Hinduism, Islam, and Judaism?

In the pursuit of a more just society, the sector represented by organized religion, which I call the fourth sector, cannot be overlooked in any strategic design for societal transformation. At times, it has offered a frame of reference and a structure for powerful action aiming at political or social transformation. Telling examples of political and religious leadership of communities under oppression are those inspired by Mahatma Gandhi and the Dalai Lama, the Basic Ecclesial/Human Communities found in different parts of the world which seek to live "Gospel values," "Buddhist values," or others in everyday life, and the metamorphosis in Central and Eastern Europe since 1989 where church involvement has had large political and social implications.

However, there are, regrettably, other cases where organized religion, especially where it represents the majority, has proved to be an impediment to desirable change and even has been instrumental in suppressing the fundamental rights of religious minority groups. For the protagonists of civil society, the issue is not whether one does or does not welcome religion's existence, influence, and involvement. They are simply there and even if religious leaders or groups, for tactical reasons, refrain deliberately from social, political, and economic engagement, such a position can have far-reaching implications for the evolution of the third sector.

A similar question can be asked in relation to political parties and their structures. In democratic countries with multiparty systems, this sector cannot be simply equated with the state or the third sector itself. Both the political sector and the religious sector have had a major influence in the dynamics of the third sector and formation of civil society organizations (CSOs). CSOs often try to influence them, but at the same time, strive for greater autonomy and reject unnecessary religious or political interference.

FAITH AND HOPE: MOTIVATORS FOR SOCIAL CHANGE

In each continent, examples abound of powerful social movements and leaders who have come up with ideas for social change, who have engaged in social action, and who were inspired by faith and vision rather than by calculated self-interest or desire for personal aggrandizement.

The civil society agenda demands concerted action at community, national, and international levels to solve global issues. Can this agenda materialize if citizens themselves are not filled with an irrational faith, belief, and hope; a spiritual vision which recognizes that poverty and injustice can be overcome; a belief that conflicts can be prevented and peace will prevail; a recognition that each person is unique and deserves respect for his/her own sake and which sees each human being as belonging to a wider, interdependent universe? Who will feed that irrational optimism and spirituality at the personal, community, and higher levels? In other words, can the aspirations of a value-driven, civil society movement be realized without due recognition of religious inspiration and motivation as underlying forces?

As a regular traveler to so-called developing countries, I am confronted by the magnitude of the problems which stand in the way of positive social and economic change. It is because I have met people driven by faith that I feel enriched and know that something can be done. Social analysis and logical thinking can make an important contribution to the design of strategy and purposeful action. Yet the belief that something can change for the better and persistently pursued efforts to realize this do not come so much from the sharpness of analysis but from an inner feeling and drive, deep within human beings and communities fed by communion with the unknown, unseen, and ultimate source of life. Religions, both as institutions and movements, have an important task of feeding that kind of irrationality which facilitates the construction of faith-based communities of hope, especially among the poor, as well as social and political change and conflict resolution by non-violent means.

The culture of the people in most parts of the world is essentially religious. This is often overlooked by protagonists of popular participation or not integrated in the practice and theories they have developed. The World Bank report *The World Bank and Participation*[4] is an eminent publication by "participation experts" from different parts of the world. It is a typical example of a religion-free approach to participation. To neglect the religious element is the opposite of participation. Grassroots people have a strong desire to improve their conditions of living, to overcome poverty, to liberate themselves from all sorts of oppression, but they are not willing to commit themselves to social change if this would imply the denial of their own culture and identity which are marked by religious practice and thinking. Secular development institutions such as international and bilateral organizations or NGOs should acknowledge that a people's perspective of development cannot be couched in secular terms alone. Project documents, which for administrative reasons may have to be written in purely secular language are, from a people's perspective, a travesty of reality.

Was Marx wrong when he said religion was the opium of the people? I think so. Religion provides the antidote against a mentality and system that values people only according to their income-generating and productive capacities. It underscores the uniqueness and dignity of each human being as a person who matters irrespective of age, gender, race, or social background. It integrates the poor, the middle class, *and* the rich in a common endeavor of transformation and does not exclude anyone.

My fear is that groups such as CIVICUS and its allied networks remain hollow structures constructed by a civil society elite and without a firm rooting in society and people's culture, if they do not engage in interaction and communication with faith communities and their leaders. What is innovative in the CIVICUS approach, however, is its strategy of dialogue. The third sector is not only a counterforce against the other sectors. By dialogue and recognizing the specific functions of the other sectors, it seeks to influence them, is open to learn from them, and tries to identify areas of common concern and coherent action. A dialogue process which does not include organized religion may turn out to be irrelevant to large sections of society.

During his nomadic life as an international scientist, the paleontologist visionary Teilhard de Chardin (1881-1955) was often confronted with situations of political turmoil and war. He concluded that to master the new times to come, it was important to recognize one basic fact: in the evolution of humankind, there is an irresistible and accelerated movement of people becoming more and more linked to one another and moving towards one another. In spite of many differences and conflicts, this movement forges people and individuals closer to one another. We live at the beginning of humankind coming together into one organized block which has become conscious of its inner coherence as a group of people.[5]

If Teilhard's vision is correct, then the challenge ahead is how to move from a United Nations concept towards a "united peoples" concept. In that perspective, the specific contribution of the third sector is to identify those issues and initiatives which can bring us together into one whole, multicultural structure which unites people and links them together in a global society.

BETWEEN SECULAR AND RELIGIOUS FUNDAMENTALISM

In this global movement towards unification, some movements and currents of thought are dangerous pitfalls. They can be grouped into two major categories, secular fundamentalism and religious fundamentalism. Both are utopian visions of society. They share the following characteristics:

- *A single, closed system of values and moral prescriptions which regulates the life-orientation and behavior of the individual and groups of people. There* is no space for questioning the premises on which the system is built. Deviant forms of thought or behavior are not tolerated and are heavily sanctioned by exclusion or other forms of social or material punishment of which execution is the most extreme form.

- *A monolithic approach towards the organization of society or special segments of it such as the economy.* Cultural, religious, political, or regional differences are not accommodated. There is a centralist style of administration. Since the ultimate cause is good, all means are used and justified, even if they cause great suffering.

Marxist-inspired regimes, most of which came to an end with the fall of the Berlin wall in 1989, were expressions of secular fundamentalism. At present, the so-called neo-liberal — in fact neo-conservative — ideology projected by leading international financial organizations and the business community also has strong fundamental traits. It puts the economy and its growth at the center as the only way to salvation and provokes the exclusion of the weaker sections of society and entire nations from mainstream development. There are heavy sanctions for non-compliance. In the sphere of religions, unfortunately, we have seen fundamentalist streams becoming stronger almost everywhere, often linked with cultural revival and reaffirmation of ethnic or national identity.

To progress, all sectors of society, including the third sector, are in constant need of reform. The third sector is not free from fundamentalist thinking and action, characterized by aggressive and oversimplified language and a "we are right, they are wrong" mentality. In cases where socio-political action has not had the desired effect, the typical reaction is "we need to do more of the same" and inject even more energy and force. The ultimate aim is to gain victory over the enemy instead of striving for harmony and the creation of a new equilibrium which will include the enemy. Korean theologian Dr. Chung Hyun Kyung[6] refers to this dichotomy as masculine energy which divides, against feminine energy which brings together. In the predominantly masculine approach, dialogue with the state or the business community is considered a waste of effort and arouses suspicion. Cooperation is regarded as co-optation.

The third sector has an important task in counteracting this kind of fundamentalist thinking and action, both in its own ranks and in society at large. To be effective, two conditions have to be fulfilled at a personal level:

- *The realization that no one and no group of people is totally free from fundamentalist thinking and inclinations.* Fundamentalism is an understandable reaction at times when one's own culture is in crisis and when life orientation and strategy have to be rethought in light of a changing environment.

• *The recognition that personal and social transformation are closely connected.* As Belgian development worker Jef Felix said at the 7th Annual Conference of the International Network of Engaged Buddhism in Thailand, March 1995:

> Both engaged Buddhism and (Christian) liberation theology lead to the cultivation of spiritual values and virtues, such as love, understanding, wisdom, and compassion in the *very midst of social engagement.* Inner and outer transformations of suffering, ignorance and violence are closely connected .... Spirituality for our times has to integrate both very closely.[7]

If we acknowledge this close relationship between inner and outer transformation, the time may have come for many persons and organizations involved in social action to reflect on their inner personal and organizational culture. By a one-sided orientation on the outer transformation of society, we become extremely vulnerable as persons and organizations. Out of frustration, we become violent in our thinking and reactions to the outer world. By just listening only to ourselves we feed our ignorance and finally we suffer. By implication, in our efforts towards the realization of basic human rights, and in our understandable rage about non-respect of the same, we should take care not to let ourselves be carried way in processes of polarization which make it impossible to effectively play mediating and negotiating roles within and between sectors.

ACTION POINTS FOR A GLOBAL AGENDA

In the quest to achieve personal and social transformation, there are many paths to follow. NGOs and community-based organizations, or people's organizations, have a key role to play in this task. Recent United Nations global conferences have highlighted the growing importance of such citizen associations and networks. They have also underscored the need for a more people-centered, inclusive global society to replace the divisive, economically-driven one we know today. I will elaborate on each of these points.

Call to the Third Sector

Participants from NGOs in the 1995 Copenhagen World Summit for Social Development produced a statement and a host of documents and declarations critical of the official texts and lack of commitment by governments. What did not come very much to the fore, even in the NGO Forum, was the cumulated valuable expertise and experience of many NGOs and people's organizations in matters of self-help promotion and social development. At these kind of events, NGOs tend to focus on what governments and intergovernmental and international financial organizations should do or should not have done, rather than putting forward their own agenda as social actors, defining their role in social development, and claiming a more suitable political climate to carry out what is primarily their contribution to social development.

From the Social Summit, several fields emerged which could be anchor points for attention of the third sector in the years to come:

- It was agreed that each country, in the South and the North, will have a defined strategy for poverty eradication by the end of 1996. The UN Commission for Social Development has been given a mandate to monitor the progress achieved and problems encountered in the implementation. The Canada-based International Council on Social Welfare plays a central role in following this on behalf of NGOs by convening regional and sub-regional forums of NGOs to pursue Social Summit issues.

- The "feminization" of poverty has been recognized — 70% of the world's poor are women. The Beijing Conference and Forum worked to produce an action plan to counteract this process. What will be the third sector's contribution to the design, implementation, and evaluation of gender-specific poverty eradication strategies?

- The so-called 20-20 proposal that states that developing countries' national budgets and donor countries' aid budgets should devote at least 20% to social development.

National and international NGOs, networks, and coalitions have set up an NGO watchdog for social development called the Social Watch initiative. Its first report was published in early 1996 by the Instituto del Tercer Mundo, Montevideo.[8] A similar sort of action has been pursued by the German NGO Forum "World Summit for Social Development" in its publication, *Social Priorities in Development Cooperation: Implementing the 20:20 Initiative.*[9]

The summit strongly recommended strengthening the role of civil society and its participation in planning, implementation and evaluation of anti-poverty programs. If governments accept this, then it would be logical that CSOs be assigned an important role in the World Bank coordinated Poverty Assessments and discussion of Country Assistance Strategies. The NGO-World Bank Committee will follow up this and also press the World Bank to increase its levels of concessional lending in the social sector up to the summit standards.

Towards an Economy of Inclusion

Virtually all national economies are permeated by the global economy. It is a gradual process of economic integration, establishing mutual interdependence between nations and people. At the same time, its mechanics drag societies inexorably in the direction of duality and social disintegration. The powerful forces of economic modernization and internationalization exclude more people from mainstream economic development, especially those from the lowest income levels. Throughout the world, the opportunity for meaningful participation in the economy is denied to more and more people. As a labor force, they become redundant. Less educated, less skilled, less gifted, too old or overburdened by family duties, they become dependent on social welfare safety nets or private charity.

This economic exclusion eventually leads to social and political exclusion and provides a fertile ground for fundamentalist and ethnocentrist streams mentioned earlier. The informal sector, a stepping stone for a few to improve their social position, is often no more than a coping mechanism to ensure a minimum standard of living. It creates its own ghettos and underclass. Upper and middle class people increasingly see those who cannot cope as a burden to society and the taxpayer. In an insidious way, this perception and the exclusion it fosters undermines the message of Christianity and other religions of the uniqueness, intrinsic value, and dignity of every human being.

The third sector has not yet developed a credible alternative to the attractive and dominant ideology of free markets, global trade, and economic growth, fueled by a vision of change which puts the economy at the center as the engine of development. Nor has it addressed neo-liberal thinking and attitudes which see and defend processes of exclusion as the unintended but unavoidable price to be paid for modernization. The current economic system divides people more than that it brings them together, it thrives more on competition than on cooperation, and in spite of its integrative impulses at a global level, it creates deep social divisions at lower levels.

Some Asian countries are often cited as models for their spectacular economic ascent, for their effective collaboration between government and private business, between local and international entrepreneurship and finance. Once a higher level of international integration has been attained, states and their governments discover they have lost control over the flow of goods, services, and capital which shape global and national economies. By 2000, the World Bank forecasts that more than 90 percent of the world's workers will live in countries with strong links to the global economy.[10] The World Bank also projects falling wages and job insecurity in rich and poor countries alike as a result of the growth of the world's labor force and the limited labor absorption capacity of growing economies. It is a considerable step forward that an institution known as a vestige of neo-conservatism admits that today, the constant search for gains in productivity leads to the loss of jobs. The well-documented 1995 report describes these trends as inevitable. Michael Walton, the report's team leader, admits that "We have not yet found the magic bullet that will take laid-off skilled workers and retrain them for the new world."[11]

Whose design is this "new world?" Who has asked for it? Where is the democratic process steering the world in that direction? The most disquieting aspect in current trends of exclusion is its presumed inevitability. Should one wait for some bright World Bank economist to invent the magic bullet that will effectively undo the ill effects of the present system? Certainly, we need bright economists in the World Bank. We also need them in NGOs, social movements, universities, and elsewhere to help to make clear to policy makers and the public at large, what the various options are and their social consequences.

THE CHALLENGE

The challenge ahead is to find a way to break out of economic determinism and to bring together economic and ethical considerations at various levels where economic decisions are being taken. We should admit that economic practice is also ethical practice and part of the process of creation; that economic practice is a way to express convictions and faith; that the economy does not get its direction from natural laws which are beyond human control but from a multitude of decisions taken by different persons acting at different levels; and that economic decisions are taken by persons acting as consumers and producers, as policy makers or policy executives, as bankers or captains of industry. There is a need for us, as members of civil society, to communicate and interact with all these persons or their representatives with the aim of transforming their, as well of our own, inner system of thinking, and simultaneously, the outer economic system which regulates and steers economic behavior.

At the micro level, there is a myriad of valuable experiences of alternative forms of consumption, production, and financing, as well as examples of human behavior and interaction which have stood the test of meaningful improvement of standards of living, economic justice, and responsible citizenship.[12] Many such examples can be found in the associative economy, that is, service-oriented, cooperative activities which are authentic expressions of a third sector economy.[13] They are not mainstream and perhaps never will be but are important signs of hope because of the principles on which they operate. As long as they are not isolated and dependent on donated funds, they influence other sectors of economic activity. An international citizen network could provide the framework for documentation of such experiences under the leadership of one or more research-oriented institutions.

The third sector cannot transform society alone. It has to build up alliances with other sectors. It has the potential to act as a credible and powerful force at national and international levels. For this, it has to appreciate and understand the close relationship that often exists between aspirations of people and their religious convictions. Organized religions and their institutions, which can be seen as the fourth sector, bring many of these people together and can provide a strong moral and ethical basis to any human undertaking. The third and fourth sectors are natural allies in development.

NOTES

1. See chapter by Brian Stanfield. "Citizen Analysis: Discerning the Signs of the Times." pp. 167-182.

2. Miguel de Oliveira and Rajesh Tandon. et al. *Citizens: Strengthening Global Civil Society.* Washington DC: CIVICUS, 1994.

3. CIVICUS is a global network of organizations promoting civil society and is headquartered in Washington, DC, USA. See reference above for more details.

4. The World Bank. *The World Bank and Participation.* Washington DC: The World Bank, 1994.

5. H. Cuypers and G. Migloire. *Pierre Teilhard de Chardin.* Kasterlee: De Vroente, 1962. Translated from the French *Presence de Teilhard de Chardin.* Paris: Editions ouvrires, 1962.

6. Dr. Chung Hyun Kyung is Associate Professor of Systematic Theology at Ewha Women's University, Seoul, South Korea. Her opening address at the Seventh Assembly of the World Council of Churches (WCC) in Canberra, Australia, in February 1991 was one of the most controversial lectures ever delivered to a WCC assembly.

7. Jef Felix. First meeting with INEB (CIDSE CLV Programme, restricted circulation) Brussels: CIDSE, 1995.

8. Social Watch Network. *Social Watch: The Starting Point.* Montevideo: Instituto del Tercer Mundo, 1996.

9. German NGO Forum. *Social Priorities in Development Cooperation: Implementing the 20:20 Initiative.* Bonn: Friedrich Ebert Stiftung, 1996.

10. The World Bank. *World Development Report 1995.* Washington DC: The World Bank, 1995.

11. Michael Walton. *World Bank News.* June 29, 1995.

12. See Mildred Leet. "Increasing Social Capital through Microenterprise." pp. 221-233.

13. Koenraad Verhagen. *Self Help Promotion: A Challenge to the NGO Community.* Amsterdam: CEBEMO/Royal Tropical Institute, 1987.

17. Core Values of Civil Society

John Epps

The strength of the civic sector is found in the number and diversity of its organizations and the speed and flexibility with which they form complex and shifting alliances around shared values and interests.

— The People's Earth Declaration:
A Pro-Active Agenda for the Future
Rio de Janeiro, Forum '92

As in many innovative undertakings, the search for civil society is blessed with a somewhat ambiguous focus. As Robert Bothwell points out in his chapter, "civil society" means many different things to its different proponents.[1] However, its most common property seems to be people's desire to improve their social environment through their own initiative. For some, this has to do with a highly developed associational practice with people routinely volunteering for civic duties. For others, it is more structural with institutions providing just and equitable care for members of the society. Some emphasize more the economic dimensions, while others focus on the political.

Far from being unfortunate, this ambiguity may be the single most provocative aspect of the entire discussion. When people try to clarify their dreams, they often enrich one another. The resulting image or concept is the product of multiple perspectives beyond what a single visionary could produce. It is what we are attempting to create from the best of the present as the world moves into a new millennium. This is why the question of common values is so relevant.

For the sake of this discussion, I will use the term "civil society" to refer to that condition or state in which the multiple processes of society or any of its units are functioning in harmony with one another. I will use a tri-polar model of society — economic, political, and cultural — as its framework.[2] When society is "in balance," its economic processes are providing adequate sustenance, its political processes are adequately organizing various interests and influences, and its cultural processes are providing a sense of meaning and significance. None of the three dominates the others.

Thinking of balanced processes, however, is no mean feat. People deeply rooted in one part of society have difficulty according respect or even recognition to those in another. For instance, those working in business tend to be anti-government and, while possibly generous to cultural pursuits, are somewhat dubious of their practical value. On the other hand, people in political life tend to regard business as something to be controlled or milked since, it is thought, greed is its primary value. Cultural advocates often harbor prejudice against business as shallow and selfish and against politicians as a power-hungry group of tyrants. These common biases hardly contribute to a situation of balance but nonetheless, are part of the landscape in the 1990s.

In this situation, is it possible to contemplate civil society in which a condition of balance exists? Are we condemned to endure a perpetual state of conflict at best alleviated by an uneasy truce? Or might it just be possible to find a perspective in which the three basic dynamics are complementary, in which respect and admiration are the rule rather than the exception? Tensions may continue but might they not be exercised in a manner that enriches the ensuing practice?

In projecting civil society as society with its economic, political, and cultural dynamics in balance, I believe such balance is possible and necessary. However, for it to occur there must be a consensus on core values that undergird those dynamics and give them direction, flexibility, and meaning.

CHALLENGES TO DETERMINING CORE VALUES

By "core value," I mean the principle(s) and/or ideal(s) at the heart of a social unit. Without them, the identity of the unit would be so altered that it would be a different social unit. There are core values to each of the social processes. In fact, the processes are external manifestations of internal values.

This is not new. Every social invention has embodied certain values; *liberté, égalité, fraternité* preceded the outcome of the French Revolution, while "no taxation without representation" preceded the invention of United States Congress. The Renaissance was preceded by the Reformation and, while its values were quite different, they were similarly opposed to the reality of the 16th century. Values sustain and provide guidance and flexibility to structures. When social values collapse, structures may endure, but with a brittleness that is dehumanizing. New social forms come from new or recovered social values. Values lend flexibility to social structures. No structure totally exhausts its value so that constant improvement is possible. Values provide direction which structures constantly attempt to follow with varying degrees of success. Values give meaning to the people who participate in social processes so they are both validated for their efforts and distanced from the particulars of the structure.

Two issues arise when the subject of values comes up:

- *Value relativism.* Are there any universal values or is it just a matter of preference? Certainly, different cultures embody different values. Should one group or culture try to impose a set of superordinate values on the world? Who gives them that right?

- *Value identification.* How do we determine core values? For whom are they core? Should we just pick a list from the dictionary or get a group of clergy together or vote for the ones we like?

First, let us examine relativism. It is manifestly true and significant that different societies embody different values. The clash of values is part of the trauma experienced by business people operating overseas for the first time. But one need not travel to recognize the relativity of values; the news brings it into our homes. When an American teenager was jailed and whipped in Singapore for defacing a car, the degree of outrage on both sides was instructive. Many Americans could not fathom how a society could condone such inhuman treatment for an essentially mischievous act. Simultaneously, sensitive Singaporeans could not fathom how a society could let a vandal get by with destroying someone else's property. Here was a classic case of individualism versus group rights and there is no easy resolution.

It will not do, for example, to say simply that all values are dependent on their social setting and "When in Rome, do as the Romans do." A whole field of business ethics attempts to guide companies that are becoming increasingly global and finding the need to operate in societies where bribery or favoritism or unsafe conditions are the norm. Nor will it do to imagine a set of super values to which everyone globally will subscribe. Social conditions and traditions vary widely around the world and values underlying social organization must honor that fact.

A good example of an effective resolution of this issue is Malaysia. The nation is populated by three distinct cultures — Malay, Chinese, and Indian. This is not a melting pot; each retains its identity through dress, religion, food, and festival. Yet there is neither competition nor rivalry nor hostility among them. It is commonplace to see a Malay woman with a veil, a Chinese woman in a miniskirt, and an Indian woman in a sari engaged in animated conversation. Each enjoys the others' food, making Malaysia a culinary delight. Furthermore, each culture celebrates the others' religious festivals — Chinese New Year, Hari Raya Puasa, and Deepavali are all public holidays, and people commonly visit their neighbors who are celebrating. Christmas and Wesak Day are also included in the panoply of holidays involving Christians and Buddhists in the festivities. It is a marvel that factors which elsewhere in the world divide people, and sometimes occasion the most appalling atrocities, are here respected and honored.

This is not by accident. Public law forbids offending members of another religion. Violators can be imprisoned. Since this is an Islamic nation, the law particularly prohibits offending Muslims, but by implication, others are included. All are Malaysians with valid membership in the body politic. This is not to say there are no inequities or tensions, only that Malaysia has something valuable to offer the world in dealing with diversity of values. The core value operative in this situation is the preservation of public order as a precondition for development which will benefit everyone. People have experienced the alternative and found this quite a reasonable position.

The dilemma of value relativism need not paralyze, nor will it guarantee a "higher synthesis." It may simply point to other factors that must be considered. Goran Hyden reminds of this in his opening chapter to this book:

> There will be a struggle between the 'universal' and the 'particular,' i.e., the idea that human values and norms are shared by all regardless of race and religion on the one hand, and that these norms and values are determined by specific cultures, on the other .... Regardless of the particular circumstances prevailing in a country, building civil society requires the ability to empathize, i.e. to see the world from the side of those not yet convinced. It requires strategy but also the readiness to make tactical concessions.[3]

Secondly, how do we identify core values and for whom? The private sector is paying substantial attention to company values as an important element of a motivating vision for staff. Typically, the most senior people are expected to name the core values and others are expected either to conform to those values or to leave. Increasingly, that is changing. Companies are finding ways to involve people in naming the core values of their work and are discovering that this involvement contributes to instilling the values in people.

In their book *Built to Last,*[4] James Collins and Jerry Porras documented 18 "visionary" companies and found each had three to five core values the company would hold even if these values became a competitive disadvantage. The values may have emerged from the founder's dream, but often they were the result of people working together over time and discerning what kept them going.

Since civil society involves the creation of social capital through the active participation of its citizens, it follows that participatory process are the most appropriate way for people to identify core values. Such processes may yield different results for different societies or social groups. Although we live in a global environment, we still live in particular cultures with particular traditions and approaches. There may be no single set of core values for civil society in the new millennium. Still, a participatory search for core values will contribute significantly to developing attitudes of respect and honor that are preconditions for civil society.

DISCERNING CORE VALUES: A MODEL

One such process was carried out at the conference on "The Rise of Civil Society in the 21st Century" in Cairo, Egypt, in September 1996.[5] Forty people from 16 nations engaged in a think-tank on core values. Through a participatory process, they developed a set of core values which for them constituted the foundation of civil society. What follows is the results of their deliberations, using the tri-polar model of society described earlier.

Economic

The core economic value was "sustainable sufficiency." It will not do to promote or perpetuate a vast disparity between rich and poor. This is not to advocate a leveling of income nor an effort to negate substantial rewards to valuable contributors. It is, however, an attempt to end the mindless race for more and more, and the equation of one's social worth with one's income. How much is enough? This is a question to be pursued with vigor.

There is clear evidence that continuing on the path of "get all you possibly can" is not sustainable, either in terms of the earth's resources or in terms of human energy. The economic sector of society must provide adequate means for people to survive and thrive; it need not provide the means for extravagance. Sustainable sufficiency demands the use of resources in a way that does not unduly deplete them; production must be undertaken with attention to environmental impact; and distribution must accord every member of society an opportunity to access its benefits.

Thorny issues remain, however. How can we provide a "floor" to income without the debilitating dependency caused by welfare programs? Is it possible to aim for full employment in a diminishing job market? Where do we draw the line between environmental protection and resource development? Within an overall value of sustainable sufficiency, these questions demand innovative solutions.

Political

The core value was "inclusive participation," within the framework of the rule of law. Members of a society are valued for their contributions to the society and are expected to offer those contributions. People are free to participate in the decisions that affect them. This doesn't mean getting one's way all the time. While consensus is cherished, there can be no tyranny of the minority where a few dissidents withhold consent and block progress. In this schema, individual license to do as one pleases is a value secondary to that of inclusive participation.

Inclusive participation raises its own questions. Would this value deny people the option of non-participation? For example, must voting be mandatory with enforcement against those who abstain? Would the value deny people the option of opposition to the notion of participation? Must dissidents be stifled to preserve the society? Does the group always have power over the individual, whose very dissent may generate creative options not yet conceived by the mainstream? The answers to these questions have to be worked out in the context of the particular society in which they are raised. Most likely, they will be different in an urban metropolis and in a rural village. Limits are always placed on individual freedom, but in a situation in which the core value is inclusive participation, those limits seem to be both tolerable and conducive to responsibility.

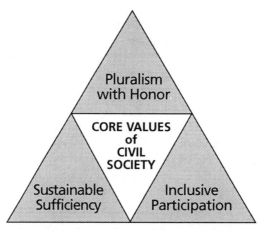

Figure 1. Core Values of Civil Society

Cultural

The core cultural value was identified as "pluralism with honor," meaning that all the diverse elements of society are worthy of value and respect. There can be no discrimination based on race, tradition, or culture. Each element of society's mosaic must be recognized, appreciated, and valued. There can be no hierarchy of traditions, but rather an appreciation for them all. This does not mean a single person must forego his or her background and merge into some sort of homogenous mass. Quite the contrary. One is expected to manifest and remain part of one's heritage as a significant contribution to the social mix.

Again, questions arise. Does this mean people are "stuck" with their traditions and discouraged from adopting another? Is criticism an anathema to civil society? Isn't globality generating a new culture that will replace some of the traditions we have honored? Certainly, culture is a dynamic and evolving reality whose future shape can only be imagined. But whatever its shape, assuming the significance of all its diverse elements will provide useful guidance.

So diverse are the world's cultures and so opposed are many of its practices that this value is extraordinarily difficult to implement. But the alternative

— ethnic cleansing and its dehumanizing corollaries — run totally counter to civilized functioning, as Susan Fertig-Dykes graphically illustrates in her chapter on building civil society in the former Yugoslavia.[6] Working out ways to live together as a diverse people in our global villages remains a challenge to be resolved. Viewing that challenge in the context of "pluralism with honor" offers a perspective that may prove useful.

Two of these three core values — inclusive participation and pluralism with honor — emerging from the deliberations of this particular group of people are remarkably similar to those commonly espoused as norms of civil society, namely trust, reciprocity, tolerance, and inclusion.[7] The values named by this group could well be arrived at by many other groups doing the same exercise, but to argue that such exercises are a repetitious waste of time would be missing the point.

The act of developing these statements of value was an act of civil society itself. It brought together a highly diverse group of people in free association, used a participatory method to elicit their input and build a consensus, and demonstrated trust, reciprocity, tolerance, and inclusion. This group of people embodied the values they identified. Similarly, people at various levels of society, from community to region, need to identify their own core values for civil society.[8] The process of identifying core values of civil society will help sharpen our focus on what we aspire to and will assist in no small measure in realizing those aspirations.

NOTES

1. Robert Bothwell. "Indicators of a Healthy Civil Society" pp. 249-262.
2. For an elaboration of this model as it was developed by the Institute of Cultural Affairs, see appendix, pp. 293-294.
3. Goran Hyden. "Building Civil Society at the Turn of the Millennium." p. 42.
4. James Collins and Jerry Porras. *Built to Last: Successful habits of Visionary Companies.* New York: HarperBusiness, 1997.
5. The Cairo conference was sponsored by the Institute of Cultural Affairs International. This particular thinktank had participants from Australia, Belgium, Bosnia, Brazil, Canada, Croatia, Egypt, India, Japan, Jordan, Malaysia, Nigeria, Taiwan, The Netherlands, the United Kingdom, the United States, and Zambia.
6. Susan Fertig-Dykes. "Sparks of Hope In the Embers of War: The Balkans." pp. 67-82.
7. These particular values are mentioned by Michael Bratton, quoted in "Civil Societies and NGOs: Expanding Development Strategies." InterAction's Civil Society Initiative. Report of Workshop #1. 9 February 1995. p. 3.
8. See appendix for a set of procedures to do this, pp. 298.

Section IV

FUTURE DIRECTIONS
FOR CIVIL SOCIETY

18. Why Civil Society Will Save the World

Alan AtKisson

*Never doubt that a small group of thoughtful, committed
citizens can change the world. Indeed, it is the only
thing that ever has.*

— Margaret Mead

In the beginning, there was civil society. Long before there were corporations or governments or even a market economy, there were self-organized
groups of people committed to the betterment of human life. Civil society
has saved the "world"[1] time and time again. I propose that civil society is saving the world now, and that the rise of sustainability — an ideal which, like
democracy, has grown out of civil society's creative ferment — is both example and proof of its central role in the advance of human well-being.

In the final analysis, "civil society" is nothing more, and nothing less, than
a fancy name for "us." *We*, the people, are civil society, and all the ways we
come together — in families and volunteer organizations, in schools and religious institutions, in amateur sports teams, in political parties, and even just
at parties — are an expression of this. Wherever human beings gather to achieve
a common purpose, outside the boundaries of government or the market
economy, there is civil society.

When the history of the 20th century is written, civil society will be cred-
ited with incubating the solutions to the enormous challenges we face, testing
those ideas in the field, and mobilizing support to spread them wherever they
need to go. Examples abound. How did we fend off mass starvation? Private
foundations funded independent researchers in non-profit institutes, who invented the green revolution and spread it, despite enormous governmental
and economic resistance at first. Human rights? Thousands of people participated in the campaigns of Amnesty International and other groups, forcing
governments and businesses to take the issue more seriously. Environmental
protection? Grassroots groups organized, became educated, protested, sued,
in some cases risked and gave their lives to protect a specific piece of land or
the integrity of the whole Earth. The great bureaucracies of the world came

lumbering after them — in some cases reluctantly, but in others with gratitude that "ordinary citizens" were willing to push the issues out of the shadow of denial and into the daylight of consciousness.

Civil society is the people, and the people know what needs to be done. More importantly, the people know what needs to be *learned*, and unlike the great bureaucracies — which must worry about protecting their status, image, funding, and power — the people are willing to risk looking foolish, or worse, in order to learn something both new and desperately needed.

Only 250 years ago, democracy was just such a foolish idea. How did it gain currency? Not as an act of government — the governments of the day were profoundly anti-democratic — but as an act of self-organized conscious-ness-raising. It happened through conversations, letters, and self-published pamphlets. It grew from individuals reading history and talking in groups about the future. It drew on close observations of other people's ways, particu-larly (in the United States) the Native Americans whose contributions to democracy in that country have never been adequately recognized. Ultimately, the fate of democracy rested with the courage of people willing to make the sacrifices of leadership, and with the more extraordinary courage of those willing to make the even greater sacrifices involved in following their leader-ship.

Bureaucracy is not a bad thing. Indeed, civil society's *modus operandi* is to create bureaucracies which institutionalize the hard-won new learnings and values. Conversations about democracy, for example, led to the American Revolution, which led to the formation of the United States Government. Bu-reaucracies are the agents of implementation, and they are often filled with people dedicated to working inside their highly complicated systems to effect change. However, the great bureaucracies, such as government, large corpo-rations, and other major institutions, are rigid by design, because they are monuments to the past. They are the institutionalized memory of the things humanity has already learned how to do, and their job is to preserve that memory from being lost or degraded. We therefore cannot expect them to lead us in charting the course to the future.

The task of designing the future is inevitably left to civil society, that is, to us. The name of that future — today's equivalent of yesterday's foolish idea of democracy — is sustainability.

Sustainability is often accused of being a vague term, but it is only vague to those who resist embracing it. Prior to the American Revolution and the founding of the new republic, democracy was subject to the same criticisms: "Its meaning is open to interpretation." "It's fine in theory but impossible in practice." "The people couldn't possibly govern themselves." "There are no working examples (since Athens)." "It's being co-opted by the power structure." The criticisms mostly emanated from those who felt they had something to lose from democracy's wide acceptance. We now have hundreds of years of history, in the United States and around the world, that proves the criticisms wrong. Not that democracy is without flaw; as Winston Churchill quipped, "Many forms of government have been tried, and will be tried in this world of sin and woe. No one pretends that democracy is perfect or all-wise. Indeed, it has been said that democracy is the worst form of government, except for all those other forms that have been tried from time to time."[2] Still, few would argue today that democracy has not been a blessing for humanity. No one can dismiss democracy — in all its forms, with all their warts — for being vague.

Complexity is often mistaken for vagueness and sustainability is, like democracy, a complex idea. A shift from monarchy or dictatorship to representative government involves the creation of a system of checks and balances, the design of constitutions and legislatures, choosing rules and procedures for voting, and countless other tasks. Many innovations have to be attempted, tested, and adopted by the nation's people and institutions. Likewise, a shift away from the primacy of economic growth toward a more balanced approach that weaves together environmental, cultural, and economic vitality as an integrated whole engages society in an enormously complex and creative challenge.

There are many definitions of sustainability, but in creating definitions, I believe the simplest is best. To continue drawing parallels with democracy, the words "government of the people, by the people, and for the people" contain all the basic principles of representative government. Its concrete expression is left to the actual practice of governing. For some years, my colleagues and I have used a similarly short, but less eloquent phrase to sum up sustainability: "long-term cultural, economic, and environmental health." The emphasis in this definition of sustainability is on *health over the long-term*, for both people and nature, and on the *integration* of the factors that constitute that health. These two concepts, followed to their logical conclusions, are enough to give birth to the broadest array of concrete sustainability practices, in all the world's different places and cultures.

The complexity of sustainability is daunting. The changes it requires of us, in order to practice it, are every bit as revolutionary as democracy was more than two centuries ago. However, just as the demand for democracy was driven by (among other things) rising levels of wealth and education among the common people, historical forces are at work that demand an embrace of sustainability. Nature, for one, is sending clear signals that something is terribly wrong, from disappearing songbirds, to falling human sperm counts, to cracks in the ice around Antarctica. There are equally dire indicators of stress in our culture, with young people bearing the harshest impact of declines in public investment, the widening gaps between rich and poor, and an increase in public insecurity. Even the economy — the growth of which has been the primary focus of human labor for several hundred years in some societies — is faltering. Official growth rates and other indicators are high and rising, but the growth is now coming at the expense of quality of life, and poverty is worsening worldwide.

These signs of stress call for nothing less than the reinvention of our economies, technologies, cities, dwellings, vehicles, and the social patterns that go with them. Redeveloping human civilization to be sustainable is the great task of our era, and it will undoubtedly take the better part of a century's effort. Fortunately, the work has already begun. At the end of the 20th century, we are approximately one generation into a process of transformation that will require at least three generations to complete. Here are some signs of the work in progress:

- Hundreds of communities around the world are instituting new measures of progress to guide their development, so they can change direction and move toward sustainability. Whole nations are following suit.

- Professional and institutional associations — from scientists, to economists, to religious leaders — are coming together to share ideas and make consensus declarations on what must happen to ensure a sustainable future. These gatherings and statements work like lenses, focusing both *at*tention and *in*tention on the challenges before us.

- Demonstration projects are bursting out on every continent, at every scale, from school yards to former industrial waste dumps, proving that economic development can be done in ways that protect, or even restore, the environment.

- New ideas on everything from tax policy to revolutionary new forms of energy production and conservation are starting to pour out of the world's think tanks, laboratories, and academic institutions.

- Governments, from the United Nations and its member states to small towns everywhere, are writing sustainability into their resolutions, policies, and even their laws.

- Several multinational corporations are putting themselves on 20-year tracks to thoroughly transform themselves into sustainable operations, creating zero emissions and net positive benefit to both society and the Earth.

- Hundreds of thousands of relatively wealthy and middle-class people are beginning to question their allegiance to the consumer economy and to practice some form of "voluntary simplicity" or "low-impact lifestyle."

Where did nearly all of these growing movements, including those in government and business, originate? Where did the inspiration, the ideas, the motivation, and first tries come from? There can be no question but that the answer is civil society. Volunteers, visionaries, and what might be called "valuaries" — people of conscience, who struggle to fully integrate their values into their professions and personal lives — created the ideas, worked in small groups to refine them, worked in ever larger settings to test them out and disseminate them more broadly, until even the great bureaucracies could no longer ignore what the rest of society took to be common sense. This process gives proof to Margaret Mead's dictum: "Never doubt that a small group of thoughtful, committed citizens can change the world. Indeed, it's the only thing that ever has."[3]

Civil society is humanity's conscience, its early-warning system, and its laboratory. It is where the world's thoughtful, committed citizens go about the business of changing things for the better. Civil society makes a transformation to sustainability possible, because it is the place where many of humanity's best traits come forth, most strongly and most reliably. Among these traits are our capacities to be:

Participatory. Civil society is a game anyone can play. There is a place for everyone at the table, and everyone has something to contribute. The more the merrier, the more diversity the better, because out of the sparks caused by rubbing our differences together come the fires of enlightenment. Civil society's capacity to welcome and channel the creative capacities of virtually everyone is the source of its energy and power.

Open. The doors to so many of our institutions are closed to new participants, new perspectives, and new ideas. Closed also, too often, are the eyes and ears of the people who work within them. Civil society is a place where we can look and listen for what is actually happening, for what other people are feeling and saying, for what is true. Participating effectively in civil society demands, and facilitates, nothing less than our full awareness and openness to the world around us.

Synergistic. When people and their differences come together, in relationships built on mutual respect and trust, their combined intelligence becomes much greater than the sum of its parts. Information jumps out of its tracks. Unexpected and fresh ideas are evoked. Chance conversations lead to improbable new realizations. Skills are combined and recombined to do impossible things. These are all examples of synergy at work, and nowhere is synergy more vitally present than in the participatory and open atmosphere of civil society.

Intuitive. The world is full of information. It's difficult to know what data, questions, and directions are most important. More difficult still is sorting out the signals from the noise. Most difficult of all is finding a way to hear what *isn't* being said — a way to invite the unconscious into consciousness. "Intuition" is a name we give to the deeper capacities of our minds to process vast quantities of information in ways we ourselves are not, perhaps cannot be, consciously aware of. The results of the mind's deep reflections are served up to consciousness in the form of a "sense," "feeling," or "hunch"; only later are rationalizations attached to them. Needless to say, intuition — perhaps our most valuable and misunderstood mental capacity — is far more at home in civil society than in the great bureaucracies of government and the marketplace.

Truthful. Given the many incentives against honesty — from pain, to profit, to power — it's a miracle that telling the truth happens at all. It is most able to happen in civil society, where the incentives against it are weakest. Civil society is where we learn to "speak truth to power," first by telling the truth to one another. Personal truth. Scientific truth. Spiritual truth. Telling the truth is the single most powerful thing we can do to change the world. When we tell it together, as a group, a community, or a society, we tear away the curtains of denial, and prepare the stage for real creativity.

Innovative. Virtually all new ideas have their genesis in civil society. Why? Trying new ideas is risky. They often fail. If you are an elected official, business owner, or the leader of any large public institution, you can rarely afford to fail. You depend, in fact, on those outside the circle of accepted authority to come up with new ideas and test them, to sort the wheat from the chaff. Civil society is the incubator of new ideas. It thrives on risk, creativity, novelty, and invention, and offers the best of what it finds to the institutions of society, as a gift.

Visionary. Among ourselves, outside the boundaries of what we do for work or what our government expects of us, we are free to dream. We are free to imagine a community, a country, a world that is better than the one we live in now. We are free to share that image with each other without fear of persecution or ridicule, and to imagine how it might come to be. We can see it all coming together in the mind's eye — the people, relationships, intuitions, bold new ideas, and honest assessments — and creating something new and beautiful. Civil society is where idealism resides. Idealism gives birth to vision. Vision is what makes any effort to serve the common good vital and inspiring.

Enthusiastic. An "enthusiast," in the word's original meaning, meant "one who is filled by God." Regardless of our religious beliefs, the work of civil society is founded in faith. Faith is not somber; it is exuberant, alive, sometimes wildly excited. Enthusiasts dedicate their lives to something bigger than themselves, as an act of radical love. They are less interested in making a fortune or a name for themselves, and more interested in making a difference. The great bureaucracies frown on enthusiasm, because enthusiasm is the harbinger of change. In civil society — among our family, friends, fellow volunteers, and colleagues in service — we are free to fully express our excitement about working for the betterment of humanity and the Earth.

You can remember these eight traits by their first letters; civil society enables us to be POSITIVE about the future. Being positive doesn't mean being in denial; indeed, overcoming denial is one of civil society's main functions. It also doesn't mean walking blithely into difficulty, unprepared for the possibility of failure. It does mean cultivating *hope*. As one of the greatest living philosophers of civil society, Vaclav Havel, has written, "Hope is . . . not the conviction that something will turn out well, but the conviction that something makes sense [to do], regardless of how it turns out."[4]

In a way, we already know how it's going to turn out. As city planner and urban philosopher J. Gary Lawrence once observed, "Sustainability is inevitable. The only question is how we get there."[5] In other words, do we consciously work together to effect a transformation? Or do we let the collapse of cultures, economies, and ecosystems force us into it? Both roads lead to sustainability. Both are fraught with challenges and difficulties. The first is infinitely preferable, because the second involves inconceivable amounts of suffering. This is why many thousands of people have already dedicated their lives to a vision of transformation — a vision of hope.

Sustainability is a natural step in humanity's evolution, the next major breakthrough in enlightenment since democracy. Just as democracy brought with it a liberation of the human spirit and an outpouring of creativity, sustainability carries with it other gifts of the spirit, gifts we can only begin to glimpse. With Havel, I believe that sustainability "makes sense."

Humanity will achieve sustainability, just as we have achieved a seemingly impossible, and nearly global, transition to democracy. The field of possible futures also includes collapse, transformation, and most likely, some mix of the two. Civil society will be the critical actor, in any event. When collapses of any kind occur, civil society will be there to pick up the pieces and rebuild. When transformation occurs, civil society will undoubtedly have hatched it. It's all but inevitable: democracy will give birth to sustainability, and civil society will save the world.

NOTES

1. The word "world" derives from the early Germanic language and is made up of two words whose Old English forms were *wer*, "man," and *ieldo*, "age." Thus, its literal meaning was "the age of man" or perhaps more appropriately, "the age of consciousness."

2. From a speech by Sir Winston Churchill in the House of Commons, London, 1947.

3. Locating the source of this popular quote has proved a challenge. It appears not to be something Mead ever committed to writing. Eric Utne, founder of the American magazine, the *Utne Reader*, reports that Mead made the remark to Robert L. Schwarz of the Tarrytown School for Entrepreneurs when Schwarz was organizing salon-type events in Tarrytown, New York. Schwarz passed on the comment to Utne, who also promoted salons as part of his magazine's concern for citizen engagement. The quotation certainly fits well into this context.

4. Vaclav Havel. *Disturbing the Peace: A Conversation with Karel Hvizdala.* Translated by Paul Wilson. New York: Alfred A. Knopf. p. 181.

5. Personal communication.

Appendix:
Tools for Building
Civil Society

THE SOCIAL PROCESS

In the midst of its community reformulation work on Chicago's Westside in the 1960s, the Institute of Cultural Affairs (ICA) discovered the need for a comprehensive model of how the processes of society work together to care for the whole. It developed a referencing system for analyzing social processes based on the economic, political, and cultural dynamics of society.

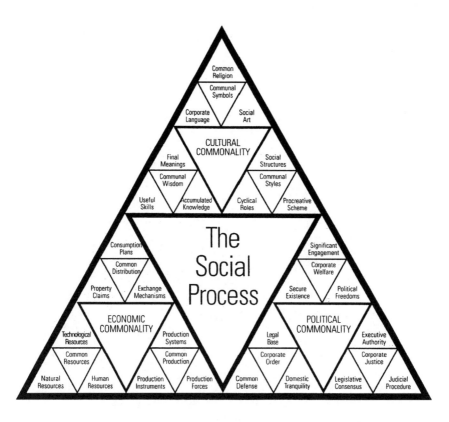

Figure 1. The Social Process Triangles

ICA began this work by undertaking a massive year-long study project involving hundreds of staff around the world. Participants read over a thousand "leading edge" books and articles covering all aspects of the workings of society and a diversity of cultural perspectives. From these sources, they selected key terms to describe those activities which appeared pivotal to the functioning of any society. They plotted this data onto a series of triangles, beginning at the first level of economic, political, and cultural triangles [See Figure 1.]. Each of these was further divided into three more triangles: economic processes into resources, production, and distribution; political processes into order, justice, and welfare; and cultural processes into wisdom, style, and symbol. Each of these was further divided into three more, and so on, down to 729 triangles, covering six levels of social processes.*

---

* A booklet of these triangles is available from the ICA Global Archives at 4750 North Sheridan Road, Chicago, Illinois, 60640, USA. Phone (773) 769-6363, fax (773) 769-1144, e-mail: icaarchives@igc.apc.org.

THE TECHNOLOGY OF PARTICIPATION (TOP)™

The hallmark of the work of the Institute of Cultural Affairs (ICA) is its use of participatory methods which help people plan together, reflect on their experience, and motivate them to action. Known as the *Technology of Participation™ (ToP),* these methods have been invented, tested, and refined over three decades of working with communities and organizations around the world.*

ICA programs demonstrate the effective application of *ToP* methods in diverse settings and assist groups of people to develop their own "culture of participation." ICA staff design and facilitate programs with businesses, community associations, public agencies, and non-profit organizations. They teach *ToP* methods in both public courses and in-house training programs. Although the names of the courses vary from country to country, the content is similar. Currently, three basic *ToP* courses are offered in the USA and a number of other countries:

- **Group Facilitation Methods** — includes a demonstration, explanation, and hands-on practice of a group discussion model, a workshop process for building consensus, and an action planning method for turning ideas into accomplishments.

- **Participatory Strategic Planning** — builds on the above in a four-step strategic planning process that elicits the group's vision, articulates the blocks to that vision, creates strategies to deal with those blocks, and ends with an accountability-based implementation plan.

- **Toward A Philosophy of Participation** — explores many of the underlying patterns and assumptions that make participation work, as well as additional tools for the adventurous facilitator.

In addition to offering the above courses and on-site training, the ICA in Phoenix, USA coordinates a *ToP* Fast-Track Trainer program, a national *ToP* faculty, and a regular International *ToP* Training of Trainers event. *ToP* Facilitator Guilds also operate in a number of cities in Europe and North America.

* For further information, contact the ICA Phoenix office: 4220 North 25th Street, Phoenix AZ 85016, USA. Phone: (1-800) 742-4032 or (602) 955-4811, fax (602) 954-0563, e-mail: icaphoenix@igc.apc.org.

COMMUNITY PARTICIPATION WORKSHOP*

The Community Participation Workshop (CPW) is an example of the application and adaptation of the ICA's participation methods in a particular setting. A detailed set of procedural guidelines for the CPW was created during the training course for government extension officers in Ethiopia. It was originally thought the workshop would take place over two days, but after the first CPW it was shortened to one day. It was found that with proper care, discussions could be completed within that time; more importantly, farmers were reluctant to commit more than one day to attending a workshop due to the heavy burden of their work. In most districts, the CPW eventually evolved into a two-session event, the first on identifying development needs and the second on constraints, then creating proposals and a local action plan.

The first session began with introductions and an explanation about the purpose of the workshop. Past development accomplishments and current initiatives within the community were listed. Then those assembled for the CPW were divided into three groups: one for women, one for youth, and one for

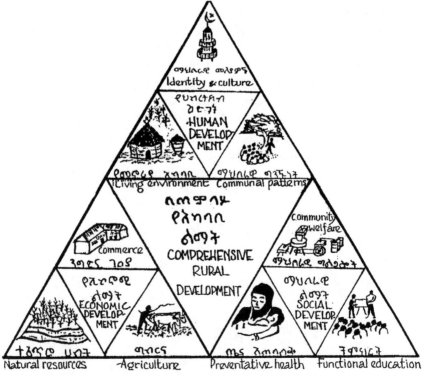

Figure 2. Comprehensive Local Development Triangles

men. In the smaller groups, the facilitators introduced the "comprehensive local development" triangles. [See Figure 2.] Using visual symbols, these triangles depicted a broad range of development topics:

- Economic development included natural resources, agriculture, and village industry and commerce.
- Social development included primary health care, functional education, and community welfare.
- Human development included living environment, communal patterns, and community identity.

People were then asked to consider the strengths and weaknesses of each major category in their own *kire*. This encouraged people to think comprehensively about development before they were asked about needs. Each group identified and prioritized five development needs which they thought were most important. Simultaneously, a special group composed of women, youth, and men created a map of the *kire*. After approximately an hour and a half, all groups reconvened to hear the results of one anothers' discussions.

Following the plenary on development needs, people returned to the three smaller groups to discuss the constraints and possible solutions to the top priority need they had identified earlier. Each group created an action plan for implementing that proposal through the use of local resources. The groups then reassembled to share their plans. As a final step to the CPW, coordinators were selected for all three community projects.

* From "Grassroots Empowerment in Ethiopian Villages" by Terry Bergdall and Frank Powell. For further information, contact Terry Bergdall, Methods for Active Participation, PO Box 34019, Lusaka, Zambia. Phone/fax: (260-1) 252825, e-mail: bergdall@zamnet.zm.

PARTICIPATORY RAPID APPRAISAL*

The main features of Participatory Rapid Appraisal (PRA) are:

Triangulation. A form of cross-checking. Accuracy is achieved through diverse sources and different kinds of information, not statistical replicability. Triangulation is done in relation to the composition of the team, sources of information, and mix of techniques.

Multidisciplinary team. The members of the PRA team should have different skills and backgrounds, so the different viewpoints of team members complement one another and provide a comprehensive picture of the situation. In this way, the team approaches the appraisal from several viewpoints, which results in new and deeper insights. All members of the PRA team are involved in all aspects of the study — design, data collection, and analysis. Ideally, the PRA team includes women and community members. PRA is a learning experience in which the participants also learn from one another.

Mix of techniques. The PRA techniques are taken from a wide range of possible tools, tailored to the specific requirements of the study.

Flexibility and informality. Plans and research methods are semi-structured and are revised, adapted, and modified as the PRA field work proceeds.

In the community. The main aspect of the PRA is learning from, with, and by members of the community. The team empathizes with the community members and strives to see their lives and their problems through their eyes. Most of the activities are done jointly with community members or by them on their own. PRAs are generally done too quickly for outsiders to become insiders. Therefore, it is important to have community members participate in the appraisal. Involving community members greatly facilitates interpretation, understanding, and analysis of collected data.

Optimal ignorance and appropriate imprecision. The PRA team avoids unnecessary detail, accuracy, and over-collection of data which is not needed for the purpose of the PRA. What is needed is decided through on-the-spot analysis. The team asks itself, "What kind of information is required, for what purpose, and how accurate does it have to be?"

On-the-spot analysis. Learning takes place in the field and the analysis of the information gathered is an integral part of the field work itself. The team constantly reviews and analyzes its findings in order to determine in which direction to proceed. It builds up understanding and narrows the focus of the PRA as it accumulates knowledge.

* From "Consulting Egypt's Local Experts" by Marlene Kanawati. For further information, contact Marlene Kanawati, Center for Development Services, 4 Ahmed Pasha Street, 6th Floor, Garden City, Cairo, Egypt. Phone (202) 354 6599 or 355-7558, fax (202) 354-8686, e-mail: cds@idsc.gov.eg.

A PROCESS FOR DISCERNING CORE VALUES OF CIVIL SOCIETY*

Step 1: Set the context.

"Like any organization, civil society is supported by core values. They lie underneath the structures and practices that constitute it. They are the invisible glue that remains stable, providing identity, cohesion, and direction to the people. Without core values, there is no civil society.

Core values are not changeable or relative; they define the social unit. If they change, the unit ceases to be, or at least ceases to be what it was. We want to try identifying some core values for civil society and begin thinking about how to propagate them.

In their book *Built to Last*, Collins and Porras suggest a method they call the MARS team: Suppose this group of people were sent to Mars to launch the best of the Earth's wisdom to initiate civil society. What values would we want them to represent?"

Step 2: Give the assignment.

Individually, then in small groups, look at each dimension of society — economic, political, and cultural — and the basic components of each of these dimensions and name the core values that dimension embodies when it is working well.

Step 3: Work as individuals and in buzz groups.

Discuss and select two or three values for each of the nine processes identified in the second level of the Social Process Triangles. Write each on a card and post it in the spot designated for that process.

(When this is done, depending on the size of the group, you will have a mess of cards with much overlap and a good deal of variety. This is not a problem.)

Step 4: Divide into three teams — economic, political, cultural.

Have each team take the cards in its arena and determine the group consensus regarding no more than three core values for that arena.

Step 5: Ask each team to develop a report to present its value(s) to the whole group.

Step 6: Discuss as a whole group.

Step 7: Identify the consensus.

* From "Core Values of Civil Society" by John Epps. For further information, contact John Epps, LENS International Malaysia Sdn. Bhd., Box 10564, 50718 Kuala Lumpur, Malaysia. Phone (603) 757-5604, fax (603) 756-4420, e-mail: icaklm@igc.apc.org.

The Institute of Cultural Affairs International

Purpose

People today are demanding a greater say in shaping their own lives and the societies of which they are a part. Shared responsibility is replacing hierarchical authority in governments, corporations, organizations, and communities. The ICA catalyzes that responsibility by teaching and demonstrating participatory approaches to leadership, planning, and action. It does this through facilitation and training programs which include strategic planning, consensus decision-making, and team building.

Why "Cultural" Affairs?

Many societies today are out of balance. Economic forces drive a global economy which has outstripped the capacities of national governments to hold it accountable. Political systems, even so-called democracies, provide little opportunity for inclusive citizen participation. Culture — those shared understandings, values, patterns, symbols, and stories that build community and provide a context for decisions — needs to be re-empowered if a more people-centered, sustainable society is to emerge from the present situation. It is the nurturing of these "habits of the heart and the mind," as Goran Hyden reminds us, that is at the core of civil society.

Origins

The ICA International (ICAI) was founded in 1977 in Brussels, Belgium. It is an international non-profit association which assists the activities and operations of autonomous national member Institutes (ICAs) and their global relationships.

Relations with Other Organizations

The ICAI has Category II consultative status with the United Nations Economic and Social Council, liaison status with the Food and Agricultural Organization, working relation status with the World Health Organization, and consultative status with the United Nations Children's Fund. It is a member of the International Council of Voluntary Agencies, a working partner with the Center for Our Common Future, and has served on the NGO Consultative Group for the International Fund for Agricultural Development. Member Institutes have their own relations with NGO networks and other bodies.

Funding

Funding for ICA programs comes from a broad base of contributors including individuals, trusts and foundations, religious organizations, companies, bilateral and multilateral agencies, and fees for service. Major grants have been received from AusAID (Australia), Caritas, CIDA (Canada), DANIDA (Denmark), the European Union, Food For All, Ford Foundation, Helvetas, ICCO, IFAD, JICA (Japan), Lutheran World Relief, Misereor, Near East Foundation, UNICEF, UNDP, USAID (United States), and Wilde Ganzen.

Locations

ICAs operate in Australia, Belgium, Bosnia, Brazil, Canada, Côte d'Ivoire, Croatia, Egypt, Germany, Guatemala, Hong Kong, India, Japan, Kenya, Korea, Malaysia, Mexico, the Netherlands, Nigeria, Peru, the Philippines, Portugal, Spain, Taiwan, the United Kingdom, the United States, Venezuela, and Zambia.

About the Contributors

Alan AtKisson is a writer, international consultant, and community organizer focused on sustainable development, cultural change strategy, and the effective management of businesses and non-profit organizations. He is the former executive editor of *In Context*, an award-winning journal of sustainability, and co-founder of Sustainable Seattle, a volunteer effort which pioneered a widely replicated model for community-based indicators. His writings have appeared in the *Utne Reader, Whole Earth Review, Environmental Impact Assessment Review, Aeropagus, Seattle Weekly*, and many other books and publications. He directs the National Indicators Program at Redefining Progress, a public policy institute in San Francisco, USA.

Terry Bergdall has been engaged in promoting grassroots development for more than a quarter of a century. His work has ranged from the inner city of Chicago to the impoverished coal fields of northern Japan. For the past 13 years he and his wife have lived and worked in Africa and presently reside in Zambia. In addition to a broad spectrum of freelance consultancy assignments, he is an active member of CARE International's Regional Resource Team for Management Development. He is also a PhD candidate at the Centre for Development Studies at the University of Wales. His book, *Methods for Active Participation: Experiences in Rural Development from East and Central Africa*, was published by Oxford University Press in 1993.

Robert Bothwell is President of the National Committee for Responsive Philanthropy, a US-based organization dedicated to changing private philanthropy to be more responsive to social justice and environmental issues. He initiated the first public examinations of community foundations and their responsiveness to the disenfranchised, and of corporate grant-making to racial and ethnic populations. His work has expanded the flow of information between foundations and grant-seekers and stimulated the development of women's funds nationwide. He is the author of numerous articles and reports on philanthropy, social justice, and urban finance.

John Epps, one of the original designers of the ICA's *Technology of Participation*, is concerned with the role of the private sector in promoting civil society. He has conducted seminars and consultations for more than 200 companies and organizations throughout Southeast Asia, the USA, and Europe on strategic thinking, customer service, quality improvement, and leadership development. In addition to chapters in *Approaches That Work in Rural Development* and *Participation Works: Business Cases from Around the World*, his articles have been published in professional journals in several countries. A resident of Kuala Lumpur, Malaysia, he is a leader of a global think tank for the recovery of meaning and values in the workplace.

Susan Fertig-Dykes, Director of the Institute of Cultural Affairs (ICA) in Bosnia and Herzegovina and founder of ICA Croatia, provides consultation and facilitation services to development and relief organizations in the former Yugoslavia. She brings to this work a long history as a writer, editor, producer, and director in film-making and television, in addition to working as a media consultant and manager in various branches of the United States government. Born in the Philippines, she has lived in nine countries in Asia, Central and South America, and Europe.

Mirja Hanson is Chair of the International Association of Facilitators and a managing partner of Millennia International, a network of organization development and facilitation companies around the world. Building on her early work as a community development consultant with the ICA in Midwestern USA and Japan, she has more than two decades of management consulting experience with local, regional, and state governments, as well as private organizations. She directed the State of Minnesota's award-winning quality improvement program, STEP, and was recently appointed Director of Transition to refocus the mission of government in Minnesota's twin cities of St. Paul and Minneapolis, USA.

Goran Hyden is Professor of Political Science at the University of Florida, USA. Before taking that position in 1986, he worked at the Ford Foundation for Eastern and Southern Africa and lectured at universities in Kenya, Tanzania, and Uganda. He has also served as a consultant to numerous international organizations and governments, including UNICEF, UNDP, the Swedish International Development Cooperation Agency, and the Tanzanian government. He serves on the Board of the Dag Hammarskjold Foundation and the African Centre for Technology Studies in Nairobi, Kenya. His many books include *Governance and Politics in Africa* (edited with Michael Bratton), *No Shortcuts to Progress*, and *Beyond Ujamaa in Tanzania*.

Saad Eddin Ibrahim is Professor of Political Sociology at the American University in Cairo, Egypt and Chairman of the Board of the Ibn Khaldoun Center for Development Studies in Cairo. Among his many other responsibilities, he is Secretary General of the Egyptian Independent Commission for Electoral Review, President of Cairo's Union for Social Professions, a Trustee of the Arab Thought Forum (Amman, Jordan), a member of the Club of Rome, the World Bank's Advisory Council on Environmentally Sustainable Development, the Board of Minority Rights Group International (London), the Middle East International Forum, and Transparency International's Council on Governance.

Janice Jiggins is Professor of Human Ecology at the Department of Rural Development Studies at the Swedish University of Agricultural Sciences, where she is exploring the relationship of food supply, natural resources, and population dynamics. Her international career has included PhD studies in Sri Lanka, working with the Overseas Development Institute in London, the Rural Development Studies Bureau in Zambia, and the Ford Foundation in Kenya as well as consulting with multilateral and bilateral donor organizations and private foundations. Her recent publications include *Changing the Boundaries: Women-Centered Perspectives on Population and the Environment* and a chapter in *Environmental and Social Impact Assessment*.

Alice Johnson is Associate Professor at the Mandel School of Applied Social Sciences, Case Western Reserve University, Cleveland, USA. In the United States, her research focuses on homelessness and the development of shelter-based services. She has been involved since 1990 in international social work in Romania, where her work has included a case study of an institution for handicapped persons, curriculum development with six new schools of social work, and management training for leaders of non-governmental organizations. In 1996, she led a community assessment of civil society development in five cities of Romania.

Marlene Kanawati is Manager of the Education for Development Unit of the Near East Foundation's Community Development Services in Cairo, Egypt. A social scientist, she has worked extensively in organizational diagnosis, training needs assessment, and training program design. She is a member of numerous local and international NGOs and is an assistant professor at the American University, Cairo. Although many of her research and conference publications remain unpublished, she is the co-author of *Women's Life and Health* (Arabic) and is preparing *Economy and Beliefs of the Cairo Urban Poor* for publication.

David Korten is founder and President of The People-Centered Development Forum, a global alliance of organizations and people dedicated to creating just, inclusive, and sustainable societies through voluntary citizen action. He brings to this work over 35 years of experience in business, academic, and international development institutions including Harvard University, the Ford Foundation, and as Asian regional advisor to the United States Agency for International Development. Among his many publications which are required university course reading are *Getting to the 21st Century: Voluntary Action and the Global Agenda, Community Management*, and *When Corporations Rule the World*. He is chair of the board of directors of Positive Futures Network, publisher of *YES! A Journal of Positive Futures*.

Mildred Leet is co-founder of the New York-based Trickle Up Program, chair of the Board of Audrey Cohen College for Human Services, and vice-president of the US Committee for the United Nations Development Fund for Women. She has served as president of the National Council of Women of the USA Inc., vice-president of the International Council of Women, and on the boards of the International Peace Academy and the Save the Children Federation. She and her husband, Glen Leet, have received countless awards for their pioneering work with Trickle Up.

Frank Powell has been consulting with the private sector, public sector, NGOs, and local communities for over 25 years in 16 countries. For the past ten years, he has lived in Kenya and worked throughout Africa. His consultancy work includes designing and managing community participation initiatives, strategic planning, human resource development, organizational development, and facilitating participatory workshops and conferences. Among his many consultancies, he is serving as the Institutional Strengthening/Training Specialist for the World Bank Urban Development Project in Swaziland and is an active member of CARE International's Regional Resource Team.

Monte Roulier is Senior Community Advisor and Director of the Good Community Initiative for the National Civic League, USA. In this capacity, he designs, develops, and facilitates community-based strategic planning processes in the United States and abroad. He has established partnerships with government officials and private sector leaders responsible for natural resource management in Russia and managed training programs for them during their visits to the United States. He has also served as president of a company specializing in education, sustainable development, and democracy projects in Russia and Central Asia.

Brian Stanfield is on the staff of The Canadian Institute of Cultural Affairs, where he edits a periodical, *Edges: New Planetary Patterns,* and is engaged in curriculum development, research, and writing. A former school teacher, he spent many years designing and teaching human development programs with the ICA in India, Jamaica, and his native Australia. He was a staff member and later dean of the Institute's Global Academy. He is currently editing *100 Ways to Use the Conversation Method in the Workplace.*

James Troxel is Chief Operating Officer of Millennia Consulting and serves on the Adjunct Faculty of DePaul University's School for New Learning, Chicago, USA. In 25 years of work in community and organizational development and leadership training, he pioneered many adaptations of the ICA's *Technology of Participation (ToP)* process and is an architect of the participative strategic planning process now installed in organizations worldwide. He is a founding member of the International Association of Facilitators (IAF) and editor of *Participation Works: Business Cases Around the World* and *Government Works: Profiles of People Making a Difference.*

Bhimrao Tupe is a consultant and trainer in Education and Human Capacities Development with the Institute of Cultural Affairs India. His work in community and organizational development, which has focused on curriculum research, design, and implementation, has taken him from India to Belgium, the

United Kingdom, and the United States. He was Assistant Dean of the Human Development Training Institute in Maliwada, India, an innovative program to train grassroots leaders in methods of community participation, leadership development, and citizen engagement.

Koenraad Verhagen is Secretary-General of CIDSE (Coopération Internationale pour le Développement et la Solidarité) which represents and coordinates the work of 17 Catholic development organizations in Europe, North America, and New Zealand. In this capacity, he represents CIDSE at the United Nations, the World Bank, various European institutions, and the Vatican. He has also worked in teaching and research capacities for the Institute of Social Studies in The Hague, the Dutch Catholic funding organization CEBEMO, the Royal Tropical Institute, and the International Labour Office. He has published numerous articles and reports on development, cooperatives, and related issues.

Paul Watson is former Executive Director of San Diego Youth and Community Services, USA. A native of Long Island, New York, he began his career in human services while a teenager. He worked for 15 years with the Training Research Institute for Residential Youth Centers, Inc. He serves on the Board of Directors for the National Network for Youth Services, is Vice-Chair of the National Council on Youth Policy, and participates in a number of local organizations including the San Diego Community Congress and the Strategic Action Committee of the San Diego Children's Initiative. He is writing a book on his life experiences entitled *The Price of Dignity*.

Barbara Wright is a Master of Social Work graduate from Case Western Reserve University in Cleveland, USA. She has worked for 18 years at Summit County Children Services Board, as a child welfare caseworker, volunteer coordinator, public speaker, trainer, and project coordinator of an abuse and neglect outreach program for teen parents. She participated in the 1996 Listening and Learning in Romania project as a team leader, and continues to explore the evolution of civil society in Romania.

Index